FOR THE SUN AFTER LONG NIGHTS

FOR THE SUN AFTER LONG NIGHTS

THE STORY OF IRAN'S WOMEN-LED UPRISING

Nilo Tabrizy and Fatemeh Jamalpour

Atlantic Books
London

First published in the United States in 2025 by Pantheon Books, an imprint of The Knopf Doubleday Publishing Group, a division of Penguin Random House, LLC.

First published in hardback in Great Britain in 2025 by Atlantic Books,
an imprint of Atlantic Books Ltd.

Copyright © Nilo Tabrizy and Fatemeh Jamalpour, 2025

The moral right of Nilo Tabrizy and Fatemeh Jamalpour to be identified as the authors of this work has been asserted by them in accordance with the Copyright, Designs and Patents Act of 1988.

All rights reserved. No part of this publication may be reproduced, stored in a retrieval system, or transmitted in any form or by any means, electronic, mechanical, photocopying, recording, or otherwise, without the prior permission of both the copyright owner and the above publisher of this book.

No part of this book may be used in any manner in the learning, training or development of generative artificial intelligence technologies (including but not limited to machine learning models and large language models (LLMs)), whether by data scraping, data mining or use in any way to create or form a part of data sets or in any other way.

Some names and identifying characteristics have been changed to protect the privacy of the individuals involved.

Every effort has been made to trace or contact all copyright holders. The publishers will be pleased to make good any omissions or rectify any mistakes brought to their attention at the earliest opportunity.

10 9 8 7 6 5 4 3 2 1

A CIP catalogue record for this book is available from the British Library.

Hardback ISBN: 978 1 80546 092 3
E-book ISBN: 978 1 80546 093 0

Printed and bound by CPI (UK) Ltd, Croydon CR0 4YY

Atlantic Books
An imprint of Atlantic Books Ltd
Ormond House
26–27 Boswell Street
London
WC1N 3JZ

www.atlantic-books.co.uk

Product safety EU representative: Authorised Rep Compliance Ltd., Ground Floor, 71 Lower Baggot Street, Dublin, D02 P593, Ireland. www.arccompliance.com

To my mom, Mina, who let me to fly, Taraneh Alidoosti, Sepideh Qolian, Mina Akbari, and my sisters who run with me in Iran's streets

—Fatemeh

For my mamani, Maman Roya, and Baba Hossein for instilling in me the strength and kindness of our people

—Nilo

CONTENTS

Introduction   ix

PART I: *JIN / ZAN*, WOMAN
   For Woman, Life, Freedom   3
   For Students. For the Future.   6
   For Not Being Afraid Anymore   10
   For the Sun After Long Nights   16
   For Dancing in the Alley   19
   For Continuous Crying   29
   For My Sister, Your Sister, Our Sisters   34
   For the Wounds of Baluchestan   40
   For Defenseless Bodies and Lives   48
   For the Imprisoned Intellectuals   53
   For Nika and the Moon   62
   For the Endless and Repetitive   68

PART II: *JÎYAN / ZENDEGI*, LIFE
   For What They Stole from Us   77
   For the Freedom of Choice   89
   For My Mom, Your Mom, Our Moms   100
   For the Women Whose Feet Were Cut from Running   107
   For the Regret of a Normal Life   111
   For the Girl Who Wished to Be a Boy   117
   For a Lifetime of Loneliness   125
   For Changing Rusted Minds   135
   For the Image of Repetition   152

For Bloody Aban and Its Fifteen Hundred Living Martyrs   157
Grief Is the Bitter Fruit They Set   166
For Not Being Ashamed of Poverty   170
What Can They Know of Our Distress Who Watch Us
   from the Shore?   186
Outside the Confines of My Body   190

PART III: *AZADÎ / AZADI*, FREEDOM
For Kian and His Rainbow   195
My Palate's Bitter with Grief's Aftertaste   200
For Hanged Heads   208
How Sweet Those Days When We Were Still   216
For the Women Who Never Express Regret   221
The Roses Have All Gone   226
Goodbye, My Beloved Homeland   234
We Wait for Light and Darkness Reigns   239
For Resistance and Hope   243

Acknowledgments   251
Notes   259
Index   295

INTRODUCTION

> For the imprisoned elites
> For feeling at ease
> For the sun after long nights
> For all the nerves and insomnia pills
> For Woman, Life, Freedom
> For Freedom
> For Freedom
> For Freedom
>
> —Shervin Hajipour, "Baraye"

NILO AND FATEMEH

ON SEPTEMBER 16, 2022, a twenty-two-year-old Kurdish woman named Mahsa Jîna Amini was killed in Tehran by the city's morality police. She was viciously beaten after having been detained by an officer who accused her of not dressing appropriately in public, in defiance of the country's hijab rule, which broadly governs what women should wear. As this horrible incident was unraveling, details were quickly disseminated by a handful of local journalists on social media. Sajjad Khodakarami, an independent Iranian journalist based in Istanbul, broke the news of Jîna's assault on Twitter, sharing that on September 13 she "was treated in Tehran's Kasra

Hospital due to severe injuries, including brain damage."* On the same day, Hamed Shafiei, a reporter who covered political and local news for *Shargh,* one of the largest and most prominent Iranian newspapers, posted an Instagram story. He wrote, "I went to Kasra Hospital. The atmosphere was tense there, and people were shouting, 'They killed someone's daughter. The police killed her. The morality police killed her.'" The accompanying image of Jîna lying unconscious in a hospital bed, with a swollen face, tubes coming out of her mouth, and dried blood on her ears, went viral.

As these threads of reporting began to come together, the regime tried to shut down coverage of the story. A police spokesperson told reporters at *Shargh* to disregard the incident with Jîna—that publishing what was happening at the hospital would only cause trouble for *Shargh* and for the police. But the regime couldn't stop what was already in motion. The news continued to be shared all over various platforms, both by media outlets and by individual reporters. And when Jîna succumbed to her injuries on September 16, the *Shargh* reporter Niloofar Hamedi defied orders to keep quiet and told the world about her death in a tweet. Alongside a photo of Jîna's grandmother and father wrapped in a tight, tearful embrace outside the closed door of the ICU, Niloofar wrote that "the black dress of mourning has become our national flag."

The Islamic Republic stood firm in its claim that Jîna had died due to a health issue, denying that the morality police had beaten her to death. But Iranians knew better, and the Friday after Jîna's death swarms of people, mostly women, congregated in front of Kasra Hospital, overflowing with rage about seeing another one of our young women disposed of by the security state with such casual cruelty.

Morality police vans, plainclothes officers of the Islamic Revolutionary Guard Corps (IRGC), and riot police surrounded the hospital

---

* Mahsa Amini's Kurdish name is Jîna, which means "life" in the Kurdish language. The Iranian state legally recognizes names of Persian or Islamic origin, meaning that many members of ethnic minority communities must have a name in their local language preceded by a state-recognized name. To honor her name and her heritage and to respect how her friends and family refer to her, we will do the same by calling her Jîna throughout this book. Jiyan Zandi, "Why It's Vital to Center Kurdish Voices in the 'Woman, Life, Freedom' Movement," *Time,* Nov. 23, 2022.

to try to prevent people from mourning and demonstrating. Authorities started to violently arrest people, shooting at and beating them. Elaheh Khosravi was one of the first journalists on the scene. After the commotion made it impossible to stay at the hospital, she walked down Alvand Street to Argentina Square nearby. There, she witnessed and reported on an act of protest and mourning that became a symbol of the 2022 movement that followed Jîna's death: a young woman, scissors in hand, cutting off her ponytail while shouting, "You [the regime] are forever dishonorable!" The image was reminiscent of "Daf," a poem by Reza Baraheni, an Iranian poet:

> *A woman was running on the rigid beaches*
> *Shouted: God, God, God, why have you forgotten Tehran's sky?*

For those of us in Iran who have lived through destruction, war, and turmoil, poetry and literature have always been our shelter. In some cultures, poetry is for the elite. Yet in Iran, it's for the masses. Nearly every Iranian, regardless of economic status or educational level, knows the great Persian poets. Even those who cannot read can recite, from memory, a favorite verse written by Hafez or Rumi. Poetry has seeped its way into our being; it's part of our very Iranianness. And it isn't only delicate or whimsical. It is now and has always been political.

It's fitting, then, that the legacy of Jîna's death and the movement it would inspire would unfurl in real time through revolutionary songs and poetic slogans chanted at demonstrations and recorded in protest graffiti that covered the walls and streets that the authorities took from our people. For centuries, narrative expression has shaped how we bring life to the most urgent issues for our people. One of the earliest poetic works that collectively shaped us is the *Shahnameh*, an epic poem by the Persian poet Ferdowsi. In AD 977, Ferdowsi began writing a story in more than fifty thousand rhyming couplets about the mythical tales of ancient Iran. He takes the reader on a journey from the creation of the world to the seventh century, when the Arabs conquered Iran and brought Islam to the Persian Empire. It took Ferdowsi more than forty-three years to complete this narrative, writing amid the Arab invasion that imposed a new language and religion on our people. Taking care to intentionally use Persian words, Ferdowsi preserved our language and history at a time when it could have been lost forever. Word by word, story by story, we have survived our oppressors by force, with narrative as our lifeline.

At the core of the slogans created and spread during the 2022 protests, the morphing of our ideas and desires into melodies and verse, is the simple human act of expression. We've been killed, imprisoned, and exiled when we dare ask for basic dignity. Expressing ourselves is how we resist repression; it's how we've resisted since *Shahnameh*. In the days and weeks after Jîna's death, Iranians logged on to Twitter by the thousands to explain why they were facing off against ruthless, violent authorities in the streets every day.

A then-twenty-five-year-old singer named Shervin Hajipour began gathering our hopes, stringing them together into a ballad called "Baraye," meaning "For." As the guitar comes in to form a sparse music bed, Hajipour's powerful and graceful voice echoes Iranians' longings. Transformed into a vessel, he runs down the endless reasons that pushed people out of their homes and into the streets in daily protest:

> *For dancing in the streets*
> *For our fear when kissing loved ones*
> *For my sister, your sister, our sisters*
> *For the changing of rotted minds.*

Perhaps accidentally, or instinctually, Hajipour joined the centuries-long tradition of verse as political commentary that is a foundational pillar of our national identity. When he posted the song to his Instagram in the early days of the movement, it was viewed more than forty million times in less than two days. In Persian we have a phrase, "khak-e pay-e mardom," which directly translates to "the dust beneath people's feet." It's a phrase used to say, "I'm with the people." Though the phrase has been co-opted by politicians like Mahmoud Ahmadinejad, a pro-regime former president, to ridicule and disparage protesters, it has since been reclaimed. In writing and sharing this song, Hajipour was not only the dust beneath our feet, standing with us firmly and completely, but also our voice, our eyes, our hearts.

Two days after Hajipour shared "Baraye" online, he was summoned by the police and questioned for "encouragement to protest," later released on bail in October 2022. He was barred from leaving Iran and lived life in limbo for two years while awaiting sentencing. In a video uploaded to Instagram on July 30, 2024, he finally informed his followers that he was ordered to turn himself in to begin serving a three-year-and-eight-month sentence for the lyrics in "Baraye." Though his travel ban had by then been lifted, Hajipour said in the video that he would serve his sentence rather than leave Iran.

"For me it's a question of how else was I supposed to protest? How else could I have critiqued what was going on?" he said, speaking directly to the camera, his voice lightly trembling. "Was there a more peaceful, civil way other than 'Baraye'?"

Even the most beautiful, nonviolent means of expression are unsafe in Iran. Songs, reporting, and the strengthening of community under unlikely circumstances threaten the regime's existence. For each Hajipour who is silenced, new words, verses, and slogans will rise, finding their ways into our bodies as we shout them into existence at a protest or write them online to live forever.

This book is, for us, our own form of self-expression. If reporters are creating the first rough draft of history by bearing witness, then it only makes sense that the story of the women-led protest movement in Iran be told by two Iranian woman journalists. Our voices and journalistic work will tell the story of Iran from the ground through Fatemeh. And like many Iranians who have left or been forced to leave, Nilo will take readers through the uncomfortable upheaval of migration and what it means to reluctantly exile oneself in order to cover an uprising. Together, we represent two perspectives combining out of necessity.

Ours are stories about Iran that will not be found in Western media, the focus of which is always tied to geopolitical issues, the extraction of our natural resources, or whisperings of a looming World War III.

At times, we will write separately in our own words. Our narratives combine when we meet each other and realize that we have to stitch our perspectives together to tell the full story of *Zan, Zendegi, Azadi*—Woman, Life, Freedom—the rallying cry and name of the 2022 protest movement. We bring these firsthand accounts to you to be the voice of our sisters. It is our life's mission now to tell these stories; to watch from afar and up close; to report and write. We have suffered from survivor's guilt, but we now realize that we are not merely survivors or estranged from our land. We are messengers.

Iranian women's fight for liberation is neither new nor completed. Women have long been rallying together to oppose oppression and injustice, and we will tell the story of those historical and recent efforts here. We have made great strides so far. We have made it impossible for the Islamic Republic to implement its desire to cover our heads and our true selves, refusing to follow its draconian laws. We have shown that the people of Iran can expand beyond the confines of the Islamic Republic and its regime. This ongoing movement represents us, our power, our solidarity and sisterhood, a people and a nation that demand everyday life, justice, peace, hope, and an existence free from honor killings, the death penalty, and executions. We, Iranian women, are not the Islamic Republic's enemy; we are its negation. In the words of Ahmad Shamlou, the contemporary poet,

> *Idiot men,*
> *I am not your enemy*
> *I deny your existence.*

This resistance has not come without consequence. Two months before the movement took hold of Iran after Jîna's death, a pro-regime woman wearing a conservative black veil confronted a young art student and poet named Sepideh Rashnu on a public bus for not wearing a hijab. In support of Sepideh, people kicked the woman off the bus. Sepideh recorded the incident on her cell phone and sent it to the media. It went viral, and in less than twenty-four hours Sepideh was arrested by security forces. They beat her and forced her to do a televised confession on the Islamic Republic's state broadcaster with her bruised face in full, painful view. She was imprisoned for three and a half years for the crime of not wearing a hijab. Sepideh is our Rosa Parks, rebelling against Iran's gender-based apartheid. We begin and end our book with her words and those of other imprisoned sisters in Iran to show that the regime cannot lock up their bright minds and free souls:

> *A person who fights knows that revolutions will take a long time, but she does not fail. Standing for freedom is more beautiful than freedom itself. The person who fights is yesterday's child. She knows that if she doesn't taste freedom, today's children will. A person who fights knows that revolutions will last, but she will not fail.*

PART I

JIN / ZAN, WOMAN

In your name, which is our secret
There is no sunrise on the night of Mahsa
Sing so that the city becomes a song
So that this homeland becomes a homeland
It's in the streets at night
It's your turn to knock on the door.

— Lyric of Zam anthem by Mahdi Yerahi

FATEMEH

FOR WOMAN, LIFE, FREEDOM

THE EVENING AFTER Jîna's death, on assignment for the newspaper *Ham-Mihan,* my friend and colleague Elaheh Mohammadi drove eight hours overnight, through winding mountains and narrow roads, to Saqqez, Jîna's hometown in Kurdistan. She arrived there at 6:30 a.m. and drove directly to the cemetery to cover Jîna's funeral, not wanting to miss a moment of the service. Half an hour later, men and women, young and old, began to stream into the Aichi cemetery wearing Kurdish outfits, waiting with crying eyes for Jîna's body to arrive. Jîna's parents, Mojgan Eftekhari and Amjad Amini, sat beside her empty grave. In Iranian culture, losing a child is considered the deepest grief, often referred to as "burning mourning." Jîna's mother filled her fists with dirt, cast them suddenly into the air over her head, and said, "Jîna, get up. Look, these people have come to see you. Our flower is gone."

Close to the funeral start time at 10:00 a.m., people were still pouring in. The security officers tried to rush the family into burying Jîna before it got crowded. But her family refused and did not allow the officers to take Jîna's body out of the ambulance. Jîna's uncle announced in a short speech, "We will not bow down." Her parents insisted that they had made an appointment with the people. And so, they waited. In the end, Jîna's body was buried by the hands of thousands of people showing Kurdish solidarity.

The funeral was the beginning of our revolution for a normal life, for justice and equality. Elaheh called Elnaz, her twin sister, and shouted, "Elnaz, a revolution has started here! I will stay longer."

On Jîna's tombstone, her father wrote, "Dear Jîna, you will not die. Your name will become a symbol," foreshadowing the important role her death would play in the movement. Her grandfather read the poem *Tehran* by the Kurdish poet Sherko Bekas, the popular contemporary Kurd poet, whose poems many of the millions of Kurdish people in Iraq, Iran, and Syria can recite by heart. The subject matter Bekas deals with is always life, love, and freedom:

> *Tehran imposed a mandatory hijab on the trees*
> *Tehran sewed a robe on the water's body*
> *Tehran put a turban on the garden*
> *Tehran forced singing to have a beard*
> *Tehran made music a widow*
> *And it made a funeral from life*
> *Tehran does not laugh at anyone*
> *Except for death*
> *Tehran does not like anything*
> *other than death*
> *The names of all women, girls, and boys in Tehran*
> *is death*
> *And life is never born from a mother*
> *in Tehran.*

The guests at Jîna's funeral chanted, "Jin, Jîyan, Azadî," or "Woman, Life, Freedom," during the service, a slogan that derived from the political writings of an imprisoned Kurdish leader named Abdullah Öcalan. Colloquially called Apo, which means "uncle" in Kurdish, Öcalan was the son of a poor farmer in Turkey. Like those of many revolutionary leaders, his theories originate from personal life experiences. Öcalan's life was forever changed after seeing his sister Hawa forced into a child marriage in exchange for money and wheat. In 2010, in an article called "The Revolution Is Woman," he wrote that calling for freedom without gender equality is futile and illusory. Öcalan presented his ideology on three axes: women's freedom, ecology and attention to the environment, and radical democracy, which together came to form the foundation of what we now know as "Woman, Life, Freedom."

NILO

FOR STUDENTS. FOR THE FUTURE.

On September 26, 2022, I got my first email from Fatemeh in nine months. She had just been summoned and interrogated by the Ministry of Intelligence, who had threatened her with two years of jail time for her journalism at the BBC that was critical of the regime. "I am not scared," Fatemeh wrote. "Something like hope is rising among us, hope for changes, for woman, life, freedom, for you visiting me in Tehran soon."

The last time I had heard from her was in 2021, when she was preparing to return to Iran after a stint in London and told me she was cutting off contact with me completely. "It's not safe to communicate with you. You won't hear from me. Take care, abji joon. Boos boos," she wrote, calling me *abji*, her sister, and sending digital kisses my way. She knew that her return meant that intelligence and security forces would snatch her up and start interrogating her about her work as a journalist abroad, which had become common practice for the regime in our increasingly dictatorial homeland.

I got her email in the middle of my workday at *The New York Times*, for which I had begun to cover the protests surging in Iran. I was working on my first story: a visual analysis of the themes of the demonstrations that were yet to swell into an uprising. My days were spent meticulously researching, organizing, and archiving videos and images shared by Iranians on social media as the street protests started to take shape. In the beginning, everything felt like a fever—nonstop, urgent, and somewhat surreal. I slept poorly and woke up with a heaviness in my body each morning, stopping myself from falling into a deep sleep for fear of missing something from a handful of time zones away. When I saw Fatemeh's name in my inbox, I couldn't believe that it was her. If the Islamic Republic found out that she was communicating with a Western journalist, Fatemeh could have been imprisoned for years for conspiring with "the enemy." But like other Iranians who were flooding the streets at the time, Fatemeh was evolving into a more defiant version of herself—one who was willing to accept the very real cost of risking her life and freedom.

By November 2022, social media continued to be full of footage of the protests. Iranians were ripping and torching posters of the Islamic Republic's cultlike leaders, women were cutting their hair while weeping in the middle of crowds, and mourners held funerals for people killed by the state during protests. In Tehran, the country's capital, elderly women marched up to the police, daring them to put them in handcuffs; members of the brave working class led historic strikes that shut down the northwestern city of Tabriz's grand bazaar; and even in Mashhad, a religious city in the northeast that has historically supported the regime, Iranians were chanting, "Death to the Islamic Republic!" in the streets.

Led by young women and other members of Gen Z, at least two million Iranians poured into the streets in the largest and most widespread uprising that the Islamic Republic has seen in its forty-six-year history. The government responded by restricting internet access to cut Iranians off from the outside world and by killing and mass arresting their own people. Since 2009, when Iran experienced nationwide protests over claims of electoral fraud, the regime has blocked access to YouTube, Twitter, Facebook, and countless other platforms. As a result, Iranians have for decades been forced into a game of cat and mouse with regime censors, finding creative ways to be online freely by using VPNs to change their IP addresses.

From afar, I monitored the drips of videos and information that Iranians managed to get out. On Telegram, an encrypted messaging app where many Iranians communicate with each other, I was particularly shocked at videos showing the rebellion of young schoolgirls across the country. One video showed a group of girls booing a member of the Basij, the feared volunteer paramilitary unit of the Islamic Revolutionary Guard Corps (IRGC), who was giving a speech about the protests at their school. The country's most powerful security, military, and intelligence institution, the IRGC was created following the Iranian revolution in 1979 to protect the new Islamic Republic and its religious ideology. Now it's a force loyal to Iran's supreme leader with massive influence over economic and political affairs. As the Basiji spoke, the schoolgirls shouted over him, chanting, "Get lost, Basij!"

In Karaj, a big city half an hour from Tehran, a group of elementary school girls without hijabs threw paper and trash at a school administrator, yelling, "Bisharaf!" (without honor) at him as they forced him out of the building. In a culture immensely concerned with honor and dignity, *bi-sharaf* is an incendiary phrase that cuts to the very core of our being. The morality police killed Jîna because of an improperly worn hijab, a perceived act of dishonor. And now these schoolgirls denounced their oppressors as dishonorable. In real time, I saw these tiny bodies rebelling against an oppressive system known for its cruelty and suffocating repression. I felt conflicted watching this from afar—proud to share a heritage with these powerful young girls but also aggrieved and resentful that their environment forced them into resiliency so early.

Watching the protests made me think and worry about Fatemeh, who I knew was at risk by virtue of her profession in a country hellbent on suppressing the diffusion of information or any form of dissent. Fatemeh endured countless interrogations after returning to Iran, and she told me that in the last one, four days after Jîna's death in September 2022, one of the intelligence officials told her that they would send her case to the often relatively harsher Revolutionary Court, which would likely imprison her for two to five years. The Revolutionary Court operates parallel to but separately from the regular judicial system, and its focus is on protecting Iran's system of clerical rule. Political prisoners are often charged through the Revolutionary Court, facing vague charges such as "waging war against God" or "corruption on Earth."

I felt helpless watching from afar. Then and now, I want to be in Iran. I don't want to be in the diaspora, watching the cruel way that we fight with one another, blaming different factions for the current regime or being judgmental when some people don't feel comfortable sharing protest videos on social media. I don't want to play diaspora literature bingo with cheesy poems about my grandmothers and kebab and saffron and the idea of home. I want to finally learn Azeri, the language of the ethnic minority to which I belong. I want to trace my father's steps in Tabriz, the place that is my namesake and the beginning of my story. I want to lose the Western accent that pains me when I speak Persian. Instead, I am banished to a digital-only sisterhood with Fatemeh. I decided that if I could not go, the least I could do was bring you their voices, their stories. I could make sure people like Fatemeh and our fellow Iranians are heard.

FATEMEH

FOR NOT BEING AFRAID ANYMORE

For the first three days following Jîna's death, I didn't attend any protests. My family and friends all worried about me, given the risks. In the Islamic Republic of Iran, journalism is like tightrope walking. In the view of the state, I've committed infraction after infraction when it comes to adhering to the rules of its society. I worked for the *Los Angeles Times* without official media credentials, wrote tweets critical of the regime, studied in the United States, and was a journalist for *BBC Persian*. The regime considers diasporic Persian-language media its enemy. Above all, I am a feminist, and the regime hates us.

I asked my lawyer what would happen if I was arrested at the protests. "Well, you would get fifteen years in prison," he responded. Though I hid it from my family, I was concerned.

Those days, walking around Tehran was fascinating. Graffiti was visible all over, each day painted over by officials, only to be rewritten again and again by young protesters. In the alley in front of my sister's place, someone wrote "Jîna Amini." After the officials covered it, the graffiti writer came back and scrawled "Woman. Life. Freedom. For

Freedom" where Jîna's name had been. It was like a hidden war on our city's walls.

On the Monday after Jîna's death, women activists called for a protest against the regime at the intersection of Keshavarz Boulevard and, ironically, Hijab Street. I did not go, but friends told me that the demonstration turned into a confrontation between several thousand people and the riot police. Keshavarz Boulevard was divided into two sides: On one side were protesters standing hand in hand, among them women and men of all ages, religious and nonreligious, facing off against a line of riot police. Late that night, after the protests had died down, I went to Laleh Park on Keshavarz Boulevard. The cats that typically roamed had been attacked by so much tear gas that their eyes would not open. One day, an old woman who went to feed them every week showed up as usual but could not find them. Even cats are not safe from the regime's cruel repression.

When the interrogators summoned me a couple of days later, it caught me off guard. I didn't think that they would summon me amid all this chaos. The day before the interrogation, my father texted me asking me not to go out. I responded that I would not, because I had an interrogation session the next day. "Good!" he responded. In my father's eyes, being interrogated was better and safer than going to protest! The session took about four hours, and it did not go well.

Ms. Maryam Sedaghat, my main interrogator from the Ministry of Intelligence or, as she called herself, "the expert of my case" at the time, started the session by saying, "Your life will be divided between before and after this moment."

"My life has been full of these moments," I replied, laughing.

"Will you decide that you are pro–Islamic Republic or an opposition?" she asked. "I need your answer to decide about your future."

"It's so unfortunate that, after all, you have not realized that I am a journalist and cannot be pro or against it," I said. I viewed my role as reflecting and reporting the truth of what I witnessed.

She never discussed Jîna by name; she talked vaguely about someone who had died and claimed that there was no evidence to back up the brutal murder. I lost my cool and yelled in response that she was *killed*. She did not die a passive death. In response, my interrogator tried to humiliate and belittle me, calling me an extremist for contradicting the regime's account.

She told me that she and her colleagues had spoken about observations I had shared in response to a question about what had changed in Iran in the year I was away. I had told them that the number of women without hijab I saw on the street had increased by four or five times. When I had shared my vision for a freer Iran for women, my interrogators had only listened in silence, but it seemed they were finally ready to respond, nine months later.

"Our religious husbands fall into sin when they see women without hijabs," Ms. Sedaghat said.

"Well, the husbands should not look," I replied.

"First, you request an optional hijab," Ms. Sedaghat said. "Later, you want to get naked and walk down the street, and then you demand a sexual revolution." She seemed to be trying to reason with me—to show me I was mistaken in calling for women's bodily autonomy.

Then Ms. Sedaghat changed course. With an expression of feigned concern, she asked, "May I come to visit you in prison? Can we see each other after your imprisonment?"

I was shocked. I recognized a new level of manipulation in her words. It was a veiled threat. *So she finally decided to send me to prison,* I thought. I was suddenly filled with hatred for Ms. Sedaghat. During our conversations, I had gone back and forth between feeling angry with her and feeling a sense of allyship with a fellow woman. When she was assigned to my case, I worried that the interrogations would become more difficult for me. When my interrogators had been men, it had been easy to lie and play the part of a blushing, subordinate little woman for protection. But it was harder to do this with Ms. Sedaghat, because I value sisterhood, solidarity, and the collective power of women. I knew it would be more challenging for me to sit in front of a woman and lie to her directly, especially one who would undoubtedly try to find common ground and build rapport and friendship with me, even if it was all an act.

Over time, I got to see a lot of Ms. Sedaghat and her collection of bright scarves, which highlighted her monochrome jackets and pants. She never wore makeup. Her hijab was always open enough so that I could clearly see her face: She had low-arched dark eyebrows that she left unplucked and unshaped, a slightly elongated nose, dark skin, and thin lips. I learned that we were the same age, and that she was married with a son. Once, we talked about feminism, and it seemed as if she were really reflecting on the injustices I was describing. There had been moments when I wondered if I was getting through to her.

But I realized in this final interrogation that any understanding she seemed to show was all a charade, not a genuine show of friendship or kindness. So I smiled coldly and, in response to her question about visiting me in prison, said, "No, ma'am. I don't want to see you anymore."

"Is meeting with me so annoying for you?" she asked. "I thought we had had friendly conversations?"

At this point, I had had enough of her pretending that our interactions were not built on an imbalanced power dynamic. "My problem is not meeting you. It is your position; my life is in your hands, and we both know that whatever you and your bosses decide, the judge will issue it," I said. "Let's switch positions. Then we will see if you like it. I have nothing to lose. Send me to prison," I said.

Ms. Sedaghat stood and said, "You will be in jail soon, and I don't have any regrets about it, because I did my best to lead you. It seems you are watching the news from women's revolution pages. You have been radicalized again. But I will meet you on Sirat Bridge."

According to Islam, after we die, there is a bridge over which every person must pass to enter paradise. It's thinner than a strand of hair and sharp as the blade of a knife. Below it are the flames of hell that envelop the bodies of sinners. It was another moment of insanity and absurdity for me: While the regime is killing people on the streets, its representatives are talking to me about theological legends. I longed to help us out of the living hell we were living through every day in Iran.

At the end of this meeting, it was my turn to manipulate her. "May I hug you for the first and last time?" I asked. That's my technique, either a last-minute ceasefire or a fight to the end. "Goodbye, Ms. Sedaghat," I said as I hugged her.

But as I opened the door to leave, I turned back and asked, "Do you know what the difference is between my generation and Generation Z?"

"What?" she asked.

"We defended, but they keep attacking," I said, before looking her in the eye for the last time and closing the door.

Leaving the building where my interrogation took place, I became more and more enraged. Thoughts raced through my head. Being threatened in this way and living a new life of imprisonment had begun to suffocate me. My rage propelled me forward. I decided that if I was going to prison anyway, I was going to do something meaningful for my people and myself first.

I took a motorcycle taxi ride to return home. And as we passed the riot police, I screamed, "Bastards!" After nine months of suffocation in these interrogation sessions, I decided to go film the protests. I wanted to prove to myself that they could not suppress us. I told myself, "Don't let the bastards grind you down." At the protest, a young teen volunteer for the IRGC stole my cell phone right out of my hand, and I almost got arrested. But when I arrived home, I opened my laptop and sent two emails, one to Nilo and another to Louise, a friend who works at *The Sunday Times*. With Louise's help, I published my first story about the movement, titled "'By the Time You Read This, I Might Be in Jail'—the Daily Terror of a Female Protester in Iran," under a fake name. An artist had added red coloring to all the fountains and water features in Tehran, leaving a trail of "blood" across the entire city, and photos of his work were published alongside my words. After ten months, I had returned to journalism and done something meaningful for my people and myself. In my email to Nilo, I told her we should write a story together about the protest movement, and she enthusiastically agreed.

Days later, I was almost arrested again at the intersection of 16th Azar Street and Keshavarz Boulevard. I was trying to take a photo of a girl with long hair walking down the street with the armed forces in the background. One riot officer stopped me and tried to take my phone. I turned to run, but he grabbed my backpack with my notes and my laptop inside. Then, at that very moment, a crazy thing happened. The passing traffic stopped, and men, ordinary men, leaped out of their cars and off their motorcycles and ran over to help. "Let her go," they shouted, pushing the officer off me. That's how these protests were different. They were not divided by class or ethnicity or gender. We were all united.

I felt Nilo's passion and love at each protest and demonstration and kept sending her, my sister, notes in New York to bring a part of her to Tehran's streets. I sent her pages and pages. As the number of protests increased, our friendship and sisterhood grew stronger. It reached the level of daily chats, and we were united in how we had both tied our love to our homeland and our people. Eventually, Nilo and I decided to write a story for *The Paris Review* together to give insight into how the protests were developing on the ground. It was the second time we had collaborated; the first was for the magazine *n+1* during another series of bloody protests in 2019. Again, Nilo and I managed to pass the Islamic Republic's walls and published a story about the Jîna movement.

NILO

FOR THE SUN AFTER LONG NIGHTS

After seven weeks, the protests were growing and growing with no sign of an off-ramp. In a desperate attempt to contain this movement, authorities were arresting Iranians daily. Thousands would be taken into custody over the course of the protests. As an Iranian journalist living in self-exile for covering my country, I believe strongly in the power of documentation, video verification, and the collection of eyewitness testimonies. Especially when covering human rights abuses and state violence, these investigative reports demand accountability by centering videos shared on social media that become visual evidence of excessive state force toward civilians. It's my life's mission to freeze moments in time before they become history, before they become forgotten and dusted with lessons that society should have heeded. And I continued to do this as the uprisings unfurled.

Every morning, I refreshed my email, hoping to hear from Fatemeh in Tehran. Toward the end of one workday in early November, as I was in the middle of an investigation for *The New York Times* into security forces co-opting ambulances to detain protesters, I finally got a message from Fatemeh. She sent a photo of two little scraps of paper, one green and one light pink, each containing protest slogans, lines of poetry, or words of encouragement written in beautiful handwriting. "These days young women without hijab put these notes in our hands secretly in the streets as we walk past them," wrote Fatemeh. "It is such a joy among all the difficulties and dangers that we choose to face every day."

"Joonam, joonam! Thank you for sending this," I wrote back immediately. "I will read your writing on Monday with my Persian tutor. You are my teacher in so many ways." I can speak Persian fluently, but being educated in the West means that I never learned how to read or write the language. I had started taking lessons, in part for my work, but even more as an intentional way to remain connected to a language that forms the basis of my identity and connection to being Iranian. Every time I fumbled around for words, I could feel myself slipping away from my culture. The lessons helped ground me.

As Fatemeh continued to go out to protests and report back her observations to me, we put a system in place. I had already lost contact with her once and couldn't go through that again, especially considering the heightened policing as the protests stretched over weeks. We decided that Fatemeh would send me two messages—one when she headed out to the protests and another when she returned home. Many Iranians no longer took their cell phones to protests for security reasons, either to protect their contacts from exposure or to keep the phones from being stolen. Fatemeh would go out to protests during the day and at night. Each time she went out, there was a high risk for danger. The state was killing people both in broad daylight and under the cover of night. Our emails were the only confirmation I had about her safety.

One morning, my phone dinged at 4:00, notifying me of an email from Fatemeh telling me that she was heading out for the evening. Hours later, the email I'd been waiting for arrived. "Joon joon, I'm back. You are my angel and hope," Fatemeh wrote, calling me one of our many terms of endearment. "I have just arrived home tonight. I went out with a group who writes slogans each night on the walls in the streets. One of them came with their 1-year-old baby and said, 'We want a better future for her.'" I closed my laptop, finally able to sleep at noon. I hoped that I would keep getting messages from her.

Today's leaders know full well the power of organizing and how surging feelings of injustice, grief, and rage can incite action that forces systemic change. Though the religious factions that took power have taken our country down a dark path, the Islamic Republic came to be through a popular revolution led by ordinary citizens. It's clear that Iranians are overwhelmingly opposed to the existing system, and fearing a public uprising, the Islamic Republic has developed one of the strongest military, security, and surveillance powers in the region. To this day, anytime the establishment sees a person or a cause that drums up widespread support, it pounces to flatten it. The streets began to clear months after Jîna's death, but this does not mean that the people were suddenly satisfied with the Islamic Republic. Rather, it reflected how effective systemic state surveillance and violence were in putting water on our flames. Yet often how something starts can foreshadow its end.

FATEMEH

FOR DANCING IN THE ALLEY

For months, I attended protests with my friend Shokat. (She has asked me to use her mother's name as a pseudonym to protect her identity.) We have been friends for eighteen years and had been going to protests together for more than a decade, since 2009—first in Ahvaz, the city where we attended college together, and now in Tehran. Often we went to Enghelab Street to pass out small notes to other protesters, even if we did so with shaky hands. Once, when I was giving a note to a young couple, the man said, "Don't be scared, you are very brave." Bumping our fists together had become a sign of solidarity, as if we would give each other courage through this simple action and the secret exchange of notes, our handwriting, our poems, and our slogans. On the small scraps of paper that I was handing out, I had written, "Hand in hand, we become the sea."

Another time, I approached a young couple sitting on a bench on Keshavarz Boulevard, which runs parallel to Enghelab Street. It had been raining and the ground was wet. I fell over in front of where they were sitting, and while I was sprawled on the ground, my fist was outstretched toward them. I couldn't stop laughing. They were a little shocked and asked if I was okay. I responded that I had lost a battle with an imaginary enemy. I gave them the note and a chocolate, and we exchanged goodbyes with a laugh. There was joy in our solidarity.

Enghelab Square, and the streets surrounding it, have always been sites of protest. Enghelab Street is about three miles long and home to many media publications' headquarters, ample bookstores, some cafés, and the top universities in Iran. There is a high-speed bus lane in the middle of the street from which security forces attack and shoot at protesters. The word *enghelab* means "revolution" in our language, and fittingly, anytime our collective rage has bubbled over and led to various movements, it is on Enghelab Street that it bursts forth. After Islamic factions declared victory in March 1979, thousands of angry women gathered there to oppose the mandatory hijab law, shouting, "We did not revolt only to regress again." Even then, we were called whores and prostitutes for demonstrating against repressive laws. In 2017, it was also on Enghelab Street that a group of women led by Vida Movahed wordlessly stood on a metal telecommunications platform and waved their headscarves in the air. Called the Girls of Enghelab Street, they were arrested with violence and beatings and sentenced to prison. Forty-five years after the Islamic Republic Revolution, we are still chanting the same slogan as the women of that time. But the revolution should not be a highway dotted with roundabouts. We're all stuck on a one-way street that threatens to lead us to a dead end rather than freedom.

These days, even with the massive presence of riot and plainclothes police forces, Enghelab Street is more alive than New York's Times Square, and the women more beautiful and stylish than in London. Once again, in 2022, it became the center of the women-led movement. On October 26 of that year, Shokat and I attended a protest on Enghelab Street. Riot police with large clear shields were standing all around the Enghelab subway station. The regime had become fearful of the subway, streets, highways, people, cars, and windows. It was afraid of senior citizens, students, teachers, workers, women, and men.

It was afraid of the country it had maintained control over by deadly force.

"It's strange. No videos or photos have come out of the past few days on Enghelab Street," I turned and said to Shokat. The regime had imposed martial rule in September and had since been trying to take our streets from us. As more of us gathered, the government began slowing down the internet so that we could send fewer images and videos to the outside world. It's a classic repression tactic. Officers then began to snatch protesters' cell phones out of their hands to arrest them later. After that, few dared to bring cell phones to protests, which made documenting the demonstrations more complicated than ever. Our bodies were the only weapons we had to fight back against security forces. We turned into human shields, in danger of being hit by bullets, batons, and tear gas. Plastic bullets could blind our eyes at any moment. But we were willing to sacrifice all we have for our freedom and that of the next generations, for our future.

The day after, as the protest progressed onto Keshavarz Boulevard, which people had begun calling Nika Boulevard in memory of a sixteen-year-old girl who had been killed there, members of the IRGC and Basij forces stood by at each intersection. Security forces lined up in two rows in the middle of the street, leaving only a narrow path for us to pass. The first officer who saw us swung his baton in our direction to intimidate us. My friend Shokat and I continued to walk through them hand in hand.

"Did you hear what he said?" Shokat asked. "He said our faces are like penises."

"Whores," said another one of the officers, looking directly at us.

"Monkeys," two others said in chorus.

"Don't say anything," said another, scolding his fellow officers. I looked down and saw that they were aiming lasers at us.

The security forces use lasers to target protesters and communicate commands to us and each other. Red signals officers to arrest the protester; green serves as a warning, such as for scaring women into wearing hijabs or leaving the street. Blue signals officers to shoot at protesters with paintballs and bullets. The officers aimed green lasers at us until we made our way farther down to 16 Azar Street, but we continued on our path, not showing any fear until we reached Enghelab Street. With a kind of stadium rhythm, both women and men chanted together, "Put your colorful laser in your ass, in your ass."

On South Palestine Street, a squad of riot police passed us. They looked like ninjas dressed in thick black vests and arm and knee pads. One of them passed us and held out his hand as if to open his fist to us.

"Pussy," he said suggestively.

This is the way that the Islamic Republic sees us women, as "pussies" for their sexual pleasure and procreation.

We went back to the other side of 16 Azar Street to a friend's bookstore to rest and use the bathroom. We often went there during protests whenever we needed to recharge or to store our belongings. A fresh blood trail was on the ground, left on the fallen autumn leaves of plane trees—the blood required for us to obtain our freedom. The traces of fresh blood continued for several meters down the street. In a revolutionary song called "Jîna," anonymous artists sang, "Jîna, look at the streets, they have come alive with our warm blood. Jîna, swear to your name. Jîna, the sun will rise again tomorrow." I wondered about the protester who was wounded here.

I saw an armored personnel carrier, which armies use in war, and a water cannon around Valiasr Square. As we reached the main streets from our alleys in each corner of Tehran, the security forces were standing with guns and shields. It made us feel as though we were living in an occupied country. Our homeland has been occupied by 10 percent of the population—regime supporters, and its army of various military groups, from the IRGC to the national police and the riot police squads. We, the majority of the population, are held hostage by them. But, at the same time, the security forces' presence made me feel powerful: It showed that the regime feared us. It was trying to intimidate us with guns and all kinds of suppression tools, from UK-made tear gas to this weird, armored tank.

The mosque perched above Enghelab Square is the headquarters of the riot police, the IRGC, and the Basij. This is the role of mosques these days, to serve as makeshift bases in the middle of our streets. "People who are arrested here are first taken into this mosque," Shokat told me.

"This is their version of Islam. This is how they see their house of God," I replied. Opposite the mosque, on the east side of the square, security forces were ready to arrest people. There were large transport trucks waiting to cart people away to prisons. From where we were standing, we could see inside one of the transport trucks. Some of our own people had been arrested and were seated in the back. We began to sing one of the revolutionary songs:

> *Hand in hand, we become the sea.*
> *We become a storm.*
> *Hand in hand, firm fists, we shout freedom.*
> *Oh, oh, Woman, Life, Freedom.*

At another protest, I was wearing a black dress with an open neckline, and I did not have on any kind of hijab. My friend Narges said she was inspired by my exposed boobs and by my not giving a shit about riot police. I never thought my boobs would encourage someone. A police commander shouted, "We have nothing to do with hijab, but are you not cold?" I shouted with a kind of joy and grimace, "No!" A line in another revolutionary song goes, "My hair is like a fire on a mullah's robe." We did not need their forced coverings to keep ourselves warm; our energy and resistance provided all the warmth we needed.

Two girls wearing T-shirts and shorts came out into the cold from a nearby building. One of them had finely braided long hair. In the first one's fist was a chocolate and a note that read, "Continue." She slipped it into my hand as we passed each other. I read the note immediately and said, "For sure," as we hugged. Then two LGBTQ+ young men with beautiful makeup and T-shirts displaying the Pride flag bumped their fists to ours. They left notes in our palms: "You're beautiful, your hair too." I replied, "You are more so."

They had brought beauty to Enghelab Street. Shokat said, "They have audacity. If they were to get caught, they could be charged with the death penalty." She's right; being queer and LGBTQ+ in this society is punishable by execution according to the law. In the past, we did not see LGBTQ+ people in the street during the daytime; they mostly just went out at night. It seemed as if all of us had been in hiding and had avoided being in public until Jina brought all of us out into the streets. It was our great reclamation of the streets and the public places so long denied to us. Just being there was a political act of great significance and daring. Passing the IRGC and riot police security forces countless times, unveiled, sends the message: "We are not afraid of you. Witness our solidarity." It's a demonstration in itself; we do not even need to chant a slogan.

On another day, a tiny young woman, about thirty, wearing a cap and long earrings and with big eyes and a pointed nose, faced us, none of us wearing a hijab, and asked, "Guys, do I look suspicious?" We laughed and said, "Do *we* look suspicious?" She answered, "I was released from prison two weeks ago. I was pardoned. In a protest, I beat the police, but the judge looked at my teeny appearance and denied my crime. It was a waste for them to accept that I beat their agent, but I did. I hit him. I kicked the first one and said, 'This is for Nika.' I kicked the second one and said, 'This is for Sarina.' I hit the third one and said, 'And this is for me, thirty years old and unemployed.'" When we said goodbye, I told her to take care of herself and she echoed the same back to us. Shokat said, "This is for me, thirty-four years old and unemployed." And I said, "This is for me, thirty-seven years old and unemployed." We both laughed when Shokat pointed out that I was unemployed despite earning two master's degrees, one from a university in the United States.

An old Basij man stopped us and asked me to open my backpack. I had bought ten grams of marijuana but had not told Shokat. I pretended that I was going to open the zipper and kept myself calm. The smell of weed wafted out. Shokat looked at me in shock and could not believe that I had dared to go to a protest with marijuana. Suddenly a young woman screamed ahead of us, and the officer became distracted and focused his attention on the noise. We silently and quickly turned from the sidewalk to the street and sprinted off.

At the end of Vesal Street, we reached the young woman who had saved us. Her name was Mehrnaz. Her bangs were short and blond, she had elongated eyes, and her hair was black and bare. She had a piece of cloth tied in her hair. She was twenty-three years old, wearing a black hoodie and black linen pants. Her face and eyes were burning and inflamed from the pepper spray that the security officer had sprayed at her face, and this pain was the reason for her having screamed.

"You know you saved our lives. We were caught, you screamed, and we ran away," I told her. It made her laugh through the pain and burning sensation she was feeling.

Mehrnaz said, "The officer swore at me and called me a dog! I went up to his face and said, 'What are you saying?' Suddenly he sprayed pepper in my eyes and face." A fruit juice seller gave Mehrnaz ice in a paste to lessen the burning and soothe her eyes. She asked if we would walk with her. We looked at each other and said yes without any hesitation, continuing forward as a group.

Mehrnaz was with a friend named Negar, whom she had met at a protest the day Negar was hit by a paintball bullet. Negar tapped the front of her denim jacket and showed us the color the paintball left on her jeans next to her vagina, and said, "I'm bruised, look where they hit me." Mehrnaz responded, "Yes, if they killed us, they would say that we were prostitutes and died because of being bitten during sex."

Mehrnaz studied theater and used to be an actress but left that vocation due to the extreme restrictions placed on the field in recent years. As hard-liners gained increasing power in Iran after the 2020 presidential and parliamentary elections, they put more restrictions on all artistic fields, which meant that there were ever-diminishing opportunities for independent artists like Mehrnaz to work. Negar, twenty-five at the time, used to come to Tehran from Gohardasht, Karaj, a suburb in the west of Tehran, every day at five in the morning. People like Negar who cannot afford to rent a place in Tehran anymore move to the suburbs. She worked in a beauty clinic in the north of Tehran. She had a beautiful and innocent face, long eyelashes, an upturned nose, and slightly big lips. She was angry that the security forces called her small and weak. Negar advised Mehrnaz not to fight the forces: "We must be smart. We have to survive out here. We need each other."

They told Shokat and me that they had been on the street every day for the past forty days. Negar usually came straight from work wearing a uniform that showed the logo of her workplace on the corner of her collar. "I come to Tehran at 5:00 a.m. and return home at 11:00 p.m. to be able to protest each evening, but it's worth it," Negar told me. Even though people are not technically allowed to gather, Enghelab Street is crowded with young women without hijabs. Negar said that one day a plainclothes officer caught her alone in Daneshgah Street and waved his baton in front of her, saying, "I'll rape you." She was scared and kept silent until he got tired of terrifying her and left.

As we walked, Mehrnaz invited another young couple to team up with us. The girl was petite; she did not wear a hijab at all. She had short curly hair and a nose piercing. The boy was wearing a green overcoat and had long light hair, and they were holding hands. Now there were six of us.

Mehrnaz suggested we sing "Baraye" by Shervin Hajipour, which was the most popular song of the Woman, Life, Freedom movement. "People will join in," she said. We decided to go to Daneshjoo Park, a fifteen-minute walk from Enghelab Square, sit down, and sing the song while riot police with shields and military uniforms stood no more than sixty feet from us. On the outer edge of the platforms facing the street, ordinary people were sitting down. We sat on the circular platform in between the officers and the people. Shokat suggested we wear a mask, but I didn't have one. The disappointment on her face was visible. Still, we began singing until we reached the line "for students, for the future":

> *For dancing in the alley,*
> *For the fear when we kiss*
> *For my sister, your sister, our sisters*
> *For changing rusted minds,*
> *For being shamed, for poverty,*
> *For the regret of a normal life*
> *For the child laborer who seeks the garbage and their dreams*
> *For this commanded economy*

For this polluted air
For Valiasr Street and the withered trees
....
For the forbidden innocent dogs
For the endless sadness
For the image of repetition of this moment
For a smiling face
For students, for the future.

Before we could finish the song, an old IRGC officer came up to us and, filming our faces, told us to "get lost."

During another protest, Shokat and I went to the bookstore owned by our mutual friend near Enghelab Street. Bahman, the bookstore owner and a former BBC journalist like me, told us that he had been summoned to an interrogation session in Espinas Palace Hotel the day before, where they asked him if he was willing to have lunch with the interrogators. "Vegetable rice and fish, the food that is used in the slogan whose second part is Motherfucker IRGC," he told them. Mona, a mutual friend who often played revolutionary songs out of a speaker in her backpack on the subway, mused that there should be a study on why there are so many names of foods in protest slogans. I do not think we need studies. All the foods named in protest chants and slogans have been removed from families' tables in recent years due to rising inflation and the cost of food—meat, chicken, eggs, fruits, milk, and more. At my lawyer's recommendation, I had always rejected interrogators' offer of having food with them, but now I think that Bahman's response was great.

Bahman and other friends in the bookstore would call us "the guerrillas of Enghelab Street." They told Shokat and me that we had revolution in our eyes. When there was a call to protest and we did not come to the bookstore, they got worried. Nafiseh, an employee, asked Shokat and me to go to different places to protest to decrease the risk of being recognized and arrested. We answered jokingly, playing with words in Farsi.

"No, we will go to the same place every day," I said through a laugh.

"I get it," said Nafiseh. "Your strategy is not giving a fuck about the security forces."

I met Amir Ali, a thirty-one-year-old, at a protest. He told me that he and his sister write slogans on the city's walls each night. Shokat and I went with them the night after we met; Amir Ali and I tried to look after Shokat and his sister Bahareh, a twenty-eight-year-old and a bank employee. Sina, Amir's friend, sat in the car with his wife and one-year-old child so that if any security officers appeared, we could get in the car and escape. Shokat wrote on a wall, "IRGC you are ISIS, you should be disarmed." By the time Shokat had finished writing, Bahareh had written on all the walls in the vicinity. She was so fast and professional. Toward the end of the night, Shokat wanted to write something in Bahar Shiraz Square, but the landlord of the building we were eyeing suddenly arrived with his wife and daughter. He told us not to bother writing anything. Every night that protesters had written something, officers would arrive and clean the graffiti the next morning. He entered his home, and after he was gone, his daughter and wife told Shokat to ignore him and write whatever she liked. Shokat again wrote, "IRGC you are ISIS, you should be disarmed." We arrived home happy about the result, but we did not take any pictures due to security concerns, so this time I had no photos to send to Nilo.

NILO

FOR CONTINUOUS CRYING

C IVIL SOCIETY has been quashed into nonexistence in Iran. The country's brightest minds who once tracked the state's human rights offenses are lining the cells and windowless rooms of solitary confinement, languishing in Iran's prisons. Journalists in the country were being snatched up right alongside them, giving Iran the unfortunate notoriety of being the world's third biggest jailer of journalists. Fatemeh told me that journalists and activists refer to Evin Prison as Evin University. Those who are lucky enough to eventually leave come out armed with knowledge and experience learned from the people inside. The correspondents for *The New York Times* and *The Washington Post* had been kicked out of the country for a handful of years by the time that the September 2022 uprising started. There were barely any journalists for international media left, and those who were there couldn't freely report on the protests any more than the jailed domestic reporters.

When I started covering Iran in 2017, I knew that I would never be able to report from inside the country. I saw how my fellow international correspondents had been forced out and even imprisoned. Doing impactful and evidentiary-based work is impossible under the draconian state surveillance of the Islamic Republic. And this time, I finally saw that being outside the country was an advantage.

Usually, I was the first to bring up Iran-related news on my team at *The New York Times,* but after Jîna's death I was frozen in place. Three years later, the image of Jîna unconscious on a stretcher in the hospital is still imprinted in my mind. It's the only thing I can think of when I recall the early days of the movement. I'm still stuck in despair and loss with her family. The Woman, Life, Freedom uprising was something that she gave to us unwillingly—a personal tragedy that became rooted in the collective but ultimately was always hers.

When I revisit photographs taken right before her death to remember what it felt like to see it for the first time, I can linger for only a few seconds. Unconscious in her hospital bed, she looked delicate and powerless. It feels like a betrayal to see her in this state when in other videos that her community posted online in the wake of her death, we saw her smiling and dancing with her family, her long brown hair hanging straight below her shoulders. Jîna's beaming smile outlined with bright red lipstick shone—her lips matching a cherry-colored dress she wore, accented with a green floral belt of fabric wrapped over her hips. She danced the Halparke, a traditional dance rooted in unity, to Kurdish music. Waving a white cloth in her hand, Jîna was the Sarchupi, or leader, of the Halparke. In Kurdish dances, no one is at the center. People knit themselves together, shoulder to shoulder, following the Sarchupi. If only Jîna knew how much of a leader she has become to all of us. *Jîna* means "life" in the Kurdish language, and based on the fluid and free way that she moved, she was clearly a bright light.

I can't tell you exactly why, but the visual posted by Niloofar Hamedi to Twitter of Jîna's father hugging her grandmother affected me the most. He's taller than the woman he's embracing, but his face is buried in her shoulder, his back curved and his hand tightly holding on to her for support. It looks as if all his weight were on her and he would topple over if he were alone. There's no cleansing image I can look at here to take me out of this moment.

But as the protests began to spring up at the hospital, at her funeral in her hometown of Saqqez in the Kurdish region of western Iran, and then in cities, towns, and villages across the country, I started to follow along online to see how Iranians in the country were reacting. Telegram channels were posting immediate updates and sharing information about the demonstrations that were quickly building on one another. I watched these for a week before I brought anything up to co-workers or editors at *The New York Times*.

I had not covered Iran for more than two years, after a tragic incident in January 2020 made it difficult for me to continue. On January 11, 2020, the IRGC shot down a civilian airliner, killing all passengers and crew aboard, during a period of heightened tension between Iran and the United States. I knew people on that plane, and any coverage related to Iran felt emotionally untenable during that moment. In my time away from reporting on Iran, I had started using a relatively new reporting tool called open-source intelligence, or OSINT, for investigative journalism that centers on accountability. I and many journalists who do this kind of reporting, which originated in the intelligence community, don't like the term "OSINT" because of its ties to intelligence agencies—bodies that many of us often investigate for misappropriating these same tools. But OSINT can be valuable for its emphasis on accountability and using openly available source material, such as videos filmed by eyewitnesses or satellite imagery, to bring new details to a story.

Human rights organizations such as Amnesty International, Human Rights Watch, and the Human Rights Center at UC Berkeley have been pioneering in their use of OSINT for documenting crimes against humanity. And nontraditional groups have led the way in developing OSINT approaches in investigations, such as Bellingcat, an investigative team specializing in fact-checking and OSINT, and Storyful, a news agency that verifies user-generated content from social media. My colleagues on the Visual Investigations team at *The New*

York Times took the lead on this type of reporting in a traditional newsroom, thanks to the work of journalists like Malachy Browne, Haley Willis, Christiaan Triebert, Christoph Koettl, and Barbara Marcolini. In fact, many of these teammates came from Bellingcat, Storyful, and human rights organizations.

I watched my colleagues use OSINT in their investigation into the IRGC's missile strike on Ukraine International Airlines, which was the first piece of reporting that was able to show definitive visual proof of these missiles being launched from an Iranian military site. I was lucky to learn from my colleagues and apply these methods to covering protest movements where I analyzed police use of force in Chile, Colombia, and the United States. And in June 2020, my colleagues and I reported on the Black Lives Matter protests, focusing on a single incident in Philadelphia. Our investigation revealed that the Philadelphia Police Department violated use-of-force guidelines in how it deployed tear gas on protesters. A traditional video or text story might have built the narrative around eyewitness testimony or described the overall protest movement. But this relatively new storytelling format used videos from the ground as pieces of evidence to analyze the police department's use of force.

When the protests began in Iran in September 2022, I knew that OSINT would be the best reporting method to analyze how Iran's security and intelligence forces were using deadly force to try to suppress their own people. The lack of access for journalists to Iran meant that there are few other ways to report on this movement. And with news organizations increasingly getting kicked out of authoritarian countries like Russia and China, this reporting method will become even more vital in the years to come.

The Islamic Republic regularly downplays its human rights violations. Even today, it still denies that Jina was killed by the morality police. OSINT as a reporting method could verify incidents that the government continues to disavow, leaving an irrefutable official account of news events. I went to the Islamic Republic for comment on every investigation that I worked on by contacting its Permanent

Mission to the United Nations. I never received any official statement from the government on any of my reporting.

As I monitored social media for what was going on in Iran in September 2022 and the months that followed, I saw countless videos of plainclothes officers on motorbikes firing handguns into crowds, and uniformed IRGC and national police using violence to contain mourners at ceremonies for people killed by the state while protesting. If I could verify these pieces of visual evidence, then I could find out exactly which security units and intelligence officers were using violence to crack down on civilians and reveal new details with eyewitness testimony. Perhaps one day these investigations could themselves turn into evidence of the Islamic Republic's crimes. Most urgently, verifying these horrific violent events would tell Iranians in the country that we're paying attention.

FATEMEH

FOR MY SISTER, YOUR SISTER, OUR SISTERS

As protests escalated, in October 2022 the Ministry of Intelligence of the Islamic Republic and the Intelligence Organization of the IRGC issued a joint statement accusing the journalists Niloofar Hamedi and Elaheh Mohammadi of espionage. The two agencies claimed the women were guilty of "collaboration with an adversary country, assembly and collusion against national security, and propaganda against the regime"—charges that could mean ten to fifteen years in prison. This was the Islamic Republic's revenge. With the nation on edge, these two warring factions of fascism finally agreed on something: the lives of Niloofar and Elaheh. Elaheh was arrested a little more than a week after publishing her report about Jîna's funeral and has been detained ever since. She hasn't been granted a single day of leave. Like Elaheh, Niloofar was arrested and remains imprisoned.

On December 19, 2022, I read that Elaheh and Niloofar were being transferred from Evin to Qarchak Prison, which is known as a real hell. It has no windows, only poor quality and salty drinking water, and no warm food or kitchen to prepare meals. Guards close and lock the ward doors at 5:00 p.m., after which the imprisoned women are not allowed out. Niloofar's husband wrote that in Qarchak Prison, Elaheh and Niloofar could see outside only from one small hole in the wall. They used to watch the moon and sky through this hole, taking turns throughout the night. For months, they were held in a room in which the lights could not be switched off.

Saba Sherdost, a former political prisoner in Evin Prison who was detained during the early months of the protests, ended up in the same solitary cell in which Elaheh was held in Evin Prison. "In all that enduring loneliness, the only thing that felt like the presence of another person's soul was Elaheh's writings on the wall. 'Be strong. Don't be afraid. These days will pass,'" Sherdost wrote on Twitter. Elaheh's words were a kind of encouragement in the darkest place in the world, the walls of which cannot contain Elaheh's strength. Her words and experience remind me of the scene in *The Handmaid's Tale* in which a handmaid discovers a sentence on the wall of her closet left behind by the room's previous resident. Written in mock Latin was "Nolite te bastardes carborundorum," which translates to "Don't let the bastards grind you down." Elaheh was sending a similar message to women who would later step into her cell, and I would like to say the same to her: Don't let the bastards grind you down, my dear Elaheh.

During a phone call to her husband, Mohamad Hosein, Niloofar read a poem by Sherko Bekas, the Kurdish poet. Mohamad recorded her voice and published it on his Instagram and Twitter accounts:

> *If within my poems*
> *You take out the flower from the four seasons,*
> *One of my seasons will die,*
> *If you exclude love,*
> *Two of my seasons will die,*
> *If you exclude bread,*
> *Three of my seasons will die,*
> *And if you take away freedom,*
> *All four seasons and I will die.*

In another phone call, Niloofar told a mutual friend, Nahid, "Elaheh and I were sad to have missed out on the street protests. When we were in Qarchak Prison and young girls were being taken in with bruised bodies and telling us where they had been arrested and what had happened, we regretted missing having been on the streets during the protests." Her words remind me of my interview with a student activist who was arrested in the first days of the uprising. He joked that he and the other detainees of the first days were like football teams dropped from the first round. He and the other protesters missed the semifinals and finals of Jîna's movement after being part of putting it in the global spotlight.

Mohammad, Niloofar's husband, wrote for Niloofar: "You call in the morning. Every day when I wake up, I stare at my phone, wait for your call, and hear your voice. It's just important to hear your voice. But at night, the night is long. You have no right to call again at night. You call to say good night every day at four o'clock in the afternoon, the last call of the day. After that, my day is over. I will wake up again tomorrow morning with the joy and excitement of hearing your voice."

On December 17, 2022, Taraneh Alidoosti, a famous Iranian actress, another friend and sister, was also arrested for her support of the Woman, Life, Freedom movement. The regime picked her up at her home after she published a post on her Instagram account protesting the execution of Mohsen Shekari, a young gamer and protester who was executed by the Islamic Republic. Taraneh had also posted a photo of herself without a hijab holding a handwritten sign that read "Woman, Life, Freedom" in the original Kurdish—*Jin, Jîyan, Azadî*, ژن، ژیان، ئازادی—an act of solidarity that showed her commitment to minority rights. There was a beautiful contrast between the flowing locks of her black hair and the floral white curtains behind her.

Taraneh was widely known for her role in *The Salesman*, which won best foreign film in the 2017 Oscars, so her arrest made international headlines. Many foreign film festivals released statements in solidarity. Despite the outpouring of support, Western media published pictures of women like Taraneh, who were on the front lines of fighting against compulsory hijab laws, wearing head coverings. It was the antithesis of the women's stated values and beliefs.

Taraneh is more than an actor for my people and her nation. She is a symbol of resistance, standing up against oppression, saying no to the regime, and fighting against the Islamic Republic and patriarchy. She represents my generation. Taraneh launched the #MeToo movement in Iranian cinema by initiating a petition that was signed by eight hundred women in the movie industry demanding a workplace free from sexual harassment and assault; many actresses opened up about horrible experiences of being raped or sexually assaulted by Iranian men, including actors and directors.

Throughout her career, Taraneh evolved from the calm and determined girl she depicted in her first role, *I Am Taraneh, 15 Years Old*, which had earned her a best actress award in Iran before she turned eighteen, to the role of the disobedient and rebellious Leila, in the 2022 movie *Leila's Brothers*. In *Leila's Brothers*, Leila does not have a husband. She is not even in love. She is busy supporting her family and brothers and is the only person in her family who stands up to her father and strikes a blow against patriarchy by slapping her father's face. For many, the father character was a symbol of the patriarchy, reminiscent of the supreme leader, Khamenei. After her arrest, both of her recent films, *Leila's Brothers* and *Eureka,* were banned.

Taraneh and Mina, the journalist and documentary filmmaker in whose home Taraneh had posed for the photo without a hijab, thought that if they published their photos at the same time, other actors would join them, and the collective attention would protect them from being arrested. After they published their photos, they turned off their mobile phones and went into hiding. They did this so the posts would be seen as widely as possible and security agents would be unable to arrest them and force them to delete their posts. Thirty actresses did join them in protest, but the collective action did not stop them from being targeted.

After two weeks off the grid, the two women turned on their mobile phones and returned to their homes. We thought they had been spared. Lawyers always tell us that the worst kind of arrest is the one that occurs as one enters or leaves the house, because the person does not expect it and is taken by surprise in what should be a safe space. They advise us—journalists, feminists, activists, actresses, and anyone else at risk of being arrested by security forces—to delete all the chat logs from our social media accounts and applications from our phones before going out so that if we are caught, there will be less evidence to use against us. Arrests can happen at any moment, during the night or day.

When officers arrived at Taraneh's house to arrest her, she was in her car about to leave. She locked the doors and calmly deleted her chats and social media accounts while the IRGC intelligence officers were banging on the windows. I thought that the Islamic Republic was so rational that it would not be willing to pay the price of arresting a super celebrity like Taraneh, but I was wrong again. I apologize, Taraneh, we were too optimistic. Taraneh was arrested while Hana, her eight-year-old daughter, was at home. Taraneh always said that she hoped they would be human enough to come to arrest her at a time when Hana would be at school, but the child's presence did not make a difference to the security forces. They locked Taraneh in one room with a female agent and her daughter in another room while they searched the whole house.

It is easy for the Islamic Republic to turn all our nightmares into reality, but we stay alive through our dreams. After Taraneh was arrested, Mina and all her friends and family members stood outside the walls of Evin Prison in snowy northern Tehran to call for her temporary release. The answer in the first days was, "Her case has not been completed." This meant that she was still under interrogation in those dirty and dark rooms, blindfolded and handcuffed, sitting on cold iron chairs facing the wall.

Despite these horrors, images and videos shared of martyrs and others who were suffering under the thumb of the regime emphasized the joyful, rebellious lives they lived. Dancing featured heavily in many videos circulated of those killed by the Islamic Republic, like Jîna's Kurdish dances and the hip-hop dances of Nika Shahkarami, the sixteen-year-old who died in the first days of the movement. Dancing is a forbidden part of Iranian society and banned according to Islam. It is never broadcast on the Islamic Republic's TV channels. Now these young people are memorialized in our hearts and minds as beautiful dancers.

Khodanur Lojei was one of a hundred people who lost their lives in a bloody massacre in Zahedan, home to the Baluchi minority group, during the Woman, Life, Freedom protests. Khodanur was shot in his kidney. As he pleaded to be taken to the hospital, he said, "My mother and seven sisters have no one but me." His friends took him to the hospital, but the medical staff refused to treat him, and he died the day after, on his twenty-seventh birthday. After he passed away, videos of his Baluchi dance went viral. His dancing was stunning and free, like the meaning of his name—*Khoda* means "God" in Farsi, and *Noor* implies light. For me, this revolution is the revolution of dancing martyrs. In the capital, a protester wrote a graffiti message on a wall in his honor: "God is Khodanour, God is Jîna, God is the end of these endless nights."

NILO

FOR THE WOUNDS OF BALUCHESTAN

WHILE THIS WAS a women-led movement, sparked by Jîna's unjust death, the uprisings swiftly grew to encompass more than just women's rights under the Islamic Republic. Iranians overall, along with oppressed ethnic minorities, took to the streets to demand the end of this dictatorship and protest the conditions of their oppression. "What's powerful with this cycle is how the issue is a crosscutting matter for all walks of life and all ethnic backgrounds in the country," Reza H. Akbari, a program manager for the Middle East and North Africa at the Institute for War and Peace Reporting, told me when we were looking at videos of Kurdish-language protest chants in Tehran. That Jîna was an ethnic minority placed the movement, *her* movement, at the intersection of various social issues.

Iran's ethnic minority groups often organized around systemic state discrimination against their language and religion, along with being denied the right to political organization. But local ethno-political organizations that would advocate for the rights of ethnic minorities were barred, with members often rounded up, jailed, and even executed over time on unjustified charges of terrorism or other harmful actions against the Islamic Republic. The nationwide protests of 2022 galvanized communities that had been systemically silenced and brought a new solidarity between far-flung regions in Iran. Kurdistan in the northwest found ties to Baluchestan in the southeast, and even widespread support in the primarily Persian-speaking capital of Tehran. And the deadliest single day for Iranian protesters in the Woman, Life, Freedom uprising was not in Tehran but in the most marginalized, impoverished, and systematically neglected region of Iran: Zahedan, the capital of the southeastern Sistan and Baluchestan province near the borders of Afghanistan and Pakistan.

On September 30, 2022, Baluchis—a minority group made up of Sunni Muslims with their own language, customs, and dress—took to the streets in solidarity with Jîna, only to be gunned down. The U.S.-based Iran Human Rights Documentation Center (IHRDC) identified at least ninety-five people killed in the government crackdown in Zahedan. And the head of the Sistan and Baluchestan judiciary told the media on November 2, 2022, that 620 people were arrested. Baluchis make up approximately 1 to 3 percent of Iran's overall population, roughly seventy million. Many have strong tribal and family ties to other members of their community who live in bordering countries. When I interviewed Baluchi people in Zahedan and outside Iran, I noticed that they have an accent in Persian, given that it is their second language. The rhythm and cadence of their speech are faster than those of the Iranians I speak with whose first language is Persian. Being able to communicate with members of a different ethnic group, which allowed us to understand and see each other while our country was going through this chaotic upheaval, connected me more than ever to our *vatan*, our homeland. We had to promise anonymity to everyone we spoke with due to fears of government reprisals.

"There's no infrastructure. All the roads are old and date back to the Pahlavi time," one resident I interviewed told me, referring to the Pahlavi monarchy that revolutionaries overthrew decades ago. "There are no gas pipelines, so we have no gas in our homes. Schools take place in makeshift huts built with the leaves and branches of date trees.

That's where [our children] study through rain, through the devastating heat of the summer, and the cold of the winter. That is where they have to go to school."

This wasn't the first time that Zahedan or other parts of Sistan and Baluchestan saw brutal violence and mistreatment at the hands of the Islamic Republic. There's a practice known as *gozinesh* that's core to the experience of Baluchi disenfranchisement. It has also been used to discriminate against other minority groups in Iran.

Gozinesh is an ideological selection framework that requires potential state officials and employees to demonstrate an allegiance to Islam and to the Islamic Republic of Iran. Notably, they must agree to the concept of *velayat-e faqih*—a concept derived from the Twelver Shia Islamic law that forms the basis of Iran's current legal system and is based on the belief that until the reappearance of an infallible prophet, clerics must govern the social and religious affairs of Muslim people. As part of the Sunni minority, Baluchi people hold different views over the succession of the Prophet Muhammad, and as such, their mere existence comes into conflict with the Islamist Shia state.

In practice, this means that a Baluchi who wants to open a shop must go to the government and have their political beliefs thoroughly examined by the IRGC and intelligence officers. They'll be asked about what they've done for the Islamic Republic, their participation in the Iran-Iraq War, and other litmus-test-type questions to suss out their loyalty to the current system. In this line of questioning, when Baluchis say that they don't believe in the *velayat-e faqih*, because it is against their Sunni beliefs, they inevitably won't be able to get their shop permit, jobs, spots in universities, and so on. Under *gozinesh* rules, non-Shia Iranians are excluded from state positions such as the president and other high-ranking roles. In fact, no Sunni had ever held a cabinet role under the Islamic Republic until Iran's current president, Masoud Pezeshkian—himself a member of the Azeri and Kurdish minorities—appointed the first Sunni cabinet member in 2024 to be his deputy for rural development and underprivileged areas.

In 2005, an armed group known as Jundallah took eight Iranian soldiers hostage, rising to notoriety. This group is based in Sistan and Baluchestan, where it operates in Iran, and reportedly has links to bases in Pakistan. The group's leaders have referred to discrimination against Baluchis in Iran as a motivating factor for their activities. The rise of this group, which in no way reflects the activities of or receives majority support from the average Baluchi, has given the Islamic Republic a cover to suppress antigovernment movements in the region by denouncing all unrest as terrorism done by separatists and criminals aiming to destabilize Iran. The Baluchi language, along with other minority languages in Iran, is not formally recognized. Children can't be educated in their mother tongue at school, instead taught exclusively in the Persian language. These factors have fused to "other" the Baluchi people in their own homeland, leading to a series of tense standoffs with the state.

In February 1994, there were riots in Zahedan to protest the destruction of a Sunni mosque in Mashhad allegedly for city planning purposes. To quell the unrest, the IRGC fired live ammunition into the crowds. The following year, members of the IRGC seemingly displaced Baluchis after an alleged attack on the villages of Saravan and Zardkoh in the province's Iranshahr district, moving them to a desert area. On June 30, 2005, in the port city of Chabahar, Baluchi homes were reportedly demolished by security forces, rendering many homeless. The aim was to reuse this land as housing for members of the state security apparatus under a plan by the Ministry of Housing and Urban Development.

Due to the lack of economic opportunities, some residents in Sistan and Baluchestan are forced to turn to the perilous job of fuel delivery to make money. Fuel is cheaper in Iran than in neighboring Pakistan, so the way this trade works is that they go to the Pakistan border with Iranian fuel and deliver it to make a profit. But this work, known as *sookhtbar,* is dangerous. The fuel isn't prepared for transport by any industry standards when it's moved across the border by hand in this underground way, so there is a very real risk of dying in an accident from fuel explosion or being shot and killed by Iranian border guards en route. At least 168 Baluchis were killed in 2022 in the trade of cross-border fuel delivery. The systematic disintegration of the place of Baluchis in Iranian society through *gozinesh* paves the way for all of these other harmful state actions.

The indiscriminate state-sanctioned killings of September 30, 2022, became known as *jommeh-ye khoonin,* or Bloody Friday. Residents in Zahedan told me that two days before, smaller demonstrations were held in Chabahar, another city in the same province. On September 29, people began circulating messages on Telegram and other apps to call for a "broad uprising" in "all the towns of Baluchestan" as an "act of solidarity with Kurdistan and in protest of the rape of the Baluchi girl," referring to a violent assault on a fifteen-year-old girl who people said was raped by a police commander in the impoverished town. A poster was shared online with details about a planned demonstration for Friday, September 30, following the Friday prayer service, to demand accountability for these mounting instances of state violence, both in their community and with others in the country. The solidarity with Kurdistan had to do with Jîna's death and the recent protests in her home province that were met with attacks by government forces.

By around 1:00 p.m., thousands of people were in the Great Mosalla, a prayer complex across the street from Zahedan's police station. Together with my colleague Cora Engelbrecht, I set out to find people who were there that day to get a sense of the timeline of events. I interviewed eyewitnesses who told me that the mood started peacefully during the prayer service as the Sunni imam leading the service, Molavi Abdul Hamid, urged people to "maintain peace" and "control their emotions" while the rape allegation of the young girl in Chabahar was under investigation. As the prayers continued, a group of about ten to fifteen worshippers left the complex and gathered outside the police station. A video that I verified with my colleague Ishaan Jhaveri showed them throwing rocks at the station while security forces stood on the roof. We geo-located the video to confirm that it was at the police station by matching up the iron gates visible in the video with the gates of the station's roof. Geo-locating is the process of confirming where and when a video or photo was taken. It entails researching the context around a singular video by looking into what was happening before this video and matching it up with other footage of the same incident. This process is what gives us confidence in the veracity of the video. Confirming the location and then matching it up with eyewitness accounts is key to the verification process. The value of this reporting method is that it supports eyewitness testimony. It's very easy for bad actors to dismiss what people say. But if there are a handful of videos and photos that support an eyewitness's version of events, then it's much harder to dismiss. As the video from the roof of the police station continued to play, we began to hear gunshots.

To get an understanding of how the day unfolded, I reached out to Shirahmad Shirani-Naroui, who runs Haalvsh, a local human rights organization. A native of Zahedan, Shirani-Naroui documents incidents of state violence against his fellow Baluchi people. He was forced to flee Iran in 2021 due to his political activism for equal treatment of the Baluchi people and now resides in a bordering country that can't be named due to his personal security concerns. "This was a wave of nationwide protests that started over Mahsa Amini and the sadness that people felt in the wake of it. This assault was another layer that added fuel to the fire," he said to me in one of our many conversations.

Shirani-Naroui sent me dozens of pieces of visual evidence that eyewitnesses had sent Haalvsh. I spent three days sorting and cataloging the brutal violence. Because I knew what a risk it was for people to document what was unfolding, each video felt precious. This imagery was our only window into what was going on in Zahedan because no media was there that day broadcasting independently. One video that we verified showed people with their heads bowed on prayer mats as the sounds of semiautomatic and automatic gunfire pierced through the soft mumbles of prayers. One of the most important videos showed three men standing on the roof of the police station. Two appeared to be in the light green uniform of the national police while the third dressed in the traditional Baluchi clothing of *shalwar kameez*, a loose tunic over fabric pants that is worn by many different people from South Asian communities. The man dressed in *shalwar kameez* is seen firing what seems to be a pump-action shotgun in the direction of the mosque. It's impossible to verify from visuals alone whether someone is a part of a plainclothes unit or not, because we rely on established uniformed insignia to determine what unit an officer belongs to. But this man in traditional clothing firing from the police station roof was in line with eyewitness accounts of the presence of plainclothes officers shooting civilians. We were able to identify the type of gunfire thanks to audio analysis done by John Ismay, a reporter at *The New York Times* who was an explosive ordnance disposal officer in the U.S. Navy. We often went to him with questions of gunfire analysis because it helped us better understand what type of weaponry was used, which could then perhaps tell us which units were present in such incidents. Another video showed the haphazard triage and medical attention that bystanders conducted. Some of the prayer mats were used as ad hoc stretchers, transporting limp bodies with dark red blood on their limbs. I asked one eyewitness who saw the scene unfold from his nearby home why the Islamic Republic has killed Baluchi people so many times and with such apparent ease.

"It's because we don't have independent media. We're based along the border. We're very removed so [the Islamic Republic] can get away with it. We're located in one of the most remote places. Not only do we not have access to satellite networks, proper media channels, the brutality and the killings don't get any international media coverage. And this gives [the Islamic Republic] the liberty to crack down and quash any uprising," one Zahedan resident told me in an interview. "Unfortunately, they're taking advantage of our marginalization."

Documenting this horrible day in Zahedan is one of the things I am most proud of even though it was grim and personally affecting. Reporting out the story had many challenges. Beyond having to rely on intermittent internet connectivity to reach eyewitnesses, and spending hours looking at gruesome images of death and dismemberment, I was most impacted by how people I interviewed opened up to me. I asked a father who lost his son how I should describe his *pesar-e gol*, or his dear son, in our article. Using the phrase *pesar-e gol* is very familial; it requires a sense of closeness between two people to use it in conversation. I have a habit of speaking informally because I was taught to speak at home with my family. Instead of being ashamed as I often was that I couldn't speak high-level, educated, formal Persian,

I found that the intimacy here seemed to resonate with the eyewitnesses to whom I spoke. The father paused for a moment. His voice strained as he insisted several times that his son, Rafeh Naroohi, who was twenty-five years old when he was killed, was *bi-gonah,* completely innocent and without any sin.

The experts we interviewed for our story highlighted a pattern of how the Islamic Republic targets minority groups during nationwide periods of unrest. "This shooting to kill—it's the same playbook," said Hadi Ghaemi, the executive director of the Center for Human Rights in Iran. He referred to the 2019 incident in Mahshahr, where the IRGC carried out a similarly brutal crackdown when they surrounded, shot, and killed forty to a hundred demonstrators seeking refuge in a marsh in the southwestern city of Bandar-e Mahshahr. These people were predominantly ethnically Arab, another minority group in Iran. Our "Bloody Friday" story was published on the front page of the newspaper and was shared thousands of times online, even being translated and reposted in Telegram channels in Iran, meaning that it reached people inside the country.

"The people of Tabriz have common pains with us," commented one person from Zahedan who wrote to me after the story. He knew what town my family is from because it is woven into my last name: Tabrizy translates to "from Tabriz." I had never experienced a moment of cross-ethnic solidarity or been seen first by my hometown heritage. It was a uniquely moving and heartbreaking moment to be seen so specifically during tragedy while also finding community because of my work.

FATEMEH

FOR DEFENSELESS BODIES AND LIVES

O N DECEMBER 6, 2022, I took a ride on a motorbike to Enghelab Street. As the driver made his way toward Valiasr Street, I saw that all the shops were shuttered. It was the same scene on Palestine Street; the shopkeepers were striking. Protesters hacked *Fars Bulletin,* an internal communications newsletter used by the IRGC to communicate with high-ranking regime officials, and published widely a memo confirming that close to 100 percent of stores were on strike in Tehran and Kurdistan. In other provinces, like Fars, the rate had reached 90 percent. It was a revolutionary civilian protest. The Islamic Republic had lost a stronghold of support in the bazaar merchants, longtime supporters who had lost faith in the regime due to its corruption and the disastrous economic situation.

After the first day, I realized that the simultaneity of strikes and protests escalated tensions and violence, because there were no open shops where we could take shelter. There were more people on the streets, and security forces no longer distinguished between protesters and pedestrians, shooting and arresting people indiscriminately. In the following days, we got used to seeing broken shopwindows that had been struck by bullets. Many shop owners placed pieces of iron or steel in front of their broken and repaired windows and, once the stores reopened, started restricting sales to be safe and hiding and covering their stores' classy windows with wood and iron pieces. The atmosphere of the streets and appearance of the shops reminded me of photos taken during the Iran-Iraq War. Nothing felt normal anymore.

We headed to 16th Azar Street to have a rest. Shokat saw a plastic bullet on the ground and wanted to pick it up before realizing, based on where it fell, that it must have been shot from behind us. Shokat turned around, and I did too. Riot police were jumping off their motorcycles and running toward us as if we were dangerous criminals. Shokat wanted to escape, but I grabbed her hand tightly and calmly told her to stay put. It was my instinct at that moment to respond as one would when encountering a wild animal. You have to stare into its eyes. You should not show fear. I thought that if we ran, they would surely shoot us. We stood in place and stared at the officers. They stopped and stood in place too. Three middle-aged and young women with headscarves were in front of us. One asked the security forces, "What's wrong? We're just passing by. What's your problem?" The officers were convinced that we were not protesters, ignored us, and left. The woman turned back and laughed, saying, "They made a mistake. We came to protest too." Not a single strand of her hair was visible because she was fairly religious.

A crowd was standing outside a pharmacy. A group of youths heading back toward the top of 16th Azar Street from Enghelab Street said, "Don't go. They won't let you go to Enghelab Street. Also, they've thrown a lot of tear gas." Three unveiled young women laughingly said, "Are you trying to scare us with a little tear gas?" They headed toward Enghelab Street, and we followed them. Some plainclothes security forces were filming the protests, and one of the young women showed a peace sign with her fingers to their camera to humiliate them. Another one said, "Please broadcast this on the *20:30* news bulletin, thank you!" *20:30* is the name of a program on state TV channel 2 that usually displays forced confessions. My generation used to hide their faces from security cameras, but this new generation humiliates them by showing victory signs right to their faces.

On December 7, Enghelab Street was more crowded with protesters than I had ever seen. There were so many of us that the view ahead was obscured by a mass of black from the protesters walking down the sidewalk.

We hadn't gone far when a group of guards started shooting at the sidewalk from the high-speed bus lane. We quickly took shelter behind a newsstand. Pedestrians and protesters who were walking in silence were shot—young, old, women, and children. It didn't matter if you were just walking on the street or coming to buy a book or attending a protest, they would shoot at you regardless. Before reaching Enghelab Square, a crowd was coming toward Valiasr and the crossroads. A man on the phone said, "Yeah, we blocked the street for some minutes until the bastards started attacking us. We are going to Valiasr Street to see what is going on." Another young boy was saying, "My back is bruised from the bullet." Shokat motioned to follow them. I said, "Yes, they seem to be chanting slogans and may be up to more." We hadn't yet reached Valiasr Street when we were ambushed again and surrounded. It was a trap. As usual, I ran into the nearest building and up the stairs to the upper floors. I ran up to the fourth floor without stopping and dragged Shokat behind me. The hall was lined with secondhand bookstores. Shokat was tired and nervous and shouted, "It is the last floor. You are going to meet God. Stop, Fatemeh, stop." The shopkeepers asked us what was wrong. "Nothing, they just attacked us," we replied breathlessly.

A young woman who had come to buy a book got scared and called her father to come pick her up. When I saw the regular customers in the entryway, I started trying to persuade Shokat to choose a book so that we could go out with it in our hands. "*The Wisdom of Life* by Arthur Schopenhauer, is that any good?" I wondered.

She shouted at me, "With books and without books, it doesn't matter to them. They will shoot anyway. Let's go." We went back to the parking lot to leave.

The shutters of the passageway were down. The riot police banged aggressively on the door, and the doorman jokingly said, "No one is here; they took me too." On our right, a young woman was sitting on the ground, a bullet had split her eyebrow open, and her face was covered in blood. She was lucky that she had not been blinded. No matter how hard they compressed the wound with a napkin, the blood flow would not stop. A young man said, "Your wound needs stitches, but don't go to the government hospital." It was common knowledge that state forces would get information on protesters in hospitals, then use it to arrest them later.

The security forces started to shoot at pedestrians again. I took shelter under a street seller's table, where a bullet missed my nose by mere centimeters. I could feel a sharp wind as it whizzed by. I sheltered from their bullets without any protection.

When we could move on, we started chanting again, "Freedom, freedom, freedom," and ran toward 16th Azar Street. Tehran University was full of security guards, because universities were the front lines of protest.

We sought refuge behind three trash bins in an alley, where we sat on the ground. Shokat asked, "Is this place safe?" I said, "I checked, there are no cameras." She replied, "I didn't mean safe for security; I meant safe for peeing." I responded, "No, the neighbors can see from the windows."

Nearby, officers arrested two young men in front of a gas station at the Vesal intersection. Some elderly women wanted to save them, so one said, "I am his mom. Let him go!" The officers responded, "If they have family, they are not here. Get lost!" Riot police were standing while the IRGC started shooting at the sidewalk and hit them too. One of them got mad, in response to which an officer shouted, "They are outrageous."

At around 7:00 p.m., the riot police fired several tear gas canisters at the sidewalk. Our eyes and the skin on our faces were burning. We could not breathe. We could not open our eyes to see, so we stood immobile, unable to escape. While we struggled to orient ourselves, pedestrians were running back and forth, moving uncontrollably and without any rhythm like zombies in a horror movie. We were trying to get to our friend's bookstore, because Elaheh had parked her car in the bookstore's yard. I thought I might die there and never reach home. The riot police charged down the sidewalk on their giant motorbikes shooting rubber bullets. I clung to two other women in the middle of the sidewalk, and we lowered our heads as the police continued to fire. My friend Elaheh instinctually shouted, "Ya Abolfazl!"—a cry of relief referencing one of the religious figures respected by Shia Muslims.

A loud voice over police speakers on a moving car boomed, "Go back to your homes. Your presence here is a threat to national security. This is the last warning."

The security forces closed off all the streets with their cars and continued to pour streams of tear gas and rubber bullets into the trapped crowd. They were firing sound grenades to scare people, and it worked—I was terrified. It was like a war, not a protest. Eventually, the air became so thick with tear gas that the crowd dispersed.

We were on the sidewalk on Enghelab Street near 16th Azar when IRGC forces suddenly came from behind us on their motorbikes and started shooting at us. One bullet hit my back. The pain was shocking. But without stopping to tend to my injury or even process what had happened, I instinctually shouted to my friends, "They are shooting; take shelter." We were on foot and had no vehicles or anything to really hide behind. We put our hands on our heads to protect our eyes. When they were gone, I found the rubber bullet that had hit me. Shokat was still cursing, "Bastards!" When I arrived home, I took photos of my bruised back and the bullet to send to Nilo. I told her I had been hit by a bullet, but I am fine, no worries, I am proud of it. A black plastic bullet the size of a thumbnail used to blind protesters was my share of our revolution, my homeland.

NILO

FOR THE IMPRISONED INTELLECTUALS

WHEN WE PUBLISHED our "Bloody Friday" story in mid-October 2022, street protests were still going strong. The citizen journalist Telegram channels kept publishing videos showing what the demonstrations looked like and how the crackdown was evolving. We started to see videos that seemed to show ambulances being used by security forces to arrest people at demonstrations—using these vehicles, which are supposed to be neutral and for medical purposes only, as a sort of Trojan horse. Beyond this feeling plainly wrong, I researched international human rights law to see if this misuse of ambulances violated anything that we could point to accountability-wise. There wasn't any international law for using ambulances in this way during a civil conflict, but experts we spoke with said that this violated international norms of impartiality. And with protests continuing at a consistent tempo, taking place in various cities and towns across the country, this showed the lengths to which the Islamic Republic was going to stamp out nationwide demonstrations. "People are going to be afraid to seek health care, meaning more people will die," said Rohini Haar, an assistant adjunct professor at the School of Public Health at UC Berkeley. "Health care has credibility because of the idea of impartiality. It's the basic idea of 'do no harm,' and misusing ambulances clearly violates that." When I shared this investigation with Jason Rezaian, who was the last Iran-based correspondent for *The Washington Post* before he was arrested and held for 544 days, he told me that the state used ambulances to transport him from Evin Prison to the Islamic Revolutionary Court.

My colleague Ishaan and I began downloading, archiving, and reviewing dozens of videos and images of ambulances near protests. We learned that the visuals were from incidents in Tehran and Rasht, a populous coastal city in northwest Iran that sits just below the Caspian Sea in Gilan province. I set out to see if I could find eyewitnesses to fill in the gaps of what we were seeing in video. Compared with other periods of national unrest, it was easier to find eyewitnesses this time. Iranians that I spoke with seemed to be bolder than ever. Still, most spoke on the condition of anonymity because Iran's security state is exceptionally skilled at tracking down and arresting people who speak with journalists, especially Western media. I put out calls on my Instagram and had my friends ask their networks of people they knew were protesting in Tehran and Rasht to find eyewitnesses. I was put in touch with a university student in Tehran named Niki who wanted to be identified only by her first name. I conducted most of my interviews with voice notes. The government was still jamming the internet then, and communicating in voice notes instead of calls meant that our audio would cut out less. Voice notes also gave people in Iran time to respond whenever they had good internet connectivity. I was able to conduct interviews in Persian while taking my time translating responses into English.

"As I'm sending you this voice note, I'm at home. I don't know if you can hear it, but the sound of the ambulances and fire trucks never stops. They use the fire trucks for this purpose too, but more so the ambulances," Niki said. I could hear the wails of the sirens clearly, a relentless soundtrack of screeches. There was barely any silence, and Niki was constantly speaking over them as she described what she saw in Tehran during the early weeks of the uprising. "There they grabbed people in the first few days of the protests. They put them in the ambulance, turned off the lights. There were lots of people in the back, and then they went down Valiasr [Street]. I didn't see where they dropped people off, but I saw that there were civilians inside, like young girls."

One particularly brutal day of protests unfolded on October 2, 2022, at Sharif University, an extremely prestigious institution in Iran. It's one of the top schools for science, technology, engineering, and math and is often called the MIT of the country. Students had gathered at Sharif because four of their own had been summoned and arrested by the Ministry of Intelligence for their participation in demonstrations the previous week. In response, their community rose up not only to continue with the Woman, Life, Freedom movement but also to protest these arrests, which they saw as unjust and an expression of state suppression. Security forces responded to the student demonstration with tear gas and paintballs and by detaining anyone they could get their hands on. Eyewitnesses I spoke with told me that they saw plainclothes police officers whom they identified as members of the Basij forcing students into the back of an ambulance during a tense standoff in a university parking lot. "What I saw was an ambulance with no license plate in a dark alley nearby the School of Economics and Management at Sharif [University]. There was tear gas and I had a really hard time keeping my eyes open, so I just stood by for a minute or two so that I could continue to walk home. That's when I saw at least two Basijis shoving one student in the ambulance van," one eyewitness said to me in an interview. Another told me that they saw the Basij beating a student with a baton as they were curled up on the ground, leaving them covered in bruises, before shoving the student into an ambulance along with another protester and driving away.

One video that we verified shows an ambulance on fire, apparently after being targeted by protesters. Someone in the car from where the video is being filmed shouts, "They're rescuing the girls! Come out!" as they near the ambulance. Then the video shows a man wearing a light green uniform, which resembles what Iran's national police force wears, leaving the ambulance and running away from the van.

We showed this video to Afshon Ostovar, an associate professor at the Naval Postgraduate School who focuses on Iranian national security. "That definitely looks like a NAJA officer," Ostovar told me, using the English acronym for Iran's national police force. "He's not a paramedic. The uniform and firearm are dead giveaways." It's difficult to see in the blurry nighttime footage, but the firearm that Ostovar is referring to could be on the holster that's clipped to the man's back as he runs away from the ambulance.

Members of Iran's medical community voiced outrage over the misappropriation of ambulances. A video posted to Twitter on October 4, 2022, shows medical workers demonstrating outside the Razi University Hospital in Rasht. Dressed in scrubs and white lab coats, a number of health-care workers held up signs that read, "Basijis are not students," in response to their attacks on universities specifically, and "Ambulances should be used for transporting patients." Weeks later there was also a demonstration at the Mashhad Medical Society. Mashhad is a conservative religious city in the country's northeast that has historically been supportive of the Islamic Republic. There, in the building's amphitheater, a speaker read from a statement about the misuse of ambulances: "We would like it to stop in order to gain social trust."

Though Iranians had long been suspicious of the government and its security and policing forces, this co-opting of what was once a neutral service added another layer of mistrust, showing another line the government was willing to cross.

"We felt most insecure when we saw police. But we have a new level of fear unlocked. Now we feel the worst pains when we see ambulances," one Tehran protester said to me in an interview. "And every time we're stuck in traffic, now the dilemma is, what if there's a real patient in there? Or what if they're going to kill us?"

Often as journalists, we cover the worst days of a community's history and stay there for just a few moments. We covered the massacre in Zahedan, and then we moved on. When I went to *The Washington Post* in December 2022 to join the Visual Forensics team, where I could exclusively focus on OSINT reporting, I wanted to find a way to revisit

Sistan and Baluchestan. This region is chronically under-covered, as I learned through the "Bloody Friday" incident. I kept in touch with Shirahmad Shirani-Naroui as he was continuing to collect videos and document the continuing crackdowns and demonstrations across Sistan and Baluchestan. If anything, the violence that Zahedan experienced on September 30, 2022, only strengthened the resolve of the Baluchi people to keep marching in the streets. "The general population is very angry and lives pretty much under military occupation with these events," Ghaemi told me a few months later, in January 2023. "[They're] very angry at 'Bloody Friday' and the killings afterwards. It's one of the biggest centers of protests in Iran right now."

Along with my colleagues Atthar Mirza and Babak Dehghanpisheh, I analyzed more than a hundred videos and photographs of the Friday protests, interviewed eyewitnesses and human rights observers, and reviewed data collected by conflict monitoring groups for seventeen weeks of protests to look at the weekly protest activity and state crackdown following "Bloody Friday." The visual evidence we examined revealed how security forces were operating in the area—specifically how the IRGC worked alongside riot police and plainclothes agents to violently suppress the uprising by carrying out arbitrary arrests and indiscriminate beatings and, in some cases, opening fire on civilians. We were the only news organization to return to this embattled region to do a deep dive of this protest hub following the deadly day in Zahedan. I asked one of our Baluchi sources why he still took to the streets after "Bloody Friday."

"We have no future, no hope. Life has become so difficult, we think to ourselves even if we get killed here, maybe there will be a better future for our children tomorrow," he said to me in a phone call. This unnamed Zahedan resident is a fifty-three-year-old shop owner near the Makki Mosque. "We have to do something. At least we can throw a stone, chant protest slogans, scream, shout, and cry so at least a few people can hear our voice."

The videos we verified showed that the deadliest Friday protest after "Bloody Friday" occurred on November 4, 2022, in Khash, a town 110 miles south of Zahedan. Khash residents refer to that day as their own "Bloody Friday." They too were violently attacked and killed by agents of the Islamic Republic after their Friday prayer service. Haalvsh recorded at least eighteen people killed that day, including four minors. One graphic video I watched showed a chaotic hospital scene where roughly a dozen people, including two small boys, were brought in with chest, neck, and head wounds. The video showed that they were transported by other civilians in their cars, who raced up to the hospital entrance with their engines still running as they cried out for help. There appeared to be three fatalities alone in this video posted on Telegram—three people brought in completely limp and immobile on stretchers, their entire bodies covered with cloth. I was unable to independently verify what happened to them.

In Iran, it's a risk for protesters to go to the hospital with injuries because state forces often obtain the names of those who came to seek medical attention and use this information to arrest them. Sources told me that many people tend to their injuries at home and if they're lucky enough are seen by sympathetic doctors and nurses who make underground house calls. Even crueler, many Baluchi people do not have national identification cards, which are required at any health-care facility to receive medical attention. There are a few reasons for this. Some Baluchi people live in remote areas of the province, are illiterate, or never applied for these cards. And Baluchi activists have reported having their documents seized when they go to renew or apply for these identification cards as retaliation for their organizing. When the state attacks Baluchis, who are already underserved in nearly all sectors as residents in the most underdeveloped province in Iran, not having these cards becomes another barrier to the universal health care that Iran supposedly provides for all its citizens.

Beyond the grisly visuals of violence, the videos that we analyzed showed how different policing and intelligence units work together to suppress Baluchi people. We verified one video in Zahedan from Friday, November 25, 2022, that shows a man dressed in local clothing beating detainees while an armed man in tan fatigues stands by, signaling the presence of plainclothes officers that many eyewitnesses told me about. "Because we wear Baluchi traditional clothing, security forces use our clothing to blend in. The folks who were arrested, they were arrested by these security forces wearing Baluchi clothing," one eyewitness said to me in an interview. We identified the presence of the IRGC's Salman Corps, a provincial unit tasked with monitoring this region, based on their uniforms and knowledge of which IRGC unit is regularly in the area. The presence of the IRGC is "a signal that police forces and their tactics are insufficient at quelling unrest," said Afshon Ostovar, and as a result "the regime turns to more violent and militarized means."

We saw heavy weapons, such as a PKM-style machine gun mounted on a truck in Khash and a likely Kalashnikov rifle wielded by a sniper on a roof in Zahedan. These weapons fire only live ammunition, highlighting how the regime's security forces used lethal force as a crowd control measure, despite also having access to less lethal equipment such as tear gas and rubber bullets. We confirmed the accuracy of these videos by verifying the location, and the gun mounted on a truck proved particularly difficult to geo-locate. The video showed the truck on an overpass in Khash, and I naively thought to myself, Well, how many highway overpasses could there possibly be in this small town? It took three days to locate it. We were finally able to do so by matching up the peaks of the mountains in the background of the video with the topography of the area and then matching up the visible buildings in the footage with visuals of Central Al-Khalil Mosque, which was the site of many demonstrations following the Friday prayer service.

Protesters began gathering in smaller groups to avoid large crowds, which provide the state ample opportunity to spot and target them with lethal force. "Instead of shooting people, when security forces saw that the protests were intentionally dispersed throughout the city, they saw that it was harder to control them," a forty-year-old healthcare worker in Zahedan told me. He had been protesting regularly since September. In response, security forces shifted their strategy too. "They began arresting large groups of people, punishing them, charging them with waging war against God and sentencing them to death." More than a hundred Baloch protesters were arrested on January 5, 2023, in Zahedan, rounded up in a joint effort with the police and the

IRGC. Based on Haalvsh's research, Shirani-Naroui estimates that at least ten thousand Baluchi people had been detained in the past year during the uprising, adding that nearly 30 percent of those are minors.

"They're suppressing us in a different way because even they themselves realize that September 30 was a huge mistake. But their pride won't let them apologize to the people. It's kind of like the Ukrainian airliner; they hit it and immediately realized it was a mistake, but they never owned up to it," said the health-care worker. "Now that they're changing their tactics, it's not because of mercy. It's just another way of pressuring people to not protest and to instill fear in them."

In the first few weeks of my new job at *The Washington Post*, while I was reporting out this story, my senior producer and editor, Elyse Samuels, asked me what it was like covering Iran. "I imagine it must be challenging but also purposeful and meaningful for you. You know, you don't always have to cover Iran and you can take a break on it whenever you need." It was the first time that an editor had brought up something like this, and it opened a door for me to be honest about what I needed. This new reporting environment allowed me to create some mental space for myself. I had my editors' support to build in breaks while reporting on Iran.

I told Shirani-Naroui that I was going to write about my Sistan and Baluchestan reporting in the book and that I wanted to ask him more questions about how things had developed over the past year. Whenever we speak on the phone, he often throws in some Azeri words in conversation, the language that my father was brought up with as a member of the Azeri ethnic group. My mother learned this language from my father's family, and my parents still speak Azeri together. I, of course, can't understand anything. All I've learned from my family is *yokh*, meaning "no," and *yashasin Tabriz*, or "long live Tabriz." Years ago, Shirani-Naroui was imprisoned in Tabriz for his political activism, and he learned my lost language from his fellow inmates. I told him once that I hope to return to Tabriz to learn Azeri, and Shirani-Naroui responded with emphatic optimism that both of us would be able to return to our homeland one day. As always, I thanked him for putting me in touch with eyewitnesses and for archiving all the visuals that were key to our reporting. Covering Sistan and Baluchestan without Shirani-Naroui as a source would be nearly impossible. Beyond his documentation work, he has the trust of the Baluchi people who speak to me only because of their respect for him and Haalvsh.

"I hope one day we can do a story that's joyful and as beautiful as Zahedan, instead of focusing on the tragedy of your hometown," I said to him.

"No, Khanum-e Tabrizy, it's even more important that we tell people of the realities of the Baloch people," he responded, addressing me with the formal *Khanum* for Ms. or Mrs., while I always use *Aghah*, or Mr., when speaking with him. "The people of Zahedan and Baluchestan know that you feel their pain, you hear their voices, and that you will tell the world of what happened to them."

FATEMEH

FOR NIKA AND THE MOON

O mother, O mother, it is wartime
My cartridge train is full of cartridges
Take my corpse to my mother and hold my mourning ceremony
Oh, my love, dress in black,
Take my corpse so that the enemy will not see it
Who would carry my body, go slowly so that my mother can see me.

A peddler sang this folklore song on a sidewalk of Enghelab Street in front of the Melli Bank building. We, the protesters caught in the rain, cried—our tears mixed with raindrops. We all sang along to this epic Luri song in memory of Nika Shakarami, a teenager killed in the protests. I'm sorry, Nika. Your enemies buried your body before your mother could see it.

On September 20, 2022, sixteen-year-old Nika Shakarami tied her hair into a simple bun, lined her big black eyes with razor-thin eyeliner, put on a headscarf cut in half (skirting the mandatory hijab rule), and headed into the war on Tehran's streets. She took her thermos, a small towel, and swimming goggles to protect herself from tear gas. The night before, Nika had spoken with her aunt Atash about the protests. "Auntie, a useless death after breathing oxygen for 90 years is not worth it. Death must also have a meaning," Nika said, according to an Instagram post from her aunt. She never made it back home.

Born in Khorramabad, the capital of Lorestan province, Nika was an amateur painter and photographer who worked as a barista at a café in Enghelab Street. She belonged to the Lur people, an ethnic group of about five million dwelling in the western mountains of Iran. After she disappeared, her family looked for her in every prison, detention center, police department, and hospital. They circulated her photo on their social media accounts, hoping to find a sign of her. On September 29, the police finally told them to go to the Kahrizak morgue. When they saw her body, family members said, Nika's face was bruised nearly beyond recognition. All her teeth were broken. With her beautiful body and face mangled by violence, her family was able to identify her only by her birthmark.

Nika's final day was captured on videos that circulated on social media. In one, she stood on top of an overturned garbage bin and set her scarf on fire, fearlessly leading chants and throwing rocks. Nika could be heard yelling, "Death to the dictator!" Then, according to a CNN investigation, she was targeted and chased by security forces. During the chase, she hid behind a car at the intersection of Keshavarz Boulevard and 16th Azar Street. "Do not move, do not move," she can be heard telling the driver in a video captured by an unknown person on the street. She was hemmed in by security forces on three sides and arrested by several plainclothes security officers. This was the last time that she was seen alive.

It was later discovered that security forces threw her body from the top of a building to try to mask her death as suicide. The residents of the building heard a loud thud in their yard at 4:45 a.m. on September 21. But Nika's body was not discovered until hours later. "At around 9:00 a.m., one of the residents saw the body of a girl with a palm-sized blood scab on the side of her head," her aunt wrote on Instagram, adding, "Joojoo, why was your life's share so much pain and suffering?"

She used a common Iranian term of endearment, *joojoo*, which means "bird."

The terror did not end there. After her family moved her body to a mortuary closer to their hometown of Khorramabad in preparation for her burial, security forces stole Nika's body and buried her in another cemetery twenty miles away to prevent a crowded funeral like Jîna's. None of her family members were present during this unceremonious burial, which took place on her seventeenth birthday on October 3. In a video, her mother held a picture of her while shouting, "Nika, happy martyrdom." While veterans of the Iran-Iraq War or those who died in support of the regime's causes are venerated as martyrs, the regime does everything it can to repress the families of dead protesters—martyrs of the people's movements. We are not permitted to mourn or honor our dead.

Nika's aunt Atash was detained and in police custody in Tehran while this was all happening. In Iran, the regime doesn't even let you rest in peace. They steal the bodies of those that they killed during protests. They bury them in remote cemeteries to prevent people from gathering and protesting at their funerals as they did at Jîna's.

On her tombstone, her family inscribed this poem:

> *I birthed you with my blood and pain,*
> *and sacrificed you for the motherland.*

In Persian, we call people like Nika *javan-e naakam*, meaning "young people without fortune." This phrase is believed to have originated from the Iran-Iraq War, the eight-year war that took place in the 1980s in which more than thirty-three thousand Iranian child soldiers and students were killed fighting on the front lines, and refers to someone who was not able to achieve their dreams before dying. To mourn those ripped away from us too soon, there are traditions to honor their lost life experiences in death. Parents who lose out on the great honor of holding their children's wedding ceremonies carry out parts of their culture's wedding rituals at their children's funerals. Among Lurs and

Bakhtiaris, for example, it is customary to cheer at weddings for young people—a loud and deep sound that comes from the bottom of women's throats and sounds like the trill of a woodwind instrument. The same is done at funerals.

Ki-li-lee lee lee lee
Ki-li-lee lee lee lee

Nika's family continued to eulogize her months after her death. "What do you want to know about Nika?" her aunt Atash wrote on Instagram. "Find everything you want to know about her in the girls around you. They need equality." Nika chose this path, with all its risks, eyes wide open. But she wanted to live. She wanted to emigrate, viewing her life in her home country as one without a future or even a window. "Our stunning Nika wanted to become a star," her aunt wrote. "Instead, she became a star in death."

Aida, Nika's sister, has two Instagram highlights dedicated to her sister. Through Aida, we learn about the weight of Nika's presence and absence. Nika liked the color yellow and chocolate ice cream. Rose was her favorite flower, and her favorite foods were pizza and *kashk-e bademjan*, the Iranian dip made with eggplant, yogurt whey, onions, garlic, and walnuts. She loved spiderwebs and used fake spiderwebs to decorate her room. Nika loved Angelina Jolie because the actress is always herself. "She does not pretend. She is not fake. She is real. Her mischief, sadness, and anger are real," her sister wrote. Nika dreamed of going to Japan. In an imagined conversation with her sister, Aida wonders if Nika has seen the bright neon lights of Tokyo's Shibuya neighborhood or tried "mochi under the cherry blossoms of Ueno Park while wearing a blue silk kimono." Aida paints an intimate portrait of the places Nika would've loved to experience:

Discovering the secret of remote foothill temples and watching the sunset at Fuji Heights.
Walking into Arashiyama bamboo groves and smelling the green

moss (moss was always more than a plant for you. It had a soul. You once said that moss, before it had become moss, was a creature with big eyes, a gentle spirit, a hybrid, and a scratchy voice).

Nika lived with her aunt Atash in Enghelab Street. She often sat on the old wooden bench on the balcony, watching the sky for hours. She talked excitedly about the moon. She put her phone on a tripod at night and took long videos of these mischievous clouds as they floated, dancing and twisting into new shapes. She chatted with her friends and ate snacks on that bench. Aida shared a poem about the moon that her sister loved:

> "Why are you sad so often?"
> Ask the moon.
> Ask what it has witnessed.

The moon was perhaps the sole witness to what happened to Nika on the horrifying night of September 20. Tehran is filled with people like Nika, who come to the city to follow their dreams. If we want to study at prestigious institutions or make careers in art, journalism, or other competitive arenas, we have no choice but to start a new life in the metropolitan capital, where all this is accessible. The desire for independence plucks us from the outer provinces and sets us on a path that passes through the capital. But while we take one step forward, we face new obstacles to our independence. The capital city is not kind to women.

The year after Nika was killed, the regime shut down the café where she worked and all the others near Tehran University and Enghelab Street. In a story about the closures in the newspaper *Etemad*, a reporter wrote that Islamic Republic officials viewed cafés as "places for the young and students to gather, and even a strategic formation space and shelter for protesters." Nika's workplace was replaced by Tehran University's Social Responsibility Headquarters, which is used to hold training camps for Basij members with the aim of representing the value of "charity, sacrifice, and martyrdom," according to officials.

On the anniversary of Nika's death, regime forces sprayed black paint over the portrait on her grave and uprooted or destroyed all its surrounding trees and benches, as well as a small pond that her family had built for birds to drink water. They're scared of the power of graves. They're afraid of cafés.

Nika and her aunt lived three minutes away from the platform where the Girls of Enghelab Street gathered in 2017. Nika's aunt Atash shared on Instagram that Nika once asked her, "Why do people often leave flowers next to this platform?" When her aunt told her about Vida Movahed and the significance of the site, Nika responded, "Such a badass woman she was." Atash told Nika's mourners and supporters, "I heard people brought bouquets in memory of her to Godar Café, where Nika worked, but the regime shut it down. Please leave your flowers in memory of Vida and Nika beside that platform."

After teenage Nika's death, many newborn children have been named after her. A father of one of these newborn Nikas wrote on his Instagram account:

You will be born in two months.

Knowing that history differs from your textbooks or street billboards is better.

It is better to know that the spots on the mother's body are not hereditary but the remnants of a great battle.

It is better to know that these people who walk in the street with blindfolds were not born with one eye.

When you ask the first important question of your life,

Why did your mother name you Nika?

Have faith. You will hear a story that will make you proud to be a woman in this land.

And with every step you take, count how much remains until reaching freedom.

I wrote this for you. You were born, and your mother named you Nika a few months ago. Make the end of this story, Nika.

NILO

FOR THE ENDLESS AND REPETITIVE

A S MORE PEOPLE posted online, I started to see something turn. Iranians began evaluating and opining about who was or wasn't posting about the uprising. It turned into a sort of intense desperation that lashed out in flames. Our diaspora is at its worst when we see unrest in our homeland. It activates and agitates us toward judgment and mistrust of one another, and many of us feel retraumatized seeing the violence that those who remain are experiencing. I spoke with one Iranian friend who grew up most of his life in California. "It's almost like everyone's looking at this moment as the last days of the Islamic Republic. And anyone who's not falling in line with the messaging or posting on social media is going to ruin the momentum for all of us," he said to me over a long phone call during which we were trying to understand the digital finger-pointing that was going on.

For those of us watching this unfold from far away, the possibility that the Islamic Republic might fall carried with it the possibility of return. Maybe we could all soon safely visit home. Anyone who wasn't posting about the uprising or publicly showing solidarity with our sisters and brothers in Iran was seen as holding us back from a collective freedom. A friend posted about this online, saying that the way that we were surveilling each other was reminiscent of the Islamic Republic. "It's like the ghost of Khomeini is haunting all of us," he wrote. This internalized authoritarianism is woven into our collective experience. With the revolution so close in our cultural memory, we have barely begun to process the trauma of everything that came with it: the imprisonment and death of our friends and family members, sudden or gradual exile, and seeing some of the darkest days of our Iran come to bear while we're powerless and far away. The regime is uniquely skilled at long-distance authoritarianism. It's created an environment in which many who've left become paranoid and paralyzed when it comes to criticism of the Islamic Republic, knowing that the consequences for it are being unable to return or being jailed and held hostage. This atmosphere makes it nearly impossible for some to trust fellow Iranians making new lives abroad. We haven't managed to come together in community to accept and see each other.

Nor have we been able to build a strong coalition to resist and fight against the Islamic Republic. The largest and most organized dissident group operating outside Iran is the Mujahideen-e Khalq (MEK), a Marxist group now based in Albania that was one of the first groups listed by the United States as a foreign terrorist organization (FTO). It has faced accusations of engaging in cultlike activities such as ideological cleansing sessions, forced divorces, and the separation of children from their parents. This group enjoys no support in Iran, partly due to its role in the Iran-Iraq War, in which it fought against Iranians on the side of Saddam Hussein's Iraq, launching attacks that killed its own people. After the United States led the Iraq invasion in 2003 and toppled Saddam Hussein, it was left with the question of what to do with the MEK. Iraq quickly grew too dangerous for the MEK, as they were seen as vestiges of the former dictator. In order to resettle the group, the United States had to delist it, which it did in 2012. I interviewed Daniel Benjamin, who was the coordinator for counterterrorism at the U.S. State Department when MEK was delisted. He told me that the group was moved off the FTO list not because its activities had changed, but due to the urgent need to move them out of the country. "MEK was still a pretty undesirable group. But we did not want to watch it be slaughtered in Iraq," said Benjamin. But this group has received support from government officials, like Rudy Giuliani; John Bolton, the national security adviser during the first Trump administration; Elaine Chao, the secretary of transportation also under President Trump; and former governor of Pennsylvania Ed Rendell—all of whom have spoken at or attend its events. Even today, the group continues its lobbying efforts by engaging in Iran policy–focused events with influential policymakers. In February 2023, the opening speaker of the congressional session to discuss the bipartisan House Resolution 100, which aimed to lend support to Iranians protesting for "a democratic, secular, and nonnuclear Republic of Iran," was Maryam Rajavi, the head of the MEK. The bill was supported by Democratic lawmakers like Representatives Brad Sherman and John Garamendi from California. Sherman, who led minority support for the bill, has a history of supporting the MEK; he vocally supported and video chatted with Rajavi in 2022 and has signed on to other pro-MEK resolutions in the past. On top of the toxic diasporic dynamics, to see that our only organized opposition to the Islamic Republic was a Marxist cult housed in a camp in Albania deflated me.

While I was still an employee at *The New York Times*, a wave of L.A.-based Iranian actors and influencers called out the paper for a news story in the early protest coverage that focused on the economic reasons driving the uprising. This story had a line that infuriated many Iranians. It stated that most Iranians wanted a return to the nuclear deal, a failed agreement between Western nations and Iran to curb its nuclear program in exchange for sanctions relief. While there were very real economic reasons that were pushing Iranians to the brink, many people online were horrified by this story. My direct messages were full of people who wrote to me to say that the story completely missed the mark by not focusing on human rights, or that the line about the nuclear deal didn't reflect the present moment. And they were right. No one was in the streets chanting, "We want the nuclear deal"; instead, Iranians were using their bodies as human shields in front of heavily armed security forces, screaming, "Death to the Islamic Republic," "I will defend my sister," and of course, "Woman, Life, Freedom." The people in the streets wanted a complete downfall of the current system. They certainly didn't want the Islamic Republic to exist, let alone negotiate anything on their behalf.

People were demanding an explanation for why we weren't reposting videos showing police brutality at street demonstrations with the ease with which they were reposting, resharing, and retweeting. As a journalist, I don't share any videos on my social media that have not been verified by me or a colleague. Taking visual evidence from uploaders at face value is sketchy at best, and the price of being wrong is astronomical. Verifying a video can be technical and time intensive. The best way to do this is to track down the original uploader of a video and ask for the metadata, which is information that is automatically stored in a video or image file that can give details on the location, time, and date. But in Iran, people share videos on encrypted messaging apps that wipe this information away. Many sources I spoke with told me that they would create onetime-use accounts on Telegram or Signal, upload the video there, share it with a citizen journalist channel, and then delete the account altogether. Given that videos are shared from Iran in this manner to evade intelligence authorities, we are left with a series of manual steps to verify any visuals that we want to report on.

First, we have to check that this video is recent and of this current round of protests. Often, the issue with videos circulated online is not that these have been manipulated or doctored, but rather that the visuals are from a previous protest and being passed off as being of the present moment. To verify how current a video is, we take a screen grab from the first frame of the video. This image is cached in Google when people search for videos, meaning that this first frame of a video is what's stored on search engines. Then I'll reverse image search the first frame on Google, Bing, and Yandex to make sure that I check it among all the search engine providers. From there, I can see the earliest time this video was posted and shared online. This is the quickest step, and it usually takes around ten minutes. Then we move on to geo-locating the video to confirm that it took place where people online said it did. This practice can take days. Not every video can be geo-located because this methodology relies on being able to see the background of the scene: store signage, aspects of the landscape like a mountain range, and other visible features to help determine the location. This means that nighttime videos of protests, often the most deadly and violent, are nearly impossible to locate and verify. Once I'm confident in the veracity and location of the video, I'll start to do research about the incident itself. I'll look for multiple angles to give more context on what led up to the moment in question, what people were posting about online, and also track down eyewitnesses.

The internet rumor mill can spread wildly, especially with a big news event showing a popular uprising in a dictatorial country that's known for brutal crackdowns. While the online diaspora mob was demanding *The New York Times* cover state violence at the protests, Haley Willis and I were in the middle of reporting out a video analysis of what we were seeing. We were looking into a video that people online claimed showed protesters setting fire to an IRGC base. When we took a closer look and were able to verify and geo-locate it, Haley and I learned that people were having a protest outside Bank Sepah. In Persian, Sepah translates to IRGC. Someone had taken that to mean an IRGC base, tweeted it in English, and off it spread. We started working on our report on September 21, 2022, and it published on October 4, 2022. Two weeks is a relatively speedy turnaround for a project like this that involves both finding and verifying videos, connecting with sources, eyewitnesses, and experts, and figuring out our thread of analysis beyond pointing our audience toward scenes of gruesome violence. Haley told me that we did this faster than usual in our two-week turnaround because I was already plugged in with the subject matter, experts, and eyewitnesses.

There are countless examples of missed context and false information that show how crucial OSINT reporting is to cover this movement. There was no way that we could verify videos as fast as people online were sharing them. And while we were working, it was very difficult for me to see my own community working itself into a frenzy about what they saw as our poor coverage. It was incredibly draining to be mentioned on Twitter twenty times or so a day when bot accounts, which were often inauthentic and could repost and retweet automatically, would tweet #NYTSucks or other hashtags. It became an endless scroll of notifications. To this day, Haley and I still get targeted by bot campaigns in response to our October 2022 story, our mentions filled with posts urging us to be the voice of people in Iran.

To deal with it, I decided to focus on the people in Iran who were at the center of the uprising, to verify what was happening to them, and to diligently document the movement. I had to turn my focus away from the diaspora, away from criticism from even friends and acquaintances about the media on Iran to stay sane. I had only so much energy, and most of it was depleted every time I looked at a graphic video. Even writing about it now and returning to memories of diaspora infighting feels particularly draining because while it was happening, I had compartmentalized it so that I could have brain space to process videos of state killings and violence. As long as I did right by the people in our investigations, our eyewitnesses, and our sources, I was happy. That was my measure of success, and not what I was seeing online from diaspora social media campaigns. I was seeing our people getting killed by security forces, so the diaspora infighting made me feel as if we were living in distant realities. Wasn't it clear that we weren't the enemy? Shouldn't we be focusing on who is being harmed? It felt like this surreal circus of secondhand trauma on top of the uprising that was sustaining its strength on the lives of our people who were being killed regularly by the regime.

PART II

JÎYAN/ZENDEGI, LIFE

In the name of woman, in the name of life
The slave clothes were torn
May our black night dawn
All whips be axed
To be called with rosebuds
Let me and you become us again.

— the students' anthem at the University of Art in Tehran, 2022

NILO

FOR WHAT THEY STOLE FROM US

MORE THAN A CENTURY AGO, the first large-scale Iranian women's movement began to take form, bubbling up following an initial wave of nationwide protests in the country's modern era. Our people were coming to terms with how the ruling monarchial Qajar dynasty was making choices that benefited the ruling class and not ordinary Iranians. These kings and princes were selling off our assets and industries to the West under the guise of bringing prosperity to the country, but only ended up lining their own pockets rather than enriching the lives of its people. Demanding a better society, brave and powerful women began to organize. Wholly breaking with the notion of a woman being destined to be a homemaker and perhaps one of many wives to a man, we burst onto the public sphere with force, using our bodies and voices for the first time. In January 1906, a group of women attacked the carriage of Mozaffar ad-Din Shah, the fifth Qajar king who ruled until his death in 1907, as he was headed to the home of a wealthy aristocrat. The carriage stopped and one woman read out a statement: "Beware of the day when the people take away your crown and your mantle to govern."

Our story stretches back to the late nineteenth century, when a sense of growth and a desire for expansion began to take root among many Iranians. Partly inspired by the Enlightenment that had swept Western Europe and the United States by the end of the eighteenth century, the country that was then known to the West as Persia was in the midst of a nationwide conversation about progress and modernization. At the core of the debate was figuring out how to adopt these European elements of technology and institutions with consideration to the country's deeply ingrained cultural and religious traditions. And anytime there's a discussion on reform, a push and pull rises to the surface: who would gain and who would lose out in this type of societal overhaul.

The tension here was between the Qajar sovereigns, who ruled Persia from 1795 to 1925, and the religious Shia Islamic ruling elite. The push for reform, which was supported by the Shia clergy, intellectuals, and ordinary Iranians, gained speed and hurtled forward, sparked by the damaging effect of Russia and Britain's rivalry over their influence in the country. The pro-reformists were of the mind that removing control of Persia's institutions and industries from the ruling class was essential for the country to survive in this Western-dominated world. The mismanagement and government corruption led by the Qajars and the poor decisions that followed were exactly what made Persia vulnerable to Western countries that took advantage of its resources.

The nation suffered humiliating defeats in the Russo-Persian Wars (1804–13 and 1826–28) and the Anglo-Persian War (1856–57). These losses meant that it was forced to give away some of its territories to these two global superpowers. Persia handed over its claim to the Caucasian provinces, Armenia, and the Caspian Sea to Russia, and it also was forced to withdraw from Herat, signing the city over to Britain. Meddling by Russia and Britain put Persia in a position to be overly economically reliant on the West, which in turn disintegrated its domestic industries; imported, cheaper products weren't subject to tariffs, tipping the balance of trade in favor of Russia and Britain.

In the late nineteenth century, the Qajars made two concessions that cleared yet another path for Western interference in the country. The Reuter concession of 1872 gave Baron Paul Julius Reuter, a British subject, free rein to develop Persia's natural resources as he saw fit. In the background of this concession were British-Russian tensions in Persia. The ruling Qajar monarch was thought to have taken this concession to get around Russia's desire and demands to build a railway in the country. He was essentially playing one great power against another with the aim of protecting his sovereignty.

It was called "the most extraordinary surrender" of the country's "entire industrial resources" by Lord Curzon, one of the most well-known figures of Britain's colonial rule—the former viceroy of India and a former foreign secretary. For a period of seventy years, Reuter had the exclusive right to create a national bank, construct all railways, dams, canals, and similar structures, regulate rivers, and exploit all mines, except for gold and silver. Then, in 1890, Naser al-Din Shah Qajar signed a secret agreement with Major Gerald F. Talbot, a close relative of Lord Salisbury, the prime minister of England. This allowed Talbot's company the exclusive right of not only the export of Persian tobacco but also its internal sale, trade, and farming for a period of fifty years. Tobacco was a major part of trade in Persia at the time, and this deal meant that domestic tobacco farmers would have to sell their tobacco to Talbot's British company and then buy it back to use it themselves.

The effects roiled Persian society. If the tobacco concession was a smooth pebble, skipping and hopping on the water's glassy surface, then the waking consciousness and growing hostility of our people were the ripples. In late 1890, a Persian newspaper in Istanbul broke the story about the concession. Months later, in January 1891, pamphlets criticizing the shah for the numerous concessions to foreign powers, in particular regarding tobacco, began to be distributed in Persia. In the spring of that year, massive nationwide protests took hold, marking one of the first antigovernment movements in the country's modern history, seen as a sharp rebuke of foreign interference. The religious clergy was vocal and began to preach against the concession. One member of the clergy in Shiraz was so outspoken that the shah exiled him to present-day Iraq. Bazaars closed in solidarity with and protest against his exile, and residents joined in to hold demonstrations, the first large-scale organizing against the concession. Mirza Hassan Shirazi, a leading Shia cleric at the time, even issued a fatwa against the concession in December 1891, also banning the use of tobacco. But a popular boycott against tobacco had already started in Isfahan before Shirazi's fatwa. *Bazaaris,* or the merchant class and people who worked in the bazaars, led this uprising, capitalizing on the support from clerics. The movement spread to Tabriz, Mashhad, Isfahan, and Tehran, and some gatherings even turned deadly when police fired on the crowd and killed participants, which only fueled further discontent and continued to ignite the movement. In response, the government tried to give up part of the concession on internal sales of tobacco, but the people wouldn't accept this measly offering. This popular movement worked; the government abandoned the concession in 1892, resulting in the shah compensating the British company and ending up with a massive foreign debt.

And yet the dismantling of the concession didn't give back what was owed to our people. My family was one of many knocked down by the tobacco concession. My maman's paternal grandfather, Taghi Hajhosseinof, made his fortune off the tobacco trade. My maman heard these stories from her grandmother, whom she called Aziz, a term of endearment that means "darling." According to family lore, my maman's grandfather Hajhosseinof was so wealthy that he would come home with wheelbarrows full of cash. His family flourished and wanted for nothing. After the concession, Hajhosseinof lost everything and went completely broke. At that time, there was no pivoting. He couldn't go to school, find a new industry to work in, and start anew. Hajhosseinof never made money again. This pushed his wife, my great-grandmother and my maman's Aziz, into the workforce. Her sister was a seamstress, and together these two resourceful women, and a small group of others who worked for them, began to sew and make clothes for people in town. The women in my family carried us through when their male counterparts lost their economic footing and never regained balance. They sewed and stitched and created out of necessity. I begged my maman for more details because this piece of family history anchors and situates us in one of the most transformational times for our people. For decades, when I would ask my parents where we came from, I heard that we were simply ordinary Iranians. This was a rare time where I could clearly see the contours of our family legacy and history. We are bazaaris—the traditional workers and traders in local markets. Yes, we had power. But as we saw from the fallout of the concessions of this time period, we are at the whim of whichever foreign country's hands wedged their way into our nation's pockets, pulling and taking from us.

My maman told me that her father changed his last name to Daneshpouy after he went to school, saying that she could only recall that he didn't like the last name Hajhosseinof. *Danesh* means "knowledge" and is the root word for *daneshgah,* which means "university." The suffix *pouy* means "seeking." My grandfather took us from the traditional, lineage-centric Hajhosseinof to a family name of those who seek knowledge. Was he ashamed of the ill fortune that befell his family? Was he wounded by the bazaari experience, thus turning to formal education to build a new route for himself? My maman couldn't answer my questions, and my grandfather, whom I adored and called Babaei, passed away when I was in elementary school.

Now, as I observe this familial transformation with a distance of three generations, it seems intentional for Babaei to put an end to the Hajhosseinof story and start anew as Daneshpouy. I selfishly wished that my maman had carried the name Hajhosseinof with her to keep our family story intact so that it could be easier for me to unravel. My maman mentioned this story briefly and in passing to me many years ago. She didn't tell me about the historical context, the tobacco concession, or the groundbreaking protest movement that followed. I took the thread that she handed me, matched it up to the historical fabric, and stitched it together to form an understanding of our family. I can't help but feel Aziz's presence in this—the act of sewing, of stitching something to completion from scraps of what was left behind. And with my babaei changing our name and thus redefining my maternal lineage, I also feel I'm living the path of a Daneshpouy, of a knowledge seeker.

From afar, this is all the information that I could find about us, one of the many families with no way to adapt without a livelihood that was ripped away in a hush deal by a ruling monarch. And yet, without being able to speak with my babaei and now writing about his father, who passed away years before I existed, I question whether I have permission to share these family hardships, to make public a private family story, to publish in the English-speaking world how Western influence directly affected us.

Iranian women overall played a crucial role in the concession's end. In the anti-concession protests in Shiraz, a mother and her young daughter were killed by security forces. Even royal women of the Qajar court refused to serve tobacco to their husbands who puffed on their ornate hookahs. The writer Ebrahim Taymouri published a book in 1982 about this movement called *The Tobacco Boycott, the First Passive Resistance in Iran*. He further emphasized the power of woman organizers during this time: "Women's perseverance in this movement was such that when the ban on tobacco was announced, they led the protestors who were marching toward Naser al-din Shah palace. As they passed through the bazaar, the women closed down the shops." The tobacco boycott is seen by many as the first nationwide uprising in Iran's modern history. It was the first time we came together. Society during this time was largely classless and fragmented. European urban societies during this period were divided in broad classes based on shared economic interests, while the urban population in Persia was made up of myriad smaller communities that were formed based on ethnicity, language, dialect, profession, or religion. These ties were much stronger than shared economic interests, which halted the formation of class consciousness. And the absence of this awareness is what historians say enabled the Qajar monarchy to dominate society so forcefully until the spillover effects of the concessions.

This awakening of the collective consciousness of a people who were suffering greatly at the hands of the Qajar monarchy set the stage for the Constitutional Revolution at the turn of the twentieth century. As a population awoke to a series of injustices, so too did our sisters. A platform emerged for Iranian women to become politically engaged, to vocalize and envision the type of nation that they wanted to be citizens of. The first modern women's rights movement formed during the Constitutional Revolution, which began in 1905 and ended in victory in 1911. Wounded by concessions that favored Britain and Russia and wars that saw Persia's lands shrink or be signed away, the revolutionaries aimed to rid the country of foreign influence and government corruption by bringing about rule of law and restricting the power of the Qajar monarchy. Powerful bazaar merchants, influential religious figures, and some reformers who had been wrestling with these issues in the preceding decades came together to push for the country's first constitution to put an end to royal corruption that was influenced by relationships with Russia and Britain. The revolution was a major overhaul for the nation, with women's organizing emerging as one of the most radical features of this post-revolution society.

Women took part in protests and formed several underground societies and semisecret organizations to ideate strategies in support of the constitutional movement. Women's participation in demonstrations was a sharp break with the patriarchal norms at the time, which dictated that women conform to a life at home, where they would take care of their family. A number of key figures emerged as leading women in the constitutional era. Sedigeh Dolatabadi was one of the first women's rights activists. A journalist and activist pushing for the Constitutional Revolution, Dolatabadi published the first women's magazine in the Persian language in 1919 called *Zaban-e Zanan* (Women's Voice). Her magazine was banned and shut down by the clergy. Not to be deterred, Dolatabadi moved from Isfahan to Tehran and began to publish *Zaban-e Zanan* again as a monthly magazine. Mohtaram Eskandari, a member of the intellectual scene, was the co-founder and leader of the first women's rights association in Persia, known as the Jam'iyat-e Nesvan-e Vatankhah (Society of Patriotic Women). Bibi Khanum Estrabadi was a writer and activist who championed girls' education and founded the first school for Muslim girls in 1907. At the time, the only schools for girls were run by American Christian missionaries in Tehran, Tabriz, and Urmia, but Muslim girls weren't allowed to attend. Religious groups issued a fatwa against Bibi Khanum, stating that schools for girls went against Islamic law and were "heresy." Despite men attacking the school and breaking the windows while young girls studied inside, and then the school closing down almost immediately after it opened due to safety concerns, Bibi Khanum's Madreseh Doshizegan reopened a year later, in 1908, for girls younger than seven.

Empowered by a society that was changing and wrestling with questions about the power and place of its citizens, many women rose to fight for change. But I want to tell you about one in particular—Bibi Maryam Bakhtiari, our first militant sister who earned the rank of sardar, meaning "commander," for her fearless leadership. As is evident from her name, she was a Bakhtiari woman—of the same tribal family and background as my dear Fatemeh. The Bakhtiari tribe, the most powerful and influential in Iran, had been highly supportive of the constitutional movement. Bibi Maryam was born in 1874, the only child of one of the many wives of the khan, a title denoting leadership. Her father, Hossein Qoli Khan, was the headman of the Bakhtiari clan, and her mother, Bibi Fatemeh Kianarsi, was a Chaharlang, one of the two major branches of the Bakhtiari. Bibi Maryam's parents' union was designed to consolidate power, and she was born into a life of privilege as the daughter of a tribal leader. The Bakhtiaris are a nomadic armed tribe that settled in the Zagros Mountains, its ridges on Iran's western border with Turkey. A self-sufficient people, many Bakhtiaris had and still have several weapons to defend themselves and their livestock against thieves and wild animals. Bibi Maryam was only forty days old when her parents arranged for her to marry Ali Qoli Khan Chaharlang in another power union between her and the branch of her mother's tribe. She was made to join her husband's tribe and live with them when she was fifteen years old, gaining the distinction of becoming the wife of the successor to the tribe's chief. Bibi Maryam became a skilled shooter and was a commander of several groups of horseback riders in the tribe due to her status through marriage.

In 1906, the Qajar leader Mozaffar ad-Din Shah signed the new Persian Constitution, which created an elected parliament. In a victory for constitutional supporters, royal power became more limited in favor of a parliamentary system. At the time of the signing, Mozaffar ad-Din Shah was an elderly king in poor health. His son and successor, Mohammad Ali Shah, ascended to the throne upon his death in January 1907 and promised to respect these new constitutional rights before assuming power. Mohammad Ali Shah enshrined himself in history as yet another leader who ruled with empty promises. In June 1908, he invited the leaders of the constitutional movement to the Imperial Gardens outside Tehran and imprisoned all except for one, who luckily escaped. Then, weeks later, Mohammad Ali Shah placed the newly formed Parliament under siege and ordered its bombardment by artillery fire.

After the bombardment, the Bakhtiaris immediately called for a restoration of the constitution, threatening to take it by force. After this violent attack on our Parliament, Bibi Maryam wrote to her brother, a sardar who had been a strong supporter of the constitutional movement, "now that you have decided to be committed and brave in this endeavor, if all the brave men of the Bakhtiari tribe become martyrs, then gather all the Bakhtiari women, steel yourselves, take up arms and march towards the despotic camp [Tehran] to defeat the enemy. I hope that with your intellect, deep thinking, and the force of the fiery swords of the brave Iranian youth, you will eradicate the roots of this rotten tyranny." In direct opposition to Mohammad Ali Shah's empty words, Bibi Maryam emphatically stood behind hers. Her home in Isfahan became a gathering spot for fighters, and she used her status to write telegrams to leaders of other tribes, persuading them with her passion and conviction to join her and her people as they rose up against Qajar oppression. Early one morning in July 1909, Bibi Maryam secretly entered Tehran with a group of Bakhtiaris and other pro-constitution rebels under the command of her brother Sardar Asad. They stayed underground, planning the attack from a safe house overlooking Baharestan Square, the site of the destroyed Parliament. As Sardar Asad swept in to fight the Qajar government's army, with some modern arms from the German Empire, Bibi Maryam fortified the roof. With a rifle in her hand, she sat on her horse with the rest of her Bakhtiari riders and attacked pro-government forces. Her position was the most crucial in disarming hundreds of government troops, allowing for a second parliament to be formed. Bibi Maryam became one of the most famous Bakhtiari women and was even given the honorary rank of sardar, just like her brother.

Women's rights and the issues they organized around shifted for decades to come—from basic needs like a government that was oriented around the well-being of its citizens, to more specific issues such as women's education during the Constitutional Revolution, gender-based segregation, the right for women to divorce their husbands, and other concerns of the modern era. And while in 2022, women lined the streets sparked by the mandatory hijab, it wasn't always a feature of their daily lives. It had been in place only since 1981, just a few years after the Islamic revolutionaries took power.

When the military commander Reza Shah took power in a coup in 1921, and established his dynasty in 1925, he ended 131 years of the Qajar dynasty. Then he took the country through a period of modernization: Large road construction projects were in progress, the Trans-Iranian Railway was built, and the education system went through a significant overhaul. At the same time, a period known as the Women's Awakening (1936–41) was under way. This movement called for removing Islamic veils from Iranian society, which of course was met by opposition by the religious establishment. Reza Shah's government supported advancements fought for by women activists, including an end to child marriage, exclusion from public society, and educational segregation. As such, one significant piece of his legacy was a ban on the hijab and any other Islamic veils, which lasted for five years. Pushed by woman organizers and inspired by a visit to the Turkey of

Mustafa Kemal Atatürk—a Turkish nationalist leader who became the founder and first president of the Republic of Turkey and was called the father of modern Turkey for implementing a series of social and political reforms that modernized the nation—Reza Shah tried to force the same type of Westernization that Atatürk had carried out, transforming his country from a predominantly Islamic nation into a modern secular state.

The reforms in Turkey were sharply focused on remaking the traditional roles of women in society, encouraging them to attend universities, obtain professional degrees, and join the workforce. Modernist intellectuals in Iran had been demanding this type of public unveiling since the Constitutional Revolution and even presently during the Women's Awakening. In 1936, Reza Shah introduced the *Kashf-e hijab*, which translates to "the unveiling," a law banning the use of the traditional Islamic veil or any traditional garb that hid the contours of women's bodies. Under the shah's mandate, Iranian women were forbidden to wear conservative chadors that blanket the whole body, modern headscarves that women would loosely drape over their shoulders, or anything in between. But in a country with a majority-Muslim population, Reza Shah's move effectively excluded religious women from public life.

Western media often uses photos of Iranian women in the 1960s to point to the Iran that could've been. The images show attractive young women with their heads falling back in laughter and wearing miniskirts with hems hitting their thighs. But this whirlpool of nostalgia is only that—familiar-looking images that draw the viewer in without telling the full story of the ripple effects of forced unveiling and, later, the economic changes instituted by his son. Reza Shah's mandatory unveiling, though supported by women's rights activists, pushed many religious women to stay at home to avoid being harassed by police for wearing hijab. Reza Shah was perhaps unknowingly falling into another modern Western trope—that of a male political figure creating a law that governs women's bodies without their consent. Women weren't allowed to decide for themselves what to wear on their heads or their bodies, or how to make their own decisions about integrating into society. Pushed and pulled. Unveiled and veiled. Their words and movements extracted for political gain. Only empowered for brief power grabs. Our place in society left up to the whims of the men who seized control.

FATEMEH

FOR THE FREEDOM OF CHOICE

THREE DECADES of massive effort by women activists seemed to pay off with the achievement of valuable and lasting gains for women, like the right to an education. But others were suppressed and further marginalized during Reza Shah's reign. Threatened by Bakhtiari resistance during the Constitutional Revolution and the minority group's demonstrable power, Reza Shah executed Bibi Maryam's eldest son and systematically forced Bakhtiari people to settle in cities under strict surveillance, effectively ending their nomadic lifestyle in the name of "civilization."

Reza Shah was pushed out in 1941, following occupation by the Soviet Union and England at the beginning of World War II, but he preserved his dynasty by installing his eldest son, Mohammad Reza, as king. After Reza Shah's departure, the compulsory hijab law was overturned, and the wearing of hijab became optional.

Mohammad Reza Pahlavi was twenty-one and too young to rule through intimidation and hierarchy as his father had. Unlike his father, he attempted reconciliation with the Islamists and gave permission and funding to Islamic schools, where the hijab was mandated. Some left-wing women adopted the use of the hijab as an anti-imperialist symbol, which increased the number of veiled women, especially in schools and universities. Leftist women viewed their priority as fighting against imperialism, even if it meant wearing a blanket. Women without hijab were attacked by radical Islamists in public.

In October 1949, a political party called the National Front was founded by Mohammad Mossadegh, a former member of Parliament. Mossadegh was calling for the cancellation of foreign contracts and nationalization of Iranian oil, a position that cemented his popularity among many workers in Iran who were paid meager salaries by the British and Soviets for grueling work in subterranean oil wells. Laborers believed Mossadegh could help them obtain higher wages and a better life. Through Mossadegh's leading role, the Parliament rejected both grants of the Soviet Union oil concession in the north and the British concession in the south. And in April 1951, Mohammad Reza Shah was forced to appoint Mossadegh as the prime minister of Iran due to his nationalist supporters' protests and unrest. Finally, Iran had a popular representative who demanded the reclamation of our historical rights. Mossadegh also, in response to activists pushing for women's right to vote and equal participation in political life, considered a bill that would—if not explicitly grant these rights to women—no longer limit them to men. He ultimately refused the proposed bill, however, terrified by death threats from Islamists.

On August 19, 1953, with the support (or silence) of Ayatollah Kashani, the most important cleric in Iran at that time, the British MI6 and the U.S. Central Intelligence Agency (CIA) staged a coup against Mossadegh known as Operation Ajax. The United States and the U.K. wanted to keep the monarchy and prevent the oil industry from being nationalized to maintain their access to cheap oil. The CIA was newly established in 1947, and this was one of its first regime change missions. Our people were its test run. The coup was successful, and Mossadegh was sentenced to three years' imprisonment for the crime of treason against Mohammad Reza Shah. He was then placed under house arrest for the rest of his life. After this shift in power, Mohammad

Reza Shah, who had left the country briefly, returned to Iran. American companies once again got their fingers into Iran's oil supply, and a consortium of seven international companies took over the extraction and management of the oil; 40 percent of it belonged to Britain, and it was decided that 50 percent of the profit would be given to Iran.

Many experts view the 1953 coup as one of the roots of the 1979 Iranian revolution, laying the groundwork for the Islamic extremism that our revolt ushered in. Mehrdad Darvishpour, a sociologist at Mälardalen University, said that "Iranian people who faced national humiliation in the coup were able to restore their national self-confidence through the 1979 revolution." The U.K. and the United States cut short our nation's opportunity for a secular and democratic establishment and ruined the future of many generations of Iranians. This is why I think whenever Western leaders talk about democracy and freedom, they address their own people. Whenever it reaches us Middle Eastern people, Western leaders put their economic and geopolitical interests ahead of everything. In March 2000, Madeleine Albright, who was secretary of state at the time, apologized for the U.S. role in the coup against Mossadegh. But did her apology bring about any change? No. Instead, she rubbed salt into our national wound, one that hasn't healed for generations.

The coup against Mossadegh made Mohammad Reza Shah deeply unpopular among most Iranians. He tried to make reforms to gain favor among the people and follow his father in putting the country on the path toward modernization. In 1963, he put forth a set of educational, economic, and social reforms known as the White Revolution. People voted yes to these reforms in a national referendum, and for the first time in Iran a new welfare system was founded to provide services to underprivileged families. The profits of all factories would be shared among workers; agricultural lands, which used to belong to feudal lords, were divided among farmers; and young, educated people, called the Health and Knowledge Corps, were sent to remote villages to increase literacy rates and provide medical services.

The White Revolution was also a big leap forward for women's rights. After fifty-five years of trying to gain the right to vote, Iranian women were finally allowed to participate in elections and in 1963 six women were sent to the Parliament. The family support bill and the legalization of abortion were also great successes for the women's movement. These changes fulfilled the long-held wishes of women activists. Mehrangiz Dolatshahi, the first Iranian female senator and ambassador, said about her efforts to get approval from the royal family, "Some people think that the king ordered these laws immediately, but it was not so. There was colossal negotiation and effort by women activists to achieve them one by one."

Despite these gains, the last twenty-five years of Mohammad Reza Shah's rule were characterized by ideological conflicts between women activists. The women's movement split off into two separate factions: The first group consolidated its activities at the official and government levels through membership in official parties, representation in the Senate, and reaching ministerial positions. They achieved significant progress, such as approving progressive family laws, voting rights, and increased education rates among girls and women. Others became members of left-wing parties. Their goal was to overthrow the Pahlavi regime altogether. These activists undermined and ridiculed the achievements of the first group as being granted by the king and not through their own efforts.

The Islamic Republic's establishment was the result of an ideological revolution that was eventually won by religious leaders. It was not a revolution for freedom or a better life but rather the result of the unification of various groups in Iran against a common enemy: the Pahlavi regime. Islamists were against Pahlavi's modernization and reforms. Communists, Marxists, Iranian students studying abroad, and other nonreligious groups were against imperialism, as reflected in the oil concessions that followed the coup that ousted Mossadegh. These various factions with competing interests and philosophies united against Mohammad Reza Shah to overthrow the monarchy. After succeeding, the Islamists gradually removed leftists, nationalists, and other groups with whom they had joined forces during the revolution and seized absolute power and control.

One of Pahlavi's most vocal opponents was Ruhollah Khomeini, a cleric who opposed Pahlavi's Western reforms, including women's right to vote. He was exiled from Iran on November 4, 1964, moving first to Turkey and then to Najaf, Iraq, the religious heart of the country. Unlike his father, Mohammad Reza Shah had tried to compromise with the clerics. The number of mosques in the country increased from two hundred in 1942 to fifty thousand in 1979, all with the financial help of the Pahlavi regime. Yet his approach only hardened the opposition, with both nonreligious communists and Islamists uniting against Mohammad Reza Shah.

Khomeini's support was not limited to religious extremists. Noureddin Kianouri, one of the most important leftist leaders, in a meeting with the press about overthrowing the shah regime said, "By our Marxist analysis, we have come to the conclusion that American imperialism is our first enemy; then our second enemy is Mohammad Reza Shah, who is the imperialists' agent. . . . Ayatollah Khomeini has reached the same conclusion with his own interpretation." Though the two parties used different language, Kianouri said, "we accept and support" the content of Khomeini's message. On October 12, 1978, Karim Sanjabi, who inherited the leadership of the National Front Party after Mossadegh's ousting, and Khomeini met in Paris and released a joint statement calling for the ousting of the shah and demanding that Iran's new regime be Islamic, democratic, and independent.

During his exile, Khomeini started formulating the *velayat-e faqih*, or guardianship of the Islamic jurist, a system of governance that places a religious supreme leader at its center, granting him wide-ranging power and final say over state affairs. Khomeini's ideas would become the foundation of the future Islamic Republic of Iran and paved the way for him to become a religious dictator. Khomeini's influence expanded after a September 1978 visit to France, where he was able to push his ideas in Western media outlets. The shah thought that when Khomeini gave interviews to Western media in France, they would see him as backward and politically unattractive. The opposite happened. Students and nationalists loyal to Khomeini managed to create a huge amount of propaganda that boosted his image. Khomeini would host reporters and other foreign guests in a room without any chairs. Sadegh Ghotbzadeh and Ebrahim Yazdi, Khomeini's two assistants, designed such a stage intentionally. They were eager to project an image of an austere and humble religious leader in contrast to the luxury in which Pahlavi lived. Guests would sit on the floor, leaning on pillows placed against the walls.

During his stay in France, Khomeini had 117 interviews with global press, radio, and television outlets over 118 days. One of the central concerns of Western countries was that the Islamists would cut off their access to Iran's oil. By then, Iran was supplying 9 percent of the United States' imported oil. Khomeini attempted to alleviate these concerns, emphasizing in his interviews, "We will not close the oil wells nor the borders." Ghotbzadeh and Yazdi often edited Khomeini's answers in the English translation. They even paid for the mass reproduction of interviews written by them on Khomeini's behalf. Yazdi wrote in his memoir that Khomeini paid $12,000 to have an interview he had done with *Le Monde* in May 1978 run as an advertisement in the *Los Angeles Times*. In it, he claimed to believe that "a woman is a man's equal."

On January 7, 1979, representatives for the United States, the U.K., France, and West Germany held a meeting to discuss, in part, the critical situation in Iran. The U.S. president, Jimmy Carter, was worried that the shah would support the 10 percent increase in oil prices put forth by the Organization of the Petroleum Exporting Countries. He had delivered a sharp warning to the shah the previous fall that the price of oil should not increase. Mohammad Reza Shah did not heed his warning. At the same time, Khomeini was on his propaganda campaign, spreading the narrative that he would be cooperative with Western needs for oil.

In January 1979, at the Guadeloupe Conference attended by leaders of the United States, the U.K., West Germany, and France, President Carter said that it was time for a change in Iran and for the ousting of the shah. Nine days later, on January 16, the shah left Iran for Egypt. A document dated January 19, 1979, later revealed that there had been confidential negotiations between President Carter and Khomeini surrounding his takeover of Iran. Ayatollah Khomeini had told the United States that if the Americans supported his ascent to power, the

Islamists would not decrease U.S. or other Western countries' access to Iran's oil and instead foster a friendly relationship with the United States.

There is an idiom in Persian that goes, "Whoever has sown the wind shall reap the whirlwind." The United States created a storm with its behind-the-scenes support for Khomeini and reaped the tornado to come. A year after the Islamic factions won out, a group of pro-supreme-leader students occupied the U.S. embassy in Tehran, holding sixty-three ambassadorial staff members hostage for 444 days. It is a lesson that the United States and the West have not learned, but we, the Iranian people, have paid dearly to understand—never trust the Ayatollah, clerics, and Islamists. They believe that they are in a higher position than us because they are closer to Allah. Islamists can reject any justice, deals, agreements, contracts, or relations due to their understanding of God's will.

When Mohammad Reza Shah and his wife, Farah, left for Egypt, people poured into the streets to celebrate. Religious and nonreligious people, with hijab and without hijab, with a beard of a religious person or a mustache like the leftists, with a veil or a skirt, hand in hand, sang revolutionary songs and rejoiced together. People cut the king's picture out of currency, and newspapers published front-page stories with headlines like "The King Is Gone." Khomeini returned to Iran in February 1979 on an Air France plane paid for by nationalists and religious organizers. On February 10, the army withdrew from the streets, and the revolution was over. The Islamists had won.

Mohammad Reza Shah and two of his children would die in exile. Though this was not the case for him, many Iranians still view Farah Pahlavi, Mohammad Reza Shah's third wife, with respect and call her *Shahbanu*, which means "empress." There is a line from a poem by Saadi, a twelfth-century poet who is one of our national symbols, that has become a regular proverb in our daily speech: "If a person will be remembered for good and goodness, it is better than bequeathing golden palaces." Farah has had a lasting legacy for her cultural contributions to the country. Born in 1938 in Tehran to an Azeri family, she studied architecture in France before marrying Mohammad Reza

Pahlavi on December 20, 1959, when she was twenty-one. She ordered and oversaw the construction of Shahr Theater, a circular building with a combination of historic and modern Iranian architecture that remains the largest theater complex in Iran. Farah also opened the Tehran Museum of Contemporary Art in Laleh Park in 1977. This museum has the largest collection of contemporary art outside North America and Europe. Farah used to buy expensive works of famous modern painters and donate them to the Museum of Contemporary Art. Roudaki Hall, a multipurpose hall for performing ballet, opera, and music concerts, was also built under her leadership before the revolution. Its design is reminiscent of the architecture of European ballet halls.

Those landmarks remained, but all other remnants of Iran's Pahlavi period were wiped away. Khomeini immediately declared war on modern women, establishing a series of reforms in quick succession to undo any progress made under the Pahlavi reign and going back on his words during interviews in France. Women kept the right to vote and education, the most lasting achievements of the women's movement. But the Islamist storm destroyed all other attainments of the preceding seven decades of struggle, including the Family Protection Law, the national work program, and the right to an abortion.

On February 2, 1979, the regime announced that women were too squeamish to be judges and subsequently fired twenty-three female judges, forcing others to either accept positions as secretaries in the courts over which they used to preside or resign. Women still do not have the right to be judges in the Islamic Republic. Khomeini established gender segregation, instructing women and men in his own cabinet to meet with him separately. The religious and revolutionary men raided the Shams beer factory and attacked sex workers in Tehran's Shahr-e No neighborhood, where these women lived with health cards and work permits. There, a mob of men set fire to the neighborhood's houses and establishments and prevented firefighters from extinguishing the flames. The revolutionaries paraded the burned body of a sex worker around the city in the midst of their anger and hatred.

Khomeini shot the last bullet into Iranian women's bodies by ordering a mandatory hijab law on March 7, just as the last winter snow had started to fall in Tehran. Women were not allowed to go to offices, schools, and universities without being covered. Thousands of angry women headed to the streets to protest. The protests lasted six days across the country, and in Tehran alone more than fifty thousand women participated. Some unveiled and some veiled, they walked off their jobs or left their homes, braving the cold to take part in these demonstrations, chanting, "We didn't make a revolution to regress"; "Our problem is not hijab; it is freedom"; "No to hijab, yes to freedom and equality"; "At the dawn of freedom, we have no freedom"; "Neither a head wrap nor a head wrap. Freedom and equality"; and "I say moment by moment, I say under torture, either death or freedom." The hijab is one of the cornerstones of the Islamic Republic's foundation—a visual signifier of control—and the Islamists defended it fiercely. Protesters were attacked by fanatic groups of men and beaten, while religious men shouted back, "Either a head wrap or a head wrap."

Hengameh Golestan was one of the few photographers at the women's demonstration. The rest had gone to Kurdistan to cover executions of Kurdish opposition activists. No media wanted Hengameh's photos. She finally exhibited her photos from those days on February 1, 2019, after forty years, in an exhibition in London titled *Hengameh Golestan: Witness 1979*. In the photos, we see hundreds and thousands of angry women. Women who were protesting with umbrellas and under the snow with faces twisted by rage. Women waving their scarves in the air in front of the judiciary building.

In one, thousands of young high school students look forward with angry eyes. In another, women tied their hands together as a sign of solidarity. One photo attracted more attention than others. In it, Golestan captured a woman standing on top of a car wearing a flowy cape and facing a mullah, or Islamic clergyman, in front of her. Her finger is raised in a sign of warning, and her mouth is half open, seemingly mid-shout. That woman became known as the Joan of Arc of Moshtagh Street, named after the woman fighter who was honored as a defender of the French nation. Journalists and women's rights activists found her, but instead of the iconic woman in the protest picture, they encountered a woman who doesn't remember much of that day. She was Maliheh Nikjoumand, an actress who had to wear a hijab to act in TV series after the revolution. "I remember that coat. It was cream. On that day, I don't remember exactly when it was, but I know that a demonstration was held near Tehran University. A few days before, thugs were in the streets chanting. They pounded pins into the foreheads of young women. The hijab was not legal and mandatory yet, but there was tension." Those six days of women-led protests and their continued resistance delayed the mandatory hijab law by two and a half years. During this time, all universities and schools were closed for two years while they underwent what the Islamic Republic called a cultural revolution. They fired all professors and teachers who were left leaning or pro-Pahlavi or who did not agree to wearing a hijab.

In 1981, the first Islamic Parliament was formed and included 276 members, only 4 of whom were women. It approved lashing and imprisonment for women without proper hijab. Amid an atmosphere of repression, executions, and cultural revolution, women who refused to wear hijab were fired from their offices and workplaces, including 950,000 women who had previously worked for the state.

The Family Protection Law, which defined restrictions on a man's ability to remarry and had been passed in 1968 as the result of immense efforts by women activists, was repealed almost immediately, giving men the right to have multiple wives again. Before the law was passed, men could have four permanent wives at the same time and endless temporary ones, called *nikah mut'ah* in Arabic and *sigheh* in Persian. The Pahlavi bill conditioned the remarriage of the man on the permission of the court and the consent of his first wife and had also set the age of marriage at eighteen for women and twenty for men. These protections were lost after the revolution. In the ten years between 1976 and 1986, the population of "men with more than one wife" increased 145 percent.

My aunt Soraya was a victim of these new regulations. Soraya is the name of one of the stars in the sky and the name of the second wife of Mohammad Reza Shah, the second Pahlavi king. My aunt shared the same doomed fate as Queen Soraya. Both women were Bakhtiari and unable to get pregnant. Like my parents and many other Bakhtiari couples, Aunt Soraya was married off to her cousin. Because she was infertile, her husband took a second wife. No agency, no choice.

This is the fate that patriarchy wants for women. There is a Persian proverb that goes something like this: "A woman enters her husband's house wearing a white wedding dress and leaves the husband's house draped in white shroud," referring to the white cloth Muslims use in burial. It means that a woman does not have the right to divorce or to separate from her husband and must endure any mistreatment, including domestic violence, until she dies. Aunt Soraya lived with her husband and his second wife and raised her husband's five children. She was forced to be a witness to her husband's sexual relationship with another woman in her own home. She had no legal right to disagree with the situation. She always told me that she liked her husband. One day Aunt Soraya woke up, and her eyebrows, the famed marker of beauty for Iranian women, had fallen off her face. We think they disappeared due to a sadness she kept within herself.

NILO

FOR MY MOM, YOUR MOM, OUR MOMS

WHEN MY MATERNAL GRANDMOTHER, whom I affectionately called mamani, passed away in 2018, she left me an old newspaper as my inheritance. It was an issue of *Zan-e rooz*, or *Modern Woman*, a weekly women's newspaper that first hit newsstands in Tehran in 1965 and remains in circulation. My mamani gave me issue number 197 from December 1968. There were only two or three other women-focused national publications like this during that time. It was a very important publication, and this issue featured a very important woman: Sakineh Soltan Nobari, my great-grandmother, known to her family as maman-bozorg, the formal way to say grandmother.

Maman-bozorg was one of three women awarded a Mother of the Year award, presented by none other than the last queen of Iran, the empress Farah Pahlavi: "These chosen and sacrificial mothers came with their bent backs to get a medal of honor from our Empress Farah." This yellowed newsprint is the only public record of my family in Iran. We existed only in private life; no one in my family is a googleable public figure. But this article freezes a moment in time for me. I'll probably spend my whole life trying to understand who we were and the space we took up before we dug up our roots and moved them to Canada.

To learn more about my maman-bozorg, I had to ask a friend to sit down with me and translate this piece of family history as I took notes. I can speak fluently, but as the first generation to leave Iran, I'm mostly illiterate in Persian. It's taken a few years of tutoring to finally read at a third-grade level, but reading this text on my own was beyond my level of comprehension. It's a deep wound for me. I call myself *bi-savad,* or one without knowledge. I give myself this useless and painful complex of disconnection. I'm constantly feeling in the dark, trying to reach anything that will help me understand where I come from. The headline for maman-bozorg reads, "I Was the Midwife for My Last Kid."

Iranians aren't known for being forthright with information. We're indirect communicators by nature, always speaking in parables. But being implanted in the West, I've turned into something of a direct agitator. I've spent years delicately pulling at the yarn of family history, my parents' experiences during the revolution, anything to stay connected. In our culture, we have an extreme deference to elders. We respect them above all else. This manifested itself in my being unwilling to ask my parents direct questions about our history in Iran for the first twenty years of my life. I didn't want to accidently upset them or disrespect them with my questions. I became accustomed to researching on my own, using only drips of stories that they told me and old magazines left to me as a starting point.

I learned so much about the women, the matriarchs in my family, from this one article. Maman-bozorg was fifty-five years old when she won this award. The article calls her an "exemplary Tabrizy." I was thrilled to read such an adjective next to the name of my father's city. Usually, people from Tabriz and other Azeris are the butt of jokes. We're seen as provincial and unsophisticated. Often we're referred to as idiots, donkeys, or other descriptors that paint us as less intellectual. But here, we are "exemplary." Maman-bozorg had nine children and was widowed when she was only forty-five years old. She studied until the ninth grade, which was exceedingly rare for that time, especially in

Tabriz, where young girls would help in the home or get married off young. Sakineh Khanum boasts about all of her children proudly in the article.

"My daughter Alam Baradari has a literature high school diploma. She is a teacher and has three kids," she said, referencing my mamani and even a nod to my mom, who was just an infant at the time the article was written. Three generations of us women were present in one sentence. We existed. We continue to exist.

I was shocked to learn that Maman-bozorg delivered her last child with her own hands. And was perhaps even more perplexed at the matter-of-fact air in her retelling of it. When I first met my mother's uncle, Dayi Firouz, as a nine-year-old child at a family party in Tehran, I had no idea he had been brought into the world quietly in their family home.

"The pain became worse. I went to the other room; I put a bucket down and put a cloth on top of it. I put my hands on a closet in the room, and a baby was born seconds later. I was very scared, but I didn't make a sound, because I didn't want my other kids and their father to wake up. When the baby was being born, I put my hand on my stomach and I pushed and pushed until he came out. Then I put a hand on my belly button. Instead of cutting the umbilical cord off, I cut a little bit, then I knotted it," she said in her own words. I genuinely cannot imagine or process this, or even understand the ease with which she recounts the memory. The only hint of any vulnerability is her admitting she was scared for a fleeting moment. "I even remember that I got up in the morning and I washed the baby. I did all of this with bravery and without any hesitation."

Perhaps my maternal grandmother, whom I always called Mamani, knew that family history would always be important for me, and she wanted me to know that I came from a long line of educated, strong, and independent (perhaps to a fault) women. I looked at the unfinished crossword puzzle in the newspaper. Was that her writing, or my great-grandmother's? My mamani always enforced the idea that we should be self-reliant. Just like her mother, Maman-bozorg, she was widowed young. I had the immense pleasure of growing up with my mamani for years at a time in Canada. She lived with us in the beginning and then years later got her own apartment. Her own independence.

In 2018, my mamani unexpectedly passed away after falling and breaking her hip. I was filled with regret that I couldn't go to Iran for the funeral because of my reporting and public profile. I knew the chance of my being arrested at the airport and held hostage as a type of dual-national, "important" bargaining chip was high. I learned about her death on a trip to Paris. I was sitting in the back of a taxi scrolling through Instagram when I saw that one of my cousins in Iran had posted a photo of her. The caption was a black heart emoji with the phrase "roohesh shaad," which means "may her spirit be joyful"—a phrase commonly used when loved ones make their final transition. In shock, my breath started to catch in sharp, shallow inhales and exhales.

My baba picked up the phone on the first ring. "We didn't know where you were. We didn't know how to tell you," he said. It was the first time I had ever heard him sound so low and empty. He was very close to my mamani. He treated her just as if she were his own mother. I hung up and couldn't stop my loud cries. It didn't feel real at all.

"Mademoiselle, Ça va? Qu'est-ce qu'il passe?" asked the nameless French taxi driver who was witnessing my breakdown.

I translated my feelings two times over, into another language that felt unfamiliar for my emotions. "My grandmother just died. I found out in this very moment. I'm sorry. I cannot stop crying," I responded haltingly.

"Oh my God, I am so sorry. Can I take you to your family?"

The processing kept going. "No, no, I am here all alone. I'm just visiting."

"Can I take you to the airport?"

Bit by bit, the grief continued unraveling. "No. My family is in Iran. I don't have my Iranian passport with me. I'm a journalist. I cannot return to Iran. I can't go see my grandmother." Each detail I gave built on top of the other, layers of cruelty at the hands of a government that doesn't even allow us to properly grieve. And saying this out loud for the first time, I felt as if I were finally coming to terms with the inhumanity of our separation.

"I am so sorry. I am deeply sorry for your loss," the driver replied, continuing to check on me through the rearview mirror.

The next morning, I spoke with my maman, who had been in Iran for about a week to be there for Mamani while her hip was recovering. My maman had a smile in her voice as she told me that my mamani was peaceful the last time she saw her. She was no longer in pain from the fall. My maman was incredibly close with her mother, and I wasn't sure how to support her through what I imagined was indescribable pain.

"Nilofar, you're in Paris, one of Mamani's favorite cities. Go take her around with you," my maman said to me. One of the many things that I shared with my mamani was a love of travel. She had been to France, Syria, Germany, Austria, Canada, the United States, and more countries that she probably didn't get to tell me about. She had always wanted to visit India, and I had hoped to take her there one day.

I walked around Paris imagining her walking alongside me. I imagined her holding her black handbag, its strap resting gently on her right forearm. I linked my hand onto her arm, remembering the tan trench coats she always wore. When I was thinking about where to go for a snack, I imagined her reaching into her purse and handing me a little sandwich she had packed and brought with her, *nan-e sangkak,* a Persian bread with feta cheese and walnuts. I took Mamani with me to a modern art museum. I walked through a Basquiat exhibit and looked at how he painted his emotions on large canvases that towered over us on museum walls. I could feel Mamani lean over to me and whisper in my ear, *What kind of art is this? I could paint this. Maybe I should paint this and put it into a museum myself. I could have my own exhibit.* I felt my right hand grow warm, as if she were holding on to it while being cheeky.

I was spiraling through regret for making the stupid decision to report on Iran. It cut me off from spending time with my family in Iran, and now, from grieving with them. The only moment of brief solace I had was when my sister told me that Mamani had been taking computer classes so she could watch my video reports. I started reporting on Iran only a year before she passed and never knew what she thought of my work. I even learned that she was in a comedy club with other old Iranian ladies. Apparently, they would meet up in her apartment in Tehran, an apartment that my family once lived in, to tell each other jokes. I wish she had shared that with me. To protect my family in Iran, I didn't tell them much about my work or what I covered. I feared that they would get in trouble if they knew too much about my reporting. Detaining, jailing, or hassling our loved ones who remain in the country is one of the key ways that the Islamic Republic suppresses us Western journalists from afar. My mamani saw so much change in her country. As much as I miss her and wish I had more time with her, I know that this uprising would make her heart incredibly heavy. Of course, she'd be inspired by the immense bravery, but I know the images of Iranians being senselessly killed and arrested would pain her as it does me. We both unconsciously hold the pain of others. It's something she passed down to me. It's almost a gift of grace that she doesn't have to keep suffering with her fellow Iranian women. It's our turn to take it forward.

For years, I've dreamed of returning to her apartment in Tehran, of living there and retracing the steps we took before we came to Canada. Even though the apartment no longer belongs to us, I know I will go back to it one day. I'll drink tea in the living room from her short, clear glass cups and sit on the balcony early in the morning. When I think of returning to her, I think of the poem "Another Birth" by the fearless and honest Forough Farrokhzad:

> *I love*
> *your hands.*
>
> *I will plant my hands in the garden*
> *I will grow I know I know I know*
>
> . . . .
>
> *there is an alley*
> *where the boys who were in love with me*
> *still loiter with the same unkempt hair*

thin necks and bony legs
and think of the innocent smiles of a little girl
who was blown away by the wind one night.

There is an alley
which my heart has stolen
from the streets of my childhood.

....

And it is in this way
that someone dies
and someone lives on.

FATEMEH

FOR THE WOMEN WHOSE FEET WERE CUT FROM RUNNING

I GREW UP hearing and witnessing stories of women around me that seemed normal. When I was a girl, I heard the stories of my grandparents' marriages. These stories were told with an air of honor. As a child, I did not have the language to understand it, but the women in my life and family were sharing experiences of child marriage, forced marriage, domestic violence, and, worst of all, lives without love. But because these had been normalized in our culture and community, it would take some time for me to understand that these women's lives were far from ordinary—or at least should not have been.

My grandmothers' names are beautiful. My maternal grandmother's name was Sangin Mah, meaning "valuable moon." She had nine children, four boys and five girls. My paternal grandmother's name was Khanum, which means "woman." She had seven children, three boys and four girls. Both of my grandmothers were tall. One towered at six feet two, taller than many men; the other was five feet nine. Both had bright skin and sparkling eyes. When Sangin Mah spoke Persian, it was full of English words. Many of the residents of Masjed Soleyman spoke this way, because the town and its people grew up around the discovery of oil, and the development of the city was in the hands of a British delegation that came to set up the Anglo-Persian Oil Company. She would use the English words for refrigerator, tomato, glass, nurse, rest, and others. Sangin Mah never prayed correctly. She pretended to pray. Even still, she would dedicate her prayers based on whoever's house she was at in that moment. She thought that being religious would bring respect in this society ruled by the Islamic Republic. She wanted to show my mother, who was religious, that she shared that with her and the rest of our traditional family.

Sangin Mah wore urban clothes, a long navy blue or black velvet dress and a scarf that was always pinned in the middle of her head, her hair showing. Her long white hair was always in a braid, peeking out from her headscarf. Sangin Mah allowed her daughters to play sports and continue their studies. Compared with other mothers who kept their daughters at home and prepared them to be good housewives, she was ahead of her time. Before the revolution, she allowed my mother to pursue competitive running. Sangin Mah was proud of her daughters, who became independent and followed their own career paths. Whenever she stayed at any of her daughters' homes, she helped them maintain their independence by doing their household chores, cooking for their children, washing dishes, and doing laundry so that her daughters could focus on their education or jobs. But to say that Sangin Mah was a liberal woman would be an oversimplification, and she certainly wasn't a simple woman. She was a woman who defied some cultural expectations while dutifully following other norms.

Khanum, unlike Sangin Mah, spoke the authentic Bakhtiari language and wore local Bakhtiari clothes. Like other Bakhtiari women, Khanum braided her hair in two sections, brought it down from the two sides of her face, and tied them with a beautiful golden brooch below her chin. My grandfathers were brothers, and the older one remained a nomad, traveling and rootless for his whole life, living the life of a traditional Bakhtiari man. The younger one was hired by the national oil company and moved to Masjed Soleyman and became a city dweller. My grandfathers chose two different ways of life, but they shared a tradition: They both bought young teenage wives. They called the amount that they paid *shirbaha:* bride price. Now my grandmas rest in peace in our family tomb beside each other's graves. Twin graves, just like their fates.

My oldest aunt died from a contagious disease when she was a teenager. I've never heard her name, and there's no photo of her. No one has ever talked about her life. It's as if she never lived, or maybe it's a family secret, kept from me on purpose. When she was young, my grandparents got lots of money from her fiancé for her *shirbaha.* Her husband was a wealthy man who worked in Kuwait. After her death, my grandparents forced their younger daughter, my aunt Zeinab, to marry her sister's fiancé. Zeinab was only nine years old. When she told me this story, she said, "I was playing with my handmade doll when they came to take me to his home."

My mother was a professional athlete who had to give up her passion after the 1979 Islamic Republic Revolution, just like thousands of other professional woman athletes. She was a runner. Her dream was to become a short-distance sprinting champion, but this became impossible under the new regime. Today, four decades after the revolution, women are allowed to participate only in sports that allow for clothes deemed proper according to Islamic principles, which means having a hijab and one's arms and legs covered in a loose way. Women are banned from sports such as swimming, gymnastics, boxing, bodybuilding, and others that can't feasibly accommodate these rules. For years, in wrestling and weight lifting, this issue was a barrier of entry for women. Women are also required to train separately from the men, which gives way to other roadblocks such as budget and infrastructure.

I don't know if it was because of repression and fear of revolutionary people or if my parents became genuinely more religious, but whatever it was, the difference between photos of them before and after the revolution is like night and day. It marks a before and an after. They were different people before the revolution, and they never returned to being those young, free, happy people that they were in those old photographs. Nowadays I can understand. After all, their generation lost their lives and all opportunity for this revolution, so I imagine religion and the idea that you would go to heaven after death provided relief. Their generation lost their real lives for an imaginary world, expected to ignore music, art, freedom, dance, alcohol, and sex to enter heaven under the promise that there they would have it all. But my generation wanted to experience all these joys in real life. The changes in my mother's life and what would come after remind me of a line from a poem by the Nigerian writer Ijeoma Umebinyuo: "Nobody warned you that the women whose feet you cut from running would give birth to daughters with wings."

NILO

FOR THE REGRET OF A NORMAL LIFE

I THINK MY DAD, whom I call Baba, is an accidental feminist. He was born and raised in Tabriz, Iran, the third son in a family of four boys. My maman said that when she went to my baba's house to meet his family during their brief courtship, my baba was the one serving everyone tea. With no daughters in his family, my baba and his brothers did all the serving and offering of food and drinks to guests. It's something he still does today. When we have guests over at my parents' home in Canada, Baba goes around with a silver tray, balancing anywhere between six and ten glass teacups, smiling and socializing as he makes his rounds.

I told Fatemeh that I didn't want to write about the early experiences that shaped me into the woman, the feminist, I am today. They feel small. Frankly, they're privileged. But Fatemeh wants to know. She wants to know the experience of the many Iranians who've left the country. My family is every part of me. They've shaped me, frustrated me, and inspired me. My maman, my baba, and I all have birthdays within five days of each other. We're extremely close. I would choose this family in any lifetime.

My baba studied in England for his undergraduate and graduate degrees. He said that it was a privilege to be able to go abroad and anyone who had the chance took it. For him, it was a chance to become fluent in English, learn engineering, and bring his skills back to his country. He had to live completely on his own means while abroad. His eldest brother, Ahmad, bought him a suitcase and overstuffed it with comforts from home, like pistachios and different canned foods. On top of all the reminders of home was a Persian carpet that was a type of insurance. His brother told him that if he ran out of money, he could sell this expensive handwoven carpet to keep himself afloat. My baba remembers landing in Heathrow Airport for the first time in 1970. As he was trying to navigate where to go, his suitcase spilled open. Out burst his carpet, and the pistachios rolled on the ground. When he retold me this story, he started laughing while explaining that a well-dressed Englishman in a smart hat helped him gather all his items and brought thick ropes to tie everything back together. This was the first time that my baba had heard the English accent, and he kept having to ask this helpful stranger to repeat himself. I smiled, picturing the visual stereotype of carpets and pistachios that is just so very *Iranian,* and felt a connection with him. If it were me, I would've hoped that the airport floor would've opened up and swallowed me whole. But my baba said that he wasn't embarrassed. In fact, he said he was grateful for that experience because the Englishman who helped him made him feel as if he were in a country full of kindness.

Despite this being his first time in the West, he didn't feel too out of place, because in his mind he had already experienced immigration and learned how to adapt to new places. My baba moved from Tabriz to Tehran when he was about eleven years old to live with his brother Ahmad, who was in his early twenties and was already living and working in the capital. The first time that my baba experienced culture shock was in elementary school. At home in Tabriz, he grew up speaking Azeri Turkish, which is the primary language of the region. He's an Azeri, the largest ethnic minority in Iran, comprising around eighteen million people today. Persian was a language he was taught in school, but he learned *ketabi* Persian, which roughly translates to "academic" or "formal." Essentially, he learned how to read and write the language, but conversational Persian was totally foreign to him.

"When you come from Kurdistan or the southern part of Iran or the Turkish-speaking community and then you come to Tehran, it is like immigration because your language is different, your culture is different, your outlook of the society is different," he told me. "England was my second time immigrating; coming to Canada was my third."

Like me as a young kid in school in our early days in Canada, my father was picked on by kids from the capital because he was different. His accent when speaking Persian made him stand out, gave him away as an outsider. For Azeris, the hard *g* is difficult to pronounce and is one of the main markers that the Persian language is not native to them. My sister's name is Nargess, with a *g* similar to the word "guess." An Azeri speaker would pronounce her name softly, swapping in the "geh" sound for a "jeh"—Nar-*Jess*. Baba told me that on one of his first days at his new school, he had to read a poem out loud in class. One of his classmates made fun of his accent, likening him to a donkey. "They picked on me and I couldn't tolerate it, so I just went and punched the guy, and they threw me out of school for a few days," he told me as he softly laughed. "But afterward, they were scared of me."

To this day, my stomach sinks and I'm on high alert whenever I feel as if I am sticking out. It's embarrassing to admit that in my thirties I still get knots in my stomach every time I introduce myself to someone new. I watch their eyes as they try to process my name, and I wait to see what shows up in their follow-up questions. Always bracing for a "Wow, where's *that* from?" or a "I've never heard *that* one before." I don't want to be a "that," a novelty, something new to be experienced. Instead, I wish that I could just melt and disappear, daydreaming of an alternate reality where no one would hitch or stumble over my consonants, always fantasizing about what it might feel like to blend, to fit right in. When I hear my name pronounced incorrectly as "Nee-Low" or "Ny-Low," it's a sharp flick on my arm. I carry with me a heaviness, a reminder that neither my name nor my body should be in the West. My first impression and introduction to this world always grind up against something uncomfortable. The hard, short "oh" in English betrays the lyrical, long "ooo" that our vowels carry in Persian—a language of slow, intentional movement where both of us belong. For some reason, every time someone gets my name wrong, I become embarrassed at their mistake. As if I were the one doing something wrong by being here. For a long time, I never corrected people, allowing colleagues, teachers, and friends to go forward confidently in their mispronunciations. This led me down the path of making myself small.

This unconscious humbleness is part of our culture. *Tarof*—a term describing various social norms of extreme politeness—rules everything. To be Iranian is to offer guests a feeling of home. Doing so weaves in a sort of deference. When I speak on the phone with my family friends or encounter them at social gatherings, they'll greet me with *fadat sham,* which colloquially is an expression of affection but literally means "may I be sacrificed for you." Our culture is shaped around shrinking ourselves to love others in large ways. And so, when the Canadians I encountered in my early years made me feel different and wholly unwelcome, I was trying to pretend that their mistakes didn't matter to me, but inside I was suffering from being a stranger.

From my earliest interactions at school, I tried to think about how I could redirect attention away from myself and my name to anywhere else. Maybe I could have a big personality to obscure my odd name. Maybe I could adopt a uniform of blue hair and band T-shirts to fit in with other non-cookie-cutter people. I tried on a thousand "maybes." Unfortunately, shrinking myself has become a mode of survival in adult life. I do it without even thinking. I struggled on the phone with Fatemeh, unwilling to even share these few sentences. I tell myself that my moments of discomfort are minor compared with what people like Fatemeh go through in Iran on a daily basis, even though the pressure of them hasn't changed. If anything, they've rooted only more firmly in me. I wonder if I can ever retell these moments to my kids with laughter the way my dad did when he shared his pistachio-carpet nightmare. But even thinking about this hypothetical conversation with nonexistent characters, I feel an uncomfortable warmth in my palms. I feel the drop of a roller coaster after it crests a hill. I think I'll be embarrassed of so many parts of myself forever.

While in the U.K., my baba was studying electrical engineering. He had about ten months left in his PhD program when the 1979 revolution interrupted his education. Hearing rumors of the Iran border closing and growing anxious about being stuck outside with no way to reenter, he abandoned his studies to return to his homeland after a decade abroad. When he returned to Iran from the U.K., my baba went into the import-export business with his eldest brother, bringing in goods from Europe and Turkey, primarily raw materials like chemicals for the paint industry and pulp for newspapers.

My parents met during the revolution after a chance encounter between their mothers at a Quran reading for women at a home in Tehran. Shokat Khanum,* my father's mother, was talking about wanting to find her recently returned son a wife. My maternal matriarchs—my grandmother Alam Khanum and great-grandmother Sakineh Khanum—began boasting about the beautiful and intelligent Roya, who had skipped two grades and was studying physics at Tehran University. My maman's name means "good dream" in our language. That's exactly what she is, a tender vision. I am here on this earth because three Tabrizy women somehow engineered a love marriage that's lasting until this very day.

Before me, my parents had two daughters whom they raised in Tehran during the eight-year Iran-Iraq War that began in 1980. In September 1980, the then-president of Iraq, Saddam Hussein, ordered an invasion of Iran based on a few key interests: countering the potentially destabilizing influence of the Shia revolutionaries who took power in Tehran; regaining the Shatt al-Arab waterway, Iraq's major outlet to the Persian Gulf, over which Iran was given partial control under the 1975 Algiers Agreement; and establishing Saddam as a leader of the Arab

---

* *Khanum* is a term of respect that translates to "Mrs." or "Ms." when we refer to elder women in our families or as a general way of being overly respectful to strangers. Even though my grandmothers and great-grandmother will never read this book because they're no longer with us, I'm sure they would *feel* a sense of disrespect if I called them only by their first names. I love them too much to ever do so.

world. There were also indications that Saddam was trying to separate the oil-rich and Arab-majority Khuzestan province from Tehran, which was Iran's main oil source.

I was born a year after the war ended. In 1980, under pressure from President Jimmy Carter's administration, European nations announced a trade embargo for all goods and services contracted before the takeover of the American embassy in Tehran in November 1979. These restrictions changed the business landscape for many trying to make a living during this postrevolutionary and wartime period of instability, including my baba, who had to find other countries for his import-export business of Iranian goods. He started to import raw materials for tiles and the paint industry, as well as granite and marble, from Dubai, one of the few places that could do business with Iran under sanctions. Eventually, he established an office and moved us there six months after I was born. We spent summers in Tehran and winters in Dubai, but my baba stayed behind to work year-round. In the early 1990s, Dubai was nothing compared with what it is today. Most important for our family, there were no universities. Because the revolution interrupted my baba's studies, he was motivated to find a situation where his three daughters could study whatever they wanted and with stability. He didn't want to send his daughters far away. When we were in Dubai, my baba heard from an immigration lawyer that if he invested in a Canadian business, our family could come to Canada as permanent residents under the investor classification. And he did just that. He invested his savings in a hotel in Saskatoon—a snowy city in the plains of Canada—promptly moving my family. Being snow averse, we settled in Vancouver, the most temperate city in the country. By luck, by accident, by fate, we had a smooth and easy journey and road out of Iran.

FATEMEH

FOR THE GIRL WHO WISHED TO BE A BOY

F ROM THE BEGINNING, I was unwelcome in this world. I was born with my umbilical cord tied around my neck and was close to suffocating. The electricity was cut off, and I was born into the darkness. That night, our city shook from Iraqi rockets. The midwife who should have delivered me went home in fear. I stand out next to my fair-skinned siblings, and my mom still thinks my dark skin has something to do with the umbilical cord.

Between 1981 and 1990, more than twenty million children were born, despite the ongoing war, including me and my three brothers and one sister. The ideological policy of our post-totalitarian country was procreation, and people were encouraged to have as many children as possible. We were meant to become the army of Islam, and parents were encouraged to give children religious names like Somayeh, Fatemeh, Mohammad, Hussein, and Mahdi. Khomeini, the post-revolution supreme leader, called women "human makers"—a sentiment that still prevails among members of the present government.

Ali Khamenei, the current supreme leader, said, "The most important duty of women is giving birth."

I was three and a half when Khomeini, the founder of the regime and first supreme leader, died on June 3, 1989. I have a blurry memory of that day. Our fourteen-inch black-and-white TV announced his death, with an announcer saying, "God's spirit joined God." My mom cried. After his death, the council of clerics, called Khobregan, nominated Ali Khamenei, another cleric and then president, to be the next supreme leader, even though he did not have the qualifications for the role. The first condition of being the supreme leader is being a *marja'*, a title bestowed on the relative few who achieve the highest rank in religious schools, and Khamenei was not *marja'*. In an address to the nation, which was recorded and is available online, he showed humility that he would not display after. "We should weep tears of blood for Islamic society, where there is even the possibility of someone like me becoming the supreme leader," he told the people. The council of clerics claimed Khomeini had been adamant in nominating Khamenei, and within a few days a religious school in Qom issued his *marja'* designation, and he was appointed to the role of supreme leader.

The Shia Islamic faith dictates that the supreme leader, or *valiye faghih*, is responsible for enacting God's will on Earth, and Ali Khamenei's life and person are shrouded in the level of mystery one might expect from such a role. There are no public photos of Khamenei's wife, Mansoureh Khojasteh, or his daughters. He has not been interviewed by the media since becoming the supreme leader. The combination of religious fervor and political power has made Ali Khamenei one of the most brutal and deluded dictators in modern history.

Today, we hear protesters chanting in the streets, "Khamenei is another Khomeini, more of a pimp than the other." The word "pimp" has no grandiose, semi-positive definition in Persian as it does in English. In Persian, "pimp," or *koskesh*, is exclusively used to describe someone despicable—men who assault and abuse women, taking what they want from us. What may seem like a simple protest chant is a sign of change. People are pushing back against the sanctification of the supreme leader. In another protest cry, people wish for the death of Khamenei's eldest son, an end to his line of succession. They chant, "Mojtaba, you will die before becoming supreme leader." On the walls of public toilets around Tehran, people repeatedly write graffiti that reads, "This is Khamenei's house."

Yet the social and gender expectations of the Islamic Republic under Khamenei's leadership cast a shadow over my life and childhood. My parents were both teachers and devout Muslims. And Babaei, my father, took care of us in so many ways that might be looked down on as too feminine. A bright memory of mine is when Babaei cut my and my siblings' hair. All five of us took turns sitting in the short, plastic chair in his DIY barbershop, which we called the salon with the sky ceiling. On the days when my mom taught elementary school in the mornings, my father would cook for us. Babaei made us tasteless food without a trace of seasoning, but he told us it was a European or Italian dish. Never mind that he has never eaten European or Italian food; he does not eat pizza and pasta. He mostly made us rice, tomatoes, and baked potatoes. Now, when I think back to those meals that really made me miss my mom, they seem like food made in haste during wartime. These meals weren't made for us to enjoy, to sit around and take pleasure from the flavor. Rather, my dad quickly made undesirable food only for sustenance.

Over the years, I realized that my father did not do any housework in the presence of men, but when we did not have guests and it was just our immediate family, he washed dishes and prepared lunch for us. It seemed to me like our patriarchal society had unwillingly forced him to accept the role of a traditional man. But despite being educated, which many people in Iran believe is the antidote to patriarchy, he eventually gave in to the weight of societal expectations. I see what society has forced him into. I still love him and view him as my hero even if I don't fit into his view of an obedient, demure daughter.

When my mom was at school, we would play a game of our own invention. We took all the beans from the cabinets, separated the beans that were different shapes from the normal ones as kings and commanders, and made the rest our soldiers. Then we brought all of my mom's dishes and bowls to make castles and territories. It was a kind of a *Clash of Clans* strategy game played with beans and dishes in real life. Now that I go back to those days, I see how deprived we were. We were still under the influence of the king's period and impacted by war, using commanders, soldiers, and wars as playthings. While children living under normal circumstances played with dolls or cars, we formed our own territories.

My parents bought us school uniforms every two years, and we had to keep our schoolbags for three or four. The school uniform was made up of wide pants in navy or gray and a long jacket with buttons called a manteau that made my body shapeless and hit just at my knees. Any other color was prohibited. Our childhood was completely gray. The worst was the *maghnaeh*, a mandatory hijab that we began wearing in first grade. Though Islam dictates that girls should start wearing a hijab at nine years old, the Islamic Republic mandates that we start at seven. The fabric of the *maghnaeh* was sewn tight up to our chins. Whenever I wore it, I felt as if I were suffocating. The *maghnaeh* is the ugliest hijab possible. It makes us an unsightly version of ourselves.

In school, midday prayer was mandatory. We all had to array ourselves behind a mullah in an orderly manner, standing, sitting, bowing. We prayed in Arabic, a language that was not our own, and had no idea what these prayers meant. They searched our bags and backpacks as we entered to stop us from bringing makeup, posters of local soccer stars, magazines, and novels to school. When we reached middle school and high school, in addition to our nails, they checked our upper lips and eyebrows to make sure no one removed a single hair from their face.

We had a discipline grade on our report cards that carried the same value as the rest of the lessons. It counted toward our overall marks. They deducted points if we wore nail polish or plucked our eyebrows; if we had magazines or novels in our bags; and for many other endless reasons. The discipline grade was based on participating in prayers and obeying school rules. The *parvareshi* teacher, whose title and role translate to being our guide down the path of Islam, told us that we would be hanged in hell by hair that was seen by stranger men. These sharia laws were not only implemented in school; they were everywhere. There was never a minute of ease for us. When I came home for lunch, starving and wondering what there was to eat, my mother would always tell me that I should pray first.

We usually went to our paternal grandfather's house in a village in Andika County one weekend and to our maternal grandfather's house in the city of Masjed Soleyman another weekend. The weekends when we went to my maternal grandfather's house in the city, it was a completely different, modern and secular world—a world that made me realize the inconsistency between school and there. The parallel worlds formed around me. One world was the home of a religious family where the only music you could hear were pious classics such as Masoud Bakhtiari and Shajarian from a cassette tape. The other world was weekends at the home of my maternal grandparents and young uncles. They had many interesting movies and cartoon tapes and posters of Leila Foruhar, Googoosh, and other modern woman singers on their walls. They had sofas and beds. It was my luxury world, full of fantasy. My great-uncle worked at an oil company and traveled often. From his trips to different parts of the world, he brought things that we did not see in our everyday lives. Their home was the place of fairy tales, Cinderella, Snow White, *The Sword in the Stone,* Mickey Mouse, and Tom and Jerry. My uncles never prayed or read the Quran. They had girlfriends whom they talked to on the home phone for hours. Each of them had a master bedroom for himself. There were souvenirs that my oldest uncle used to bring from his foreign trips, from Buddha statues to glamorous pictures of Bollywood stars, everywhere in the house. But the world of weekends and fairy tales and cartoons ended with the end of our childhood and the marriages of my uncles. Now it is an abandoned house with faded posters and piles of dirt.

When I was ten, my parents bought bicycles for Hossein and Ehsan, my older and younger brothers. But because we were girls, according to religion, society, and my family, my sister and I did not have the right to have or ride bicycles. Little by little, I faced gender inequality not only in my own family but out in the world as well. I played soccer with the neighbor's children in our alley. I was a good goalkeeper. I had short hair and wore sweatpants like the boys and often had small holes in the knees of my pants from falling many times. Once my appearance changed and my breasts started to develop, Mamani conveyed to me a message from Babaei: I could no longer play soccer with boys. I couldn't make sense of it. I was still a good goalkeeper.

We had a big mulberry tree that my brother Hossein and his friend Pejman always used to climb. Once, I tried to climb the tree. Snaking up the branches, I felt a short-lived victory until I couldn't come down. My family had to call the firefighter to get me down. My second attempt to climb a tree was even worse than the first. This time, I climbed a narrow eucalyptus tree. The branch broke under my foot in the middle of climbing and wounded me deeply, tearing my abdomen skin from top to bottom. It was bloody. I did not tell my parents, because, whenever we hurt ourselves playing or for any other reason, my mother beat us. To her, our childhood injuries meant that we were not careful with our bodies and our clothes. I disinfected and cleaned the wound myself. I had that sore for years. I looked at it with a smile—my own secret stupid mark. It was easy to hide it because our parents rarely held or touched us, and we usually wore loose clothes that covered most of our bodies. The only time they hugged or kissed us was on Nowruz, Iranian New Year, and our birthdays. I realized over time that I had no childhood photos of myself being hugged by my revolutionary parents.

When I was in the fourth grade, I told my family that I had decided to wear a black veil. Our school administrators called all the students who wore veils from our morning line to the tribune and gifted them every week. I wanted to be one of them. This made my babaei happy, because he would no longer have to force me to wear it. My mom, however, said no, her reason being not my freedom but her belief that I am a clumsy person and would not be able to wear the veil correctly. She also thought that I was absent-minded and would lose it monthly, just as I used to tear my pants at the knees every month, and she would have to pay for it. I insisted and said, "I don't want an expensive veil. I will buy a light and cheap one. I promise I won't lose my veil."

After that, for a few years, I became like the Ninja Turtles. I put my big backpack on my back, then wore and pulled the veil down to my eyebrows and pulled the elastic behind my head to fix the veil and my *maghnaeh* on my head.

We used to go to Ahvaz to my aunt Fariba's house during the Nowruz holidays. She bought us pizza and took us to cafés and cinemas in Kianpars, the most high-class and luxury neighborhood in Ahvaz. But nothing was as fun as when we went to an amusement park called Island. It had a huge chain swing. My cousins, siblings, and I bought tickets and stood in line. We got on. It started to rotate and fly. The young boys began to jump down with dramatic gestures from the moving swing. I decided to jump like the boys while wearing a long black veil. I jumped and spread on the ground like a black pancake. They didn't open the door until the end of the ride, and I had to stay until the end of the turn. I heard people's words:

Kangaroo.

Zorro.

Is the girl jumping?

How dare you jump with your veil!

Another problem was my loud voice. My mom used to tell me that I must have swallowed a microphone. She always told me that I would lose my hearing by talking so loudly, adding, "A woman should not speak loud." Yet even now I continue to speak as loud as ever and I am not yet deaf, in spite of my mother's prediction.

In our schools, there was no education about periods or sexual hygiene. Our mothers often did not tell us anything about periods. In Islam, a menstruating woman is considered impure. Women do not have the right to enter religious places, pray, or even touch the Quran while on their periods. I had no idea about menstruation, but luckily my cousin Roya got her period first and told me all about it. When it was my turn, I hid it from everyone for months. Instead of sanitary pads, I bought diapers. After using them, I would wrap them in paper and hide them in a cardboard box in the pantry. I was embarrassed at the idea that others would know that I got my period. I did not want others to consider me impure. We did not learn that this is part of the natural life cycle for women. One day when I was at school, my mother arrived home and found the house full of bloody diapers. My two younger brothers had found them and played with them like balls. I will never forget my mom's reaction when I arrived home. Physical punishment was common in our generation. My mother often beat us and then collapsed into pools of tears after. She suffered from severe depression, but my father did not let her take medicine. Even today, there's resistance in our family to going to a psychiatrist or a therapist. They think you must be crazy to go talk to someone about your problems.

I loved jumping, but my mom once told me I should not jump. I said, "Why?" and she said that jumping might break my hymen and make my future partner think I was not a virgin. Then she spoke to me about the importance of being a virgin, scaring me about the possibility of not appearing to be "pure." "You should keep it until marriage. You cannot get married without it. Your virginity is your symbol of chastity," she said. My parents still think that I am a virgin at the age of thirty-seven.

NILO

FOR A LIFETIME OF LONELINESS

I GREW UP WATCHING the BBC with my baba. He instilled in me a love for the news. My baba has always loved strong women. He would always talk about Christiane Amanpour and Zeinab Badawi in awe; we looked up to these intelligent, well-spoken news anchors together. One of his favorite TV shows is *Suits*, and he loves the Jessica Pearson character, the head of the law firm on which the show centers. Every time she comes on-screen, my baba turns to me and says some version of "Look how smart and tough and strong she is. Did you see how she handled this situation? She's made these men look like little idiot boys." In the same way that my baba encouraged me to be strong, my sisters, my mother, and I reflected that strength back at him, reinforcing each other's feminism simply by being in a woman-dominated family and having the ability to explore that freely.

I had the space and freedom to grow into a strong woman. I was always outspoken as a child. Always a tomboy. Always bossy. Never as femme and by the book as my two older sisters. Frequently getting in trouble for talking back to authority figures. I was lucky to grow up in

Canada, where gender wasn't my roadblock. My maman never made me feel as if I couldn't be myself. She took me to Tehran in 2000, when I was ten years old. I didn't have to wear hijab in public then; I think I was too young. But my maman remembers me fighting with taxi drivers, demanding to know why women couldn't wear dresses or why men couldn't wear short sleeves. Why couldn't women and girls be on the back of motorcycles? Why only boys? The taxi driver told me that women are fragile and could fall off the motorbike. I told him that would never happen to me. I was strong. My maman let me argue with all sorts of people when I didn't understand why I was treated differently as a little girl.

I wish I could go back to that summer in Tehran when I spent nearly every hot afternoon swimming in a family friend's pool and each night playing hide-and-seek and climbing up metal gates with the boys, casting shadows onto the sidewalks. My mom would drop my cousin Shirin and me off in the mornings and scoop us up again at the end of the night. It was on these rides that my arguments with taxi drivers began. When I'm reminded that I can't return to Iran, I feel my throat start to tighten. To try to ground myself in this emotional upheaval, I recall the feeling of those tiny stones in the gray cement of the pool deck. I close my eyes and try to remember how hot they'd get and how long I'd try to sit on their warmth before plunging myself into the water. The kids I used to play with would call me Nilofar-e abi, or water lily. My maman had told me that my name means "lily" in Persian, but my refusal to come out of the pool led my summertime friends to add an extra layer to my name, a nickname of sorts—though I didn't know at the time what it meant. After being called Nilofar-e abi all summer, I wondered, Did my name really mean "water lily" all these years? Was I so disconnected from myself and where I came from that I didn't even know what my name means in my own language?

Just recently, I learned that nilofar flowers are carved all over the ruins of Takht-e Jamshid in Shiraz and Taq-e Bostan in Kermanshah. In ancient Iran, this water lily was a symbol of immortality. It represents the suffering and hardships of people who've gone through a difficult period and are moving toward peace. We bloom out of swamps, our vibrant green lily pads floating on the surface of murky water. We become full of life. The flower opens when the sun rises and closes back up when the sun goes down.

I turned eleven that summer. I was thrilled to keep climbing into double digits like Saam and Milad, the two older boys with whom Shirin and I spent all our time. I was already feeling far too impatient in my scrawny body. Shirin was born a week after me. My maternal grandmother, whom I always called Mamani, used to say that the first week of July was the best week of her life because, all of a sudden, she had two granddaughters. The family's two youngest cousins appeared out of thin air in a matter of days. Shirin was much more feminine than me. She moved delicately and wore pastel matching clothes, and her light brown hair was always neatly combed. I wonder if I would be more like her had we stayed in Iran. Maybe I would be easier to be around, more likable, maybe I'd get in less trouble. In our summer quartet, I dressed much more like Saam and Milad. My summer uniform was baggy Adidas track shorts, a boxy oversized T-shirt, and black athletic sandals. I never strayed from this aesthetic. They all said I looked like a boy, and I felt immensely proud of that.

One pitch-black night, the four of us were playing a high-stakes game of hide-and-seek. Each evening our reputations were on the line—who could be the bravest, the fastest, the quietest. Even at night after dinner, the air was hot and scorching, cloaking us in a damp heat of around ninety-five degrees Fahrenheit. In the north Tehran neighborhoods that we roamed, all the homes had metal gates and intercoms in front of the main doors. And thankfully for us, these gates were perfect to climb all over. The metal irons crossed each other, making little squares and diamonds, giving us perfect holes for our tiny feet. Whenever it was my turn to hide, I'd scramble to the top and try to blend into the background. I moved like a spider, with my skinny limbs wrapping around the metal that was still warm from the day's heat. Shirin stayed back and would hide behind cars. She never climbed up the gates, leaving that to the more reckless members of the group. During one game, I slashed my left forearm open, scraping it while climbing down. They took me to a neighbor's home to get it looked at. I think he was a doctor, but I couldn't be sure, because almost every older man I was introduced to told me he was Doctor So-and-So. Were there that many doctors in Tehran, or was this a cultural nuance that I didn't understand?

"Nilofar, what happened? What were you doing?" the nameless doctor asked me, using my full first name. But it wasn't just an innocent question, he was asking me with an air of disappointment. "Obviously I was playing hide-and-seek. We were climbing on those front gates," I quickly replied. I had a habit of snapping back and being frustrated with anyone who tried to impose authority on me. He looked up at me while he was cleaning the blood off my arm and dressing my wound. "That is not an activity for little girls, Nilofar."

"Well, I'm not a little girl," I said. "I'm actually eleven."

I don't think he knew quite what to do with me—a lanky young girl, giving an elder, a stranger, attitude. Unknowingly, I was crossing lots of cultural lines. I don't think he was ready for my instinct to be confrontational. I certainly wasn't ready for a man I didn't know to tell me what to do or where to climb.

My summers in Vancouver, Canada, were much more organized. I'd go to volleyball camp, swim on the club team, or go to weeks-long ballet intensives. I never had a problem making friends or being social. But the friends I made that summer in Tehran were different. We weren't bound by sports or an activity; it was our family or friends or proximity that brought us together. We chose to play. We created our own little teams. We'd buy these plastic balls that were made up of layers and layers of striped colorful thin material and kick them to each other on side streets as boxy sedans puttered by. When we had downtime in our summer camps in Canada, my friends would excitedly talk about their crushes. That was the only time that talkative me would fall silent. No one ever had a crush on me, at least not until very late in high school. I once showed a photo from kindergarten to an ex-boyfriend. He laughed and asked if I went to school in Norway, shocked at how different I looked from my classmates. In the photo, I'm smiling at the edge of the frame. I stick out immediately—a mop of thick black hair chopped into a sharp bob, squeezed into a row of blondes with light hair that floated down to their shoulders. My peers were holding on to dolls and Barbies, and I had my hands tucked behind my back, wearing a velvet dress that my maman had sewn for me. My body was subtly hidden behind the young girl right beside me. I was inching to disappear.

I never got to share any news of a crush or a playground "marriage" with my friends. But that summer in Iran, a boy finally looked at me. Milad had dark hair and thick eyebrows just like me. We had the same deep brown eyes and olive skin that turned golden brown in the sun. I was always jealous of my Canadian friends with hazel, blue, or green eyes, while mine looked like pools of ink. I would catch Milad looking at me while we were swimming. Once, during hide-and-seek, I know he saw me in my hiding spot but didn't call me out or tag me. Our short-lived young romance peaked during the hottest afternoons when we'd retreat inside to the only room with air-conditioning. While the adults took naps in their bedrooms, Saam, Milad, and I would play *Resident Evil* on PlayStation. I wasn't really a video game person, but I'd watch Saam and Milad play game after game, counting the number of zombies that would slowly crawl all over the screen. In these quiet moments, Milad's knees would touch mine. Neither of us pulled away. I felt a flush on my face that I felt only when I was embarrassed by someone mispronouncing my name, but this warmth didn't carry with it an urge to want to run and hide. Rather, I felt joy and embarrassment dancing together in my stomach. This must be the feeling of crushing and liking that my Canadian friends would fall all over themselves about.

As an adult looking back at photos of my first few years in Canada, I feel so sad for small Nilo. I can still feel how much I hated what I looked like. Even at five years old, I felt that I was a sheepish, disposable accessory compared with the kids I grew up with. Maybe I would be unlovable forever. I have no idea where these big feelings came from, but the self-wounding happened easily for me. Milad was the first person to change that. When I didn't like myself, he showed me that he did, simply by paying attention to me. We never kissed, never dated. Our entire romance took place in a chlorinated swimming pool, in the world of PlayStation, and between our little knees as they held warmth with each other. This sprinkle of confidence and external validation from my summer in Tehran was a perspective shift. I started to learn where my self-wounding came from, but it would take years to fix that myself and without depending on someone else's gaze.

The only time I felt unease because of my gender in Iran was when we went to the passport office. That's when I had to wear hijab for the first time. I wore my cousin's hijab from her school uniform. It wasn't a regular headscarf that I could loosely wrap and throw over my shoulder as I saw with fashionable young girls in Tehran. This was a *maghnaeh*; it was conservative and tight, my chubby cheeks constricted by the thick black fabric. I had my little toes painted bright red, sticking out from my flip-flops. I had never seen police wearing huge rifles across their bodies and stared up at them, unable to look away. One of them got in my face, screaming, "Why are your toes out? Wearing nail polish is un-Islamic!" I was staring up at his bearded face, watching him with my huge eyes, feeling the presence of a giant weapon very close to me.

I was confused. It was the middle of summer in Tehran, and the heat was scorching. Why wouldn't I be wearing flip-flops? I was hot enough wearing this uncomfortable hijab. My cousin Shirin, who'd lent me her *maghnaeh,* moved to stand between us. With light brown hair that fell in soft curls under her hijab, she was about three inches shorter than me, and I was surprised to see her as the confrontational one. "She's a guest. My cousin is from Canada; she doesn't know any better. Don't you know how to treat guests in our country?" she snapped at him.

As she pulled me away, she told me to stop being a little mouse and to stick up for myself. No one had ever accused me of being a tiny, demure thing ever in my life. I realized I stood out everywhere. In Canada, white kids would bully me about my thick eyebrows and peach fuzz mustache that sprang up far too young. I had no idea I was "brown" until my high school boyfriend told me I was, offhandedly saying, "Isn't it wild, as a white man I'm at the top of the ladder of society, and as a brown woman you're at the bottom." I had no idea my name was "weird" until I came home crying every day in elementary school to my mom, begging her to change my name to something easier for them to pronounce, like Sara. I didn't know how to share what was going on with me with my family. As a young child who started experiencing this crippling self-hatred in kindergarten, I didn't have the language to communicate what was going on with me. Instead, I would often come home sick from school in the middle of the day, calling my maman from the phone in the principal's office, telling her that I had yet another stomachache. My therapist told me that this is common; this is exactly how anxiety shows up in young children. I held a feeling of loneliness and isolation for much of my childhood. Yes, I was social and made friends easily, but I didn't know how to share with them what was going on with me. I knew that they didn't have the experience to understand either.

I never even told my sisters how much I was struggling. My sisters are two years apart, and they were nine and eleven years old when we immigrated. I'm sure they had similar pains of readjusting, but they had each other. I felt completely alone and became used to navigating everything by myself in my small body. I look back at old family photos, and there's a marked difference before we came to Canada. In my photos as a baby and toddler in Tehran and Dubai, I often have a giant grin pasted on my face, my eyes crinkling as I smile, with dimples on either side of my round cheeks. And then in the Canada chapter, my eyes are wider. My smile strained. I'm clasping tightly on my mother's arm or holding her hand. At home, my parents were supportive, caring, and nurturing, always sympathetic and attentively listening on the rare days that I could put into words what I was feeling. I learned this behavior of self-hatred from my outside environment, and it's taken decades to dismantle it piece by piece. I thought I could blend in in Tehran. That summer I learned I'd forever be a stranger no matter where I was.

As long as the current regime is in place, I'll remain a stranger to Iran. I made the conscious choice to start reporting on Iran in 2017, knowing that I would cut off this connection. I had been working as a journalist since 2012 and never wanted to report on Iran, because I knew how lucky I was having the privilege to return. While living in New York, I met many Iranian Americans, recent asylum seekers, and a few lucky émigrés who were pained that they couldn't go back to Iran due to being from political families who were a part of the opposition during the revolution or due to their activism against the current regime. This made me even more protective of my ability to go back to Iran. I don't come from a political family. I never had stories of torture or imprisonment passed down to me. I felt grateful to be ordinary. Donald Trump's presidency raised the stakes on reporting on Iran. A year after his inauguration, he signed a presidential order proclaiming the travel ban. This ban meant many of my fellow Iranians were barred from coming to the United States to lawfully study or reunite with their loved ones. Talk of war with Iran became increasingly real, and I felt I had to use my privilege of being one of the only Iranian reporters at *The New York Times* to bring Iranian voices and our humanity to news stories. The difficulty of reporting freely in Iran often highlighted the necessity of doing journalism from outside the country. Those reporting from inside were under constant surveillance and at the mercy of security officials whose red lines for what was permissible and not permissible to cover changed on a whim. My language skills and ability to form genuine connections with Iranians became key. It made sense to sacrifice my hope of returning for my *hamvatan*s, for the people of my homeland. Every time I publish something, it's a paper cut. It's a prick of loss. A confirmation that I can't return. I'm stuck here watching from afar. My therapist labeled these post-publish feelings as grief. When I hear about Fatemeh's experience of being interrogated, I know my fate could be much worse. If I landed in Iran, I would likely be grabbed immediately, taken to prison, and held as a hostage—the very thing that happened to my colleague Jason Rezaian as the Iran correspondent for *The Washington Post*. The newspaper hasn't had anyone based in the country since that incident.

This grief shows up in unexpected ways. In July 2023, I was visiting my friend Martina, who moved back to Rome after a decade in New York. We met while working at *Vice* in 2014. Martina and I used to talk about me reporting on Iran, but I always told her it was too risky. I even refused to be on email chains with the regime's media representative in New York when someone on our team was interested in going to Iran to film different video stories. We were having dinner on my last night in a neighborhood called Monti with our friend Lorenzo. I was nothing but happy and felt so lucky to be in this moment with two people who've known me for years, eating my comfort food, a haram plate of carbonara. Then, sitting at the table, I grew quiet and went within myself. My introverted, contemplative self comes out in front of others only when I'm at my most comfortable. When my guard is fully down, I go back to the internal universe I created as little Nilo where I could safely go inside my own thoughts and feelings in a self-protective way. Silently, I started to cry. I was hoping that these tears would fall and dry before anyone noticed. I was hoping that I was somehow invisible to my friends. Lorenzo asked me if I was sad because it was my last night. I couldn't hold it in, and I started to audibly sob.

"For me, it is so special to see someone in their home element. There's nothing I appreciate more. And here, I can see Martina being fully Italian. The way she's taking me around, translating for me, introducing me to her family, taking care of me, riding around together on her scooter. I've loved being here, but there is a huge part of me that is so sad that none of you will ever see me this way. I'll never be able to take you to Iran and translate for you, introduce you to my family, and show you where I'm from. None of you will ever fully see me. And it's my fault. It's because of a choice I made to report on Iran. And I don't regret it, but sometimes it just shows up like this and I feel horrible."

My words and sobs hung in the silence for just a moment. "Well, first, life is long, and you never know what will happen and that you might be able to go back at some point. Your work, what you've been doing with your reporting, is in and of itself an act of love toward your country that will bring you even closer to it," said Martina. "Sharing your culture, the way you've been doing with such pride and passion since literally the minute I met you, is such a beautiful and active way of being a citizen, and you do it in a way that's potentially even more intense than what someone who lives there could experience."

"We can see you at home. We can visit you in Canada and see you being Iranian with your family. Your home is with them too," Lorenzo added.

A few days later, I texted Lorenzo a photo that Milad had sent me of a red yo-yo I had left behind that summer in Tehran. I used to take it everywhere, snapping it down from my hands, trying to make the red plastic hover above the sidewalks and light up. I couldn't believe that Milad had found it after all this time. "I love that there's this part of me still in Iran from my favorite summer that I spent there," I wrote to Lorenzo.

"It's kind of incredible and symbolic that a yo-yo is what represents you in Iran right now. Because the thing about yo-yos is, they always come back," Lorenzo responded.

FATEMEH

FOR CHANGING RUSTED MINDS

MY FAMILY WOULD sometimes travel to larger towns to visit my father's eldest brother, who was a governor. All of the country's newspapers were delivered to his home, so instead of playing *Super Mario* with my cousins and siblings, I read newspapers until it was time to return home. My uncle always told all the children, "Look at Fatemeh, she will become someone."

Those newspapers were, for me, windows to a better world, to freedom. I looked at the big fonts of headlines in the first pages and saw the names and photos of woman reporters. Most of them had makeup, were smiling widely, and wore colorful loose headscarves with some hair around their faces exposed. I decided then that I wanted to be a journalist.

At the time, we were living under a brief period of freedom in the press, cinema, and book publishing. Upon becoming supreme leader, Khamenei removed from power leftist clerics and officials with obvious socialist ideas regarding the economy. Nearly a decade later, this group of clerics, who had a more liberal view of modern Islam, banded together and were able to elect a reformist president, Mohammad Khatami. He came to power in 1997 after gaining twenty million votes—70 percent of the electorate. Many who voted for him were young people exhausted with the regime's ideological strictness, demanding freedom, democracy, and gender equality.

Under Khatami's administration, film directors who were banned from working started making movies, and film festivals became crowded with spectators again. Khatami's cabinet expanded freedom of speech and tried to improve relations with the West. The circulation of reformist newspapers reached a million copies, and journalists, especially woman journalists, found their identities again, publishing their photos alongside their bylines. Many banned books like *One Hundred Years of Solitude* by Gabriel García Márquez got published for the first, and maybe last, time without censorship. I read it. The circulation of books reached thousands of copies, and they were reprinted dozens of times over. Khatami's presidency recorded the highest economic growth and lowest inflation rate among the postrevolutionary governments.

But, despite all the hopes we had for him, this golden era under Khatami did not last. After April 20, 2000, Khamenei, the supreme leader, reversed all of Khatami's reforms. Reformists were publicly terrorized by the IRGC, removed from power, and disqualified from running in any future elections. Intellectuals like writers and translators were killed by the Ministry of Intelligence. The supreme leader ordered the seizure of reformist newspapers, and twenty newspapers were shut down by the judiciary. All the freedoms of expression we thought had become permanent—in the press, cinema, literature, theater—were once again lost. In one of his speeches at the end of his presidency, Khatami criticized the limited powers of the presidency in Iran, claiming that the position does not hold enough power or authority to make decisions that will stick.

Still, I benefited from this brief period of cultural expansion. When I was sixteen, a bookstore called Bamdad, meaning "early morning," opened in our small town. That bookstore and *Chelcheragh* magazine changed my life. This weekly magazine published cultural, sports, artistic, social, literary, cinematic, and satirical content. Its tagline was that it was a magazine for the third generation born after the revolution. It was meant for me and others who were born in the 1980s, growing up among all the limitations of postrevolutionary Iran as we demanded reform and changes. All the journalists and writers were young. It allocated its leading article to writings from its audience. I was eighteen when my writing was published as its leading article. I was flying in the clouds. I looked at my name in disbelief. I read my article over and over again. I was heard and seen for the first time in my life. I wrote a piece that was critical of my family's strict limitations on my life and their pressure on us to study. I started to regularly submit my writings to *Chelcheragh*. I did not have access to computers or the internet at the time, so I wrote my book reviews by hand and sent them by mail, all the way from Masjed Soleyman to Tehran.

Literature and reading books saved me. I adored Annette and her courage in *The Soul Enchanted* by Romain Rolland. I fell in love with Tolstoy's *Anna Karenina*, and I remember how meaningful its beginning was for me: "All happy families are alike; each unhappy family is unhappy in its own way." I was consumed with Anna and Annette's independence and how they swam against the current and didn't give in to the fate that patriarchy wanted for them. *A Room of One's Own* by Virginia Woolf always stuck with me. Woolf gave Shakespeare a fictional sister, Judith, who didn't have room to write or a chance to become a writer. At that time, my father had told my mother not to let me read so many books. He said these books would corrupt my mind. I often placed novels among schoolbooks and pretended to study or went to the public library to read books. I read *The Second Sex* by Simone de Beauvoir with my flesh, skin, and bones. It gave me the answers to so many questions. We women belong to the men of our families under sharia law. There is some kind of "honor" that we are supposed to feel by being controlled by men. I realized over time that I do not belong to anyone. No one has the right to control me. My body belongs to me.

Growing up, I was always rewarded for my good grades. I was sixteen when Sangin Mah, my grandmother, gave me a thick gold bracelet that my mamani took and wore herself. We still did not have a sofa, and no matter how much we insisted, my father refused to buy one. I was embarrassed, because all my friends had a sofa in their home, so one day I cut the bracelet from Mamani's hand with pliers and sold it. I used the money to buy a sofa and dining table. My father did not talk to me for the next six months. I had become a stubborn girl who behaved against his will.

I was accepted to study clinical psychology in Tehran thanks to my marks on the national university entrance exam when I was nineteen years old. But my father did not want me to go. He understood he could not convince me by force, so he found his way through another door. He made me feel tormented and guilty. He said, "If you study at Chamran University in Ahvaz and our province, I will be relieved." I decided to stay home and chose an agricultural engineering major at that university. It was the first time that I sacrificed my dreams for my family.

When I was twenty, I saved money to buy a flight to Tehran to attend the anniversary ceremony for my favorite magazine, *Chelcheragh*. But at the airport, a female IRGC officer did not let me in, because she said my manteau was not appropriate. A manteau is kind of like a loose-fitting trench coat we wear for "modesty" under the Islamic dress codes for women. I did not have any other manteau. I tried to plead with her to let me in, but she didn't care. I missed my flight. I missed the ceremony. I was humiliated and lost my dignity. In September 2006, Reza Alipour, the head of the Tehran police, said that in one month 63,693 women with improper hijab were summoned and 1,149 cars seized. In 2007, the head of the country's airport police announced that they had prevented 128 women from traveling and issued 171,151 women warnings due to an improper hijab; 6,799 women had to produce a written commitment to not repeat this crime. I do not know if I counted as one of them.

In my sophomore year, my friends and I decided to go on a two-day camping trip to the countryside in Lorestan province. I told Ehsan, my younger brother, to come. On the day we were set to leave, we all gathered at our shared apartment entrance at eight in the morning in Ahwaz's Golestan neighborhood, then took a taxi to the railway station and went to the Bisheh Waterfall by local train. When we—Ehsan, Amin, my boyfriend, and my friends and their partners—reached our destination, we were so far from the city that we had no mobile service. My phone rang when we were near Ahwaz on the way back. It was my father. When I answered, he was shouting, "Where are you? I will come and set you on fire." I did not understand what happened nor that he meant "fire" literally, to immolate me. I quickly gave the phone to Ehsan. We realized the neighbors had called the landlord and got my father's number. Then they called my father and told him that his daughter had gotten into a car with some men and left. I don't know what would've happened to me if I hadn't asked Ehsan to come with us. Would my father have actually burned me?

In Iran, honor killings, forced marriage, and domestic violence are not limited to any one class, educational level, or region. It can happen to any of us. Even my educated father wanted to burn me to protect his honor. According to an investigative report by the newspaper *Shargh*, from 2021 to 2023 a woman was killed by one of the men in her family every four days across Iran; forty-three were shot with hunting rifles, Colts, and even Kalashnikovs. Forty were stabbed to death. Thirty-five were suffocated by hand or with scarves and bedding. Six were burned to death as the men poured gasoline directly onto their flesh. Four were murdered by multiple hammer blows. Thirty more women were murdered in other unusual, violent ways such as being mutilated or thrown from the roof of a building. This regular violence isn't exclusive to outer provinces. A quarter of these murders happened in the educated, urban, and "progressive" Tehran province.

Some women can escape from the men of their families and honor killings through financial independence, but not every woman has this chance. In Iran's economy, discrimination against women is starkly evident in comparison to the world average. The workforce participation rate of Iranian women is 17 percent, while the global average is 50.6 percent. Even university education has not been able to compensate for this inequality in recent years. The government began to impose gender quotas and restrictions on the admission of women to universities in the early '00s, claiming that "women's education threatens the institution of the family." After that, the government started to restrict the employment of women. According to a Human Rights Watch report from 2017, even though Iranian women make up half of university graduates, they make up less than 15 percent of the workforce in this country.

In my last semester of college, I was closely watching the news at night. It was the 2009 presidential election. Mahmoud Ahmadinejad was running for his second term, and his opponent was Mir Hossein Mousavi, the popular prime minister during the Iran-Iraq War. One of Mousavi's main election promises was to shut down the morality police. The Islamic Republic News Agency (IRNA) called the election for Ahmadinejad with 62 percent of votes. None of us believed it. We were furious at the result. I had an exam the next morning. When I was heading to the university, I wore my green fabric bracelet, a symbol of Mousavi's campaign. I was surprised when I saw all the students wearing their green bracelets. It showed our solidarity and was a sign of protest. Then we learned that security forces attacked all of Mousavi's campaign buildings, and all the reformist figures were arrested. We skipped the exam and instead ran to the streets to protest. This became known as the 2009 Green Movement; widespread national unrest broke out due to allegations of electoral fraud, with thousands marching in the streets demanding, "Where is my vote?"

The Ministry of Communications blocked texting to prevent protests. At that time, we did not have internet data on our phones, and SMS text messages were the only communication tool that we had. In his victory speech, Ahmadinejad called the protesters "dust and trash." Then protesters chanted the slogan "You are dust and trash. You are our land's enemy."

In addition to demonstrating against election fraud, women were demanding the abolition of the morality police. A video of a young woman's killing captured on a citizen journalist's phone would become an iconic image of the demonstrations. Neda Agha-Soltan, twenty-six, was killed on June 20, 2009, by a security force officer's bullet in the Amir Abad neighborhood, on North Kargar Street near Enghelab Street. Neda had studied theology for one year at Islamic Azad University but had dropped out due to pressure from the university officials to wear a hijab. The young woman, who came to the street to protest dressed beautifully, was killed seeking a better life. After thirteen years, the former U.S. president Barack Obama said he made "a mistake" by not supporting the Iranian people during the Green Movement against the Islamic Republic.

After the suppression of text messages, Facebook, and Twitter during the Green Movement, Persian-language media abroad in London and Washington, D.C., became the main source of news coverage of the protests. Many Iranian families, even in remote villages, installed satellite television to access diasporic Persian-language media, and four years later, according to the minister of culture and Islamic guidance, 71 percent of Iranian people were consuming this foreign content. These news channels and shows exposed and led to the normalization of forbidden behavior, like wearing somewhat revealing clothes, having boyfriends, kissing, and having sex with partners, cohabitation, and the loss of the importance of virginity. Although the Islamic Republic and its extremists won the 2009 election, they had lost another strategic point. Later, the police began to attack and collect satellite dishes. The police's war against satellite dishes reached a new level when they crushed them with the IRGC's tanks.

I was accepted to Allameh Tabataba'i University, the best journalism school in Iran, in 2009 to pursue my master's degree in journalism. At that time, we did not have the internet at home, so I had to go to a café to check my exam results. When I learned I had been accepted, I ran and screamed with joy all the way from the internet café to my home. In my first year as a graduate student, in January 2010, I became a reporter for the Islamic Students' News Agency (ISNA) in Tehran. My first job was as a social desk reporter, which really changed my life. I always wrote stories about the working classes and women. But it was not enough for me. I wanted to write features, long and deeply reported stories. I wanted to work at the newspaper *Shargh* but did not know how.

At the university, some classmates had begun introducing themselves as One Million Campaign members. I learned that women's rights activists had launched the "one million signature campaign to change discriminatory laws," especially family-related laws, on August 27, 2006. They were demand-oriented activists of the fifth generation of Iranian feminists. This campaign aimed to collect one million signatures through face-to-face conversations to present to the Parliament. They were accused by some officials of being U.S. mercenaries and trying to destabilize the regime. Many of the campaigners were imprisoned and forced into exile, but their legacy of raising awareness about the impact of laws on the lives of women and men is still preserved. My classmates were expelled from the university because of their participation in the one million signature campaign.

Some hijab rules are really strange. There are no clear boundaries. For example, putting sunglasses on our head is a violation. Wearing boots is a violation. Applying makeup is a violation. Having nail polish is a violation, and if we are traveling, female IRGC officers at the airport give us tissues to wipe off our lipstick and mascara before letting us fly. It was the same at university too; female officers were on patrol to inspect whether we had nail polish or makeup on or were not following dress code and would not let us into the university if we were in violation of the rules. Our anger was not only about the hijab; it was about daily humiliations we endured in the name of hijab.

When I was in the second year of my master's degree in 2011, university officials announced that women and men would no longer sit in classes together. I didn't take it seriously until the first day of classes, when I witnessed the division. Not surprisingly, the best professors were assigned to male students. Once, I was stopped by a female university Herasat officer. Herasat is a branch of policing responsible for enforcing Islamic principles in people's public and private lives. Its officers, stationed in every university and state department office or organization, are tasked with reporting infractions back to the Ministry of Intelligence and the IRGC Intelligence Organization. I was surprised to be stopped because I was wearing a long *maghnaeh* and a long manteau. She told me to take off my gloves. When I asked why, she responded that she wanted to make sure that I wasn't wearing nail polish.

As the regime has tried to impose sharia rules in our lives, we have distanced ourselves from it. I found some of my friends during Ramadan not in mosques but in cafés, which stay open all night to accommodate those who fast during the day. Ramadan was not a month of fasting for us. Muslims believe that Ramadan was the month when the Quran was revealed to Muhammad, the Prophet of Islam, but it is not known whether this revelation happened on the nineteenth, twenty-first, or twenty-third day of Ramadan. On these three nights, Muslims stay awake and pray in mosques until morning. The next day, all offices, schools, universities, and organizations start working late to give fasting Muslims enough time to rest.

But for many female students in dormitories, these three nights were an opportunity to be outside the dormitory with their boyfriends until morning prayers without anyone contacting their families to inform them of their absence. The regular prohibition on entering the dormitory after 8:00 p.m. and leaving it before 7:00 a.m. was broken during these three nights of Ramadan. The subway was open and in service throughout the night and until the morning. For my classmates and me, Ramadan was for enjoying nightlife and having the right to be on the streets of Tehran after dark as a woman. It was a month of café tours, where we would watch live concerts by female singers and piano players from night to morning. We could experience friendship without gender separation, just being in each other's company experiencing the streets of Tehran at night—streets that are taken from us throughout the year. The city was alive. The next day, all the news agencies would have photo reports of women in loose hijabs and wearing heavy makeup who had put the Quran on their heads in mosques, but there was no trace of us in any of the reports.

In December 2012, *Shargh* was up and running again after a temporary stoppage due to having published a cartoon depicting several people covering each other's eyes with ribbons. The conservatives said it insulted Iranian fighters in the Iran-Iraq War. Iranian soldiers usually wore ribbons with holy words on their foreheads like "Fatemeh" and "Mahdi." Once it reopened, I went to a job interview for a social desk reporter position. I bought a colorful scarf and put on makeup in the public toilet on my way from ISNA to *Shargh*. The atmosphere was completely different from ISNA. Women wore colorful skirts and scarves and smoked freely in the yard. There was no strict enforcement of the women's hijab like at ISNA. At the end of the interview, the social desk editor said, "We will let you know." I knew this meant no. I knew that other experienced and famous journalists interviewed for this position. But it was my dream job, and I knew I was qualified for it, so I tried to pitch myself one last time before leaving. "Being a journalist is not just a job for me. It is my whole life. I left my family, my city, and everything behind to come to Tehran and study journalism and work as a journalist." The interviewer was convinced. "Take off your coat and write your first report. You will have a trial week before I decide," she responded.

My first report became the leading headline of the front page. She told me at the end of the day that I didn't need to pass the weeklong trial and that I was hired. As a journalist for *Shargh*, I could finally afford to rent a place with my younger brother Ehsan's financial help. I had achieved financial independence from my parents. My apartment was in the Majidieh neighborhood in the east of Tehran at the end of an alley. When my friend and her partner moved in together, her boyfriend gave me his sofas and a bed. I bought a desk and chair from a secondhand store. Ehsan bought me a small table, a twenty-one-inch TV, and a bookshelf. I painted the walls in yellow, green, and blue. I had my own house. Its windows opened to the walls of other homes in the alley, but I liked it. It was my first home.

The regime's interference in our lives can be on vital issues like the citizenship of our children, or it can ruin a wedding that disobeys mandatory gender segregation because of the Amaken Police, a sector of the police that monitors establishments like cafés, event venues, and restaurants by imposing Islamic rules. The way to get around the latter requires cash bribes. The author, poet, and playwright Václav Havel once said, "The post-totalitarian system touches people at every step, but it does so with its ideological gloves on." I felt its touch one night in September 2012 while running up the stairs at a colleague's wedding. I had red hair, wore a lot of makeup, and was trying not to lose my balance while running with high heels. We had been dancing and having fun at our colleague's wedding in a garden in the northeast of Tehran when the local police attacked us. If weddings are held in an official venue space, they must be segregated by gender. Those who have more money can rent a garden, which does not have built-in segregated rooms. But there is always the fear of the police attacking a mixed wedding. We women quickly went to the upper floor to serve the dinner and to pretend that the wedding was separate. Dozens of women in high heels and long gowns with hands raised were running to the second floor. In the end, our colleague Farhad, the groom, had to bribe the local police with five months of his salary so that his wedding night would not be disturbed. If he had not given the bribes, all of us would have been arrested and put on trial for the crime of participating in a mixed party.

I did many reports about IRGC corruption at *Shargh*. But instead of corrupt officials being held accountable, it was often I who ended up in court. That was when I realized it does not matter how hard we work to shine a spotlight on government misdeeds, because the judiciary system was one of the IRGC's most powerful and entrenched supporters. As such, it began to feel as if rather than effect change, our reports could only serve to document and archive our present reality for future generations. And the IRGC's influence often seeped into the newsroom as well. One of the most important investigative reports I wrote covered a contract between the IRGC and the Tehran municipality that let the IRGC take over all of the municipality's projects. At the team editorial meeting, it was decided that it would be a front-page story. But later, our newspaper's manager, Mr. Rahmanian, took the whole report out due to his fear of backlash from the IRGC. The editor in chief, Mr. Mohamadi, and I marched into Mr. Rahmanian's office to make our case. I showed him all my documents, and we argued and bargained to return every sentence of the report. At the end of the one-hour meeting, though he still agreed to run it on the front page, only 450 words were left of my 1,500-word article.

The IRGC was formally established in the first few months of the revolution. Ayatollah Ruhollah Khomeini, the first supreme leader and the founding leader of the revolution, feared that any remaining loyalists who opposed the Islamic revolutionary cause could try to grab power during this unstable period. On April 22, 1979, he issued a command to the Council of the Islamic Revolution to establish a unit to safeguard the revolution and his ideology. This militia group didn't even have our country's name in its title. Its formation, its name, and Khomeini's paranoia all show that from its very inception no part of the IRGC would be working on behalf of the Iranian people—the very same people who flooded the streets for a popular revolution.

The IRGC played a central role in the Iran-Iraq War, serving as a paramilitary force that fought back against Saddam Hussein's attacks. And after, at this crucial moment, the decision-makers of the Islamic Republic of Iran turned to the IRGC to steer the country's postwar economy, reconstruct the damage from the war, and provide jobs for IRGC forces. President Rafsanjani first enabled the IRGC to enter the economy through the establishment of Khatam-al-Anbiya Construction Headquarters in 1988. In less than twenty years, what started as a paramilitary force became the country's main economic contractor. No one could have predicted that the IRGC would gradually become a greedy octopus that would take control of the entire economy and become a shadow state.

At first, the IRGC was given only construction contracts. Then, slowly, the military group began to bleed into every sector of our society. On May 11, 2004, just one day after Khatami opened the shiny new Imam Khomeini International Airport, for example, the IRGC occupied it until a management contract with a Turkish company was canceled and handed over to the IRGC. Now, in addition to exclusive construction projects with Tehran Municipality and many other cities, it owns airports and telecommunications services and also has a hand in the oil and gas industries and automobile manufacturing. It has swallowed all industries and the economy, without any oversight or competition. The IRGC has benefited the most from sanctions by becoming the replacement for international companies. In 2006, *BBC Persian* reported that the IRGC's revenue from "legitimate sectors of the economy" reaches up to $12 billion a year. And the IRGC is now a main obstacle to the free future of Iran, with millions of Iranians inside and outside demanding sanctions on and the disarming of this brutal militia group.

After four years at *Shargh*, I had written 272 stories and held the record for the most front-page headlines for two consecutive years. I had thirty-five thousand followers on Twitter, and I also received several journalism awards. Despite the controversy my reporting often stirred, our newspaper manager, Mr. Rahmanian, called me the future of Iranian journalism. In a Facebook post from October 2014, I shared a deeply personal moment: I vividly recalled the first time I cried with one of my subjects. Barbod, a four-year-old boy, had been set on fire by his father. As I wrote the report, tears streamed down my face. It was just before a holiday, and my editor warned me that the boy would likely pass away during the break, so I needed to finish the story quickly. I hesitated, taken aback by her urgency. "Didn't you hear what I said? Hurry up!" she snapped. The second time I cried was during an interview with a pregnant sex worker at Khaneh Khorshid, a center providing food and medical aid to homeless women and sex workers. She didn't know who the father of her child was. As she recounted a recent miscarriage, she asked if I thought her baby would be okay. Her body bore the scars of years of drug use, and her vulnerability brought me to tears. She dreamed of owning makeup and borrowed lipstick from other women every day. I gave her my makeup bag, unable to forget her quiet hopefulness despite her circumstances.

Some of my most meaningful assignments came from immersing myself in my subjects' lives. During an undercover story, I posed as a street vendor in the Tehran metro. At first, it seemed simple, but I soon realized how daunting it was. In the metro's female-only carriages, I felt the weight of the women's stares as I began shouting to sell my goods. Despite my shyness, I pushed through. The story I wrote about these hardworking women—who earn a meager living to feed their children while navigating the Tehran metro's dark tunnels and fast-moving trains—remains one of my favorites. During my two-day journey, I met various metro vendors, including middle-aged women, struggling mothers, and young sellers, each with their own stories of hardship, resilience, and motivation for joining the trade. Many of these individuals from diverse backgrounds turned to metro vending after losing stable jobs or due to financial struggles. Despite their efforts, they face numerous challenges, including physically demanding labor, dealing with indifferent passengers, and evading metro security, who frequently seize their goods.

But not every moment was filled with sadness. I've also shared laughter with my subjects. I remember visiting Khadijeh, a middle-aged sex worker, who spent two hours carefully curling her six-centimeter-long hair. After all that effort, without adjusting a single curl, she asked me, "Is it good?" I smiled and said, "Yeah." I spent a night with her to document the lives of sex workers under the patriarchal regime of the Islamic Republic, gaining insights I could never have imagined otherwise. I shared a deeply empathetic and unflinching account of a night spent with sex workers in Tehran, uncovering their struggles, routines, and resilience. Khadijeh relied on drugs like meth to stay awake and safe, introducing me to a hidden world of addiction, homelessness, prostitution, and survival. She lived in an eight-square-meter room with Behnoush, her twenty-two-year-old daughter who was a sex worker. Despite her challenges, she created a semblance of normalcy for her family. Many sex workers like Khadijeh come from deeply troubled backgrounds shaped by abuse, addiction, and abandonment. Drugs often become a coping mechanism for their harsh realities. I aimed to highlight sex workers' humanity, pain, and resilience, shedding light on a marginalized and frequently ignored community in society. I continued reporting about Khadijeh and her daughter for two years. Her story, along with that of her daughter Behnoush, is one of resilience and transformation. Behnoush, once a sex worker like her mother, overcame addiction and rebuilt her life, working with organizations like Doctors Without Borders to support the homeless and prevent diseases like HIV. Khadijeh, by then on methadone, also helps others recover. These experiences have deepened my passion for social journalism, teaching me to find hope even amid the bitter realities of life. Despite the hardships, I can still smile at life.

In another story, I exposed the heartbreaking trade of newborn babies by drug-addicted mothers in Tehran's parks. The story revealed the immense struggles of these women and their children, including the complete absence of government or societal support. In a moment I'll never forget, Hanieh, a homeless mother battling addiction, sold her newborn to me for 4 million *toman*, roughly $1,000.

In June 2014, the world volleyball championship games were held in Tehran. Since the revolution, women had not been allowed to enter the stadium to watch the matches. In 2004, women had launched a campaign called White Scarves to protest the ban on entering the stadium. Since then, women wearing white scarves would show up at Azadi Stadium during matches of the Iranian team to show discontent with the ban. When the world volleyball championships came to the city, President Hassan Rouhani ordered Shahindokht Molaverdi, the vice president of women's affairs, to provide arrangements for the presence of women in stadiums. Honestly, I had no hope that they would let us into the stadium even with the order of the president. The ban on women entering the stadiums had stronger opponents than the president and his vice president. The mullahs in Qom, called *marja's*, are religious referees. But the editor was hopeful and gave me an assignment to go. He said, "Today is a historic day, and your report will be the front-page headline." When I arrived, ten officers, men and women, severely beat me and then arrested me. I got slapped in the face three times. I was in complete disbelief. They dragged me on the ground to the police van while punching and kicking me. I closed my eyes. I wished that I was only having a nightmare. The police officers took us to the morality police building on Vozara Street, where they would kill Jîna more than a decade later.

There, I met fifteen young women who were severely beaten while being arrested in front of the stadium. The police broke one of the women's glasses while they were on her face; she was lucky not to be blinded. Some were bitten by female officers, and the trace and marks of their teeth were left on their bodies. All of us, sixteen women, were severely beaten. My clothes and bag were torn apart. The police officers told us that we do not have proper families. One officer took pictures of us while holding a paper with the title of our accusation: "participation in the stadium's protest." After the end of the game and around midnight, on the condition that we signed a paper stating that we were healthy and had not been beaten, they released us. If we did not sign the paper, they said we would be sent to Evin Prison. My report was never published in the newspaper, but I wrote it on my Facebook. Over the next few days, my post was reproduced in Al Jazeera and other media platforms.

Even though I was arrested, beaten, and humiliated, I continued reporting on what happened at the stadium. A few months later, Shahindokht Molaverdi, the vice president of women's affairs for the government, had a press conference. Her public relations manager warned me not to ask about the stadium, adding that doing so would lead to my being expelled from the meeting. I asked about it anyway, because I figured even getting kicked out was news in itself. On my way back to the newsroom, I tweeted about what had happened. When I arrived at the office, my colleagues told me Mr. Rahmanian, our newspaper's manager, was waiting for me. I deleted my tweet on my way to his office, where he started to shout at me. "You are trouble, Fatemeh!" he yelled.

"I do not know what you mean," I said.

"Your tweet," he said.

So, I pulled out my phone and showed him my spotless Twitter!

The women who were arrested that day are still friends. Later, we planned and ran a Twitter storm that gained attention for the right of women to enter stadiums in Iran. FIFA got involved, and international pressure on the Islamic Republic increased. When I saw the series *The Handmaid's Tale*, a line of dialogue by one of the main characters, June Osborne, resonated with me: "They shouldn't have given us uniforms if they didn't want us to be an army." In one of my interrogations, the officers asked about Ghoncheh Ghavami, a women's rights activist and former prisoner, and her relationship with me. I answered with a laugh, "Yes, we are friends. We became friends in your detention center. If we had not been arrested, we would never have become friends."

NILO

FOR THE IMAGE OF REPETITION

FATEMEH AND I have met only once in person. We spent several hours together in the cafeteria at *The New York Times* in 2017. Back then, she was a student at Northwestern University studying journalism, finishing her second master's degree, and was in New York after receiving the prestigious Reham al-Farra Memorial Journalism Fellowship from the United Nations. Toward the end of her time in the United States, she set up meetings with editors and fellow reporters to find opportunities to write for international outlets from Iran. A coffee meeting that would usually have been an innocuous formality felt like fate. We clicked instantly, each feeling a deep trust for the other. Fatemeh's dark curly hair had a streak of teal blue in it. It reminded me of when I used to dye my hair in my friend's basement in high school. It was my way of expressing myself, of playing with the boundaries of independence. This was the first and last time I saw Fatemeh's bright sparkling smile, heard her cheeky laugh, or listened to her express her passion and incredibly nuanced understanding of Iran.

Our relationship has grown and developed over Signal, WhatsApp, and other messaging apps, where we are connected by tiny pin-like pixels on a phone screen. Over the years, she sent me pages and pages of details about her experiences and daily life over email. I read her messages as soon as they come in and without stopping, often wondering if we'd ever be in the same room again. In November 2021, she sent me a voice note on WhatsApp, telling me that she was going back to Iran to be with her father, who was just diagnosed with cancer. Fatemeh knew what was waiting for her on the other side. "It doesn't matter to me if they arrest me, take me to jail, put me on trial. To hell with them," she said. I responded immediately with concern but didn't hear anything from her again until September 2022. We went from regular chats and check-ins to zero contact. She disappeared. I couldn't hold Fatemeh's voice messages or texts in my hands anymore. Even after contacting a mutual friend a few months later, I never heard any updates about what happened to her when she returned to Iran.

After she got in touch in September 2022, Fatemeh and I began to message daily, and then, after she had her phone stolen by plainclothes officers during a protest the next month, less regularly over email. It was a far less secure way to communicate, but she took the risk, accepting the possibility of imprisonment to make sure she would have a voice and cement herself in a reality in which the regime was no longer drowning her.

Beyond just focusing on my reporting on demonstrations on Iran, I found my friends in the country became a comfort. I knew there would be no infighting with people with whom I always felt a closeness. Fatemeh and I communicated as regularly as there was internet connectivity. As the demonstrations stretched into their third week, the government began jamming the internet as a shameful way to try to put water to our flames. It didn't work. Even though there were delays, videos, images, and communications still found ways to reach outside Iran's borders. Despite not having strong enough internet connection for voice notes, let alone a call or a video chat, Fatemeh and I communicated through emails. I felt so at home with her. I didn't have to parse through the diaspora and the bickering. I stayed connected with her and with our people by being with her in the present moment. The videos I was seeing online and that sources sent me left me with a blurry and incomplete view of what daily life was actually like there. She sent me pictures of protest graffiti scrawled on the walls and metros of Tehran, the less lethal pellets that security forces would shoot at her and her friends as they swarmed the streets, and small observations she made each day.

Our bond over the year of the protests has turned into a sisterhood I could never imagine. It's funny to think that we met only that one time in person. Fatemeh and I were both in awe of this. Imagine a Bakhtiari woman meeting her Tabrizi counterpart in one of America's most elite institutions. We laughed at how we even made it here, running past all of the bright minds of Tehran. Two halves of a whole. Rarely allowed to be in the same place, brought together by our complicated country that we both so deeply love. We talked about the news, story ideas, the protests. Slowly we grew out of our journalism comfort zones, and we began to share and talk about our families, our heartbreaks, our budding romances, and our friends.

When I look back in my email, we have more than two hundred pieces of correspondence—pinging each other back and forth with stories, jokes, and updates. Never online at the same time, we left notes for the other to wake up to, small experiences and anecdotes that I could hold in my hand as I looked at my phone every morning. There were times that Fatemeh's phone wouldn't work, or it wouldn't be secure to be on a messaging app, and we felt that email was better. We were always jumping onto the next available avenue to stay connected with each other. I started to post part of her messages anonymously on Instagram. And then we wrote together again, this time for *The Paris Review*.

"I read your piece while crying. It is impactful. You put away your dream for your people," she wrote to me after reading a draft of our essay about the protests. "I am really proud of having you in my life, you are brave and fearless."

"Mah keh raftim kharej shodeem, tarsoo hastim. But you're not," I wrote to her in Persian but using the English keyboard to sound out the words, meaning, "We who left, we've become afraid."

"Do not say that. You are my brave juje," she responded, referring to me as a bird, which is a term of endearment for us.

Our very bond continues to be a form of resistance. The fact that at the height of the protests we communicated despite the risks that she faced in being associated with me, a journalist for an American publication, was defiance. The Islamic Republic could keep me from returning to Iran, but it couldn't keep me from reporting on my home country and from making a sisterhood with Fatemeh, a courageous and talented journalist whom it tried to silence for months. Without her, I felt alone in the diasporic comments section online. And the regime succeeded in isolating Fatemeh as well by taking away her ability to report and work freely. But together we formed an unbreakable team, a sisterhood in which often I felt more understood than in the Iranian community in the West that I've been a part of for nearly thirty years. To communicate securely, she would delete our messages and empty her trash after contacting me. I have so much privilege here: the privilege to have had a relatively easy route out of Iran, to work for top media organizations where I learned from incredible colleagues, and now to keep the messages that Fatemeh was forced to wipe. I get the space to reflect on her words while she moves in survival. Until recently, I used to look at Fatemeh as a mirror of what it would've been like if I had stayed in Iran.

Being a journalist in Iran is quite different philosophically and structurally from being a journalist in the United States. Whereas in the United States we are firmly tied to the idea of impartiality, the stakes and the dictatorial climate in Iran are such that being a journalist is inherently political. Journalists are often viewed as being just as political as human rights activists in the country and are jailed right alongside them in Iran's sprawling prison system. Many newspapers in Iran reflect a political party or faction. There are reformist organizations, like the newspaper *Shargh*, that reflect the opinion of those who want to reform the Islamic Republic to have a more open relationship with the West. There are hard-line organizations, like the Islamic Students' News Agency, that tout a pro-regime standpoint. At first, ISNA was managed by reformists, but after the 2021 presidential election of

Ebrahim Raisi, supporters of the regime have taken more control of media outlets to espouse their conservative views. There's even the newspaper *Kayhan*, which is seen to publish the perspective closest to the supreme leader, and Tasnim News Agency, which is closely linked to the IRGC. There's no room to be "unbiased" in the Western definition of journalism as a reporter in Iran when the abuses by the government are so clear—especially in the context of the Woman, Life, Freedom uprising, where we have countless visual examples of Iranians killed while protesting.

As we grew closer, I stopped seeing Fatemeh as my alternate life and instead as a part of me. She is the bolder voice in my head; she pushes me out of the fear I carry from coming from an apolitical family background. When I'm exhausted and unsure if I can do any more reporting on Iran, she keeps me going. I know her tie to Iran is stronger than mine, so often I don't burden her with my gnawing sadness at not being able to return. And still, she senses it. She can feel me saying it in our silence. And whenever one of our calls hangs in that moment of stillness, Fatemeh reminds me of our dreams: We will go back to Iran one day, we will open a journalism school, and we will create a space for minority languages that have effectively been banned from formal education. We take turns living in each other's hopes because, given the state of our country and how it has cracked down on our people, neither of us can remain starry-eyed for too long. Despite the Islamic Republic's trying to keep us apart and trying to silence our fellow journalists and activists, we have each other. It's an indescribable gift from whichever deity was on duty that day in 2017 that put us in the same room in New York. We were brought together to fuse our voices to tell the stories of our homeland's darkest days, and it's a personal mission that we have no choice but to continue with.

FATEMEH

FOR BLOODY ABAN AND ITS FIFTEEN HUNDRED LIVING MARTYRS

I WAS WATCHING Nilo's wooden reed dip into a pot of deep black ink as she practiced her Persian-language calligraphy on her Instagram story, squeaking and screeching as the reed dragged letters along the page. What I saw was much more than the creation of a work of art. I saw Nilo's love for the Persian language and her roots. Her reed twists to create the letters *h, n, s,* long and bold; the reed did not slip between her fingers while moving. She wrote down poems. Our interest in Forough Farrokhzad's poetry brought us closer together. Later, I sent Nilo the only documentary that Farrokhzad directed; it's considered the best documentary in the canon of Iranian cinema. It is primarily a visual poem about deprived people. Nilo also fell in love with her. We talked to each other about our daily lives—dates, family issues, and other stories—for hours and hours despite the regime's walls, time differences, and language barriers. Meanwhile, around me, the suffocating reality of living in the Islamic Republic of Iran dealt us another blow.

On December 28, 2017, protests against the economic situation started in Mashhad, the most important religious city in the northeast. The hard-liners triggered that protest against Hassan Rouhani, the moderate president, and his cabinet, but they were unaware that the fire they were lighting would soon spread to the entire country and burn them too. It was the first national protest after the Green Movement in 2009. Each popular uprising in the Islamic Republic's history has gotten increasingly more anti-regime, calling for a wholescale dissolution of this system that serves only a handful of ruling elites. Long gone are the days of reform. We are no longer living in 2009 asking our "leaders," "Where is my vote?" We are demanding, "Death to the dictator."

I felt that the streets were calling me, so I decided to go and cover the protest. "If I do not return home at night, cover my laptop in a plastic bag and bury it in our small garden," I told Mohamad Mehdi, my youngest brother, before leaving home. I arrived at Enghelab Square at 3:30 p.m. Protesters were walking toward Tehran University and chanting, "The fundamentalists, the reformists, it is over," and "This is the last message; the goal is to overthrow the whole regime." It was the first time the slogans took aim at the whole regime. I held my cell phone behind my scarf and started to film as the crowd passed Tehran University, where students were gathering and chanting. The security forces locked all the university's entrances to prevent the students from joining the protesters. We reached Vesal intersection, where I stood on a cement platform beside a gas station and filmed how the protesters attacked the riot police and forced them to retreat. I filmed all the angles, long shots, medium shots, and close-ups, amid all that chaos. There was no trace of the Fatemeh who hid her phone and was scared at the beginning of the protest, though the atmosphere soon began to change. The IRGC forces and riot police arrested some young men and beat them heavily in front of the crowd to scare other protesters. Young men screamed from the pain of the punches and kicks to their heads and bodies.

I headed into the alleys and interviewed protesters—two young women and one male student. I thought I had enough material and almost prepared to go home, but I decided on a whim to interview an older protester too. I found a retired male protester in front of Sepideh Cinema on Enghelab Street and started interviewing him. Before long, plainclothes officers arrested both of us. Walking with the officers, I remember my knees were shaking because I was so afraid. It seemed to take hours to arrive at the police van.

I waited for a chance to delete the videos and chats with Nilo from my phone. After I did, the van got filled up with female protesters, all handcuffed and beaten up. We did not know where we were being taken. As the van got closer to Argentina Square, we realized the destination was the morality police building on Vozara Street, where they would later detain and beat Jina. The van that took us returned immediately to the site of the protests to arrest more people, and they did not hand over any papers or information to the officers at the police headquarters. At that moment, I realized that these new police officers might not know that I had been filming. A female officer gave us a paper on which we were meant to write our personal information, including our home and work addresses, our reasons for attending the protest, and which channels we watched on TV. They took our mug shots—I was the second one—then police officers took us woman protesters to the interrogation room three by three.

They called my name and those of two other women, and we went to a small room. In the left corner of the room was a bench; in the right corner was a small desk with two chairs on either side, one for the interrogator and one for the criminal. The first woman questioned was young, about thirty. After looking at her information, the officer asked her, "What were you doing wrong in front of the Nawab metro station in Azadi Street?" He pointed out that her workplace was in the Molasadra neighborhood, a rich neighborhood in the north of Tehran, and her home in Shahriar, a poor, marginalized neighborhood two hours away from Tehran. Neither was near where she had been arrested.

"Haj Aghah," she said, using a respected religious title for men, "I got my period on the train and wanted to buy a pad."

I could barely control my laughter. Haj Aghah was surprised and said, "You should write this for the judge."

"Of course," she said.

I could not believe my ears. I realized then that we could lie. When it was my turn, I sat in front of Haj Aghah.

"What do you do?"

"I am a videographer of marriage ceremonies, Haj Aghah."

"Why did you attend the protest?"

"I did not; I had a job interview near Enghelab Street, and then I saw people and stayed to watch because I had not seen this before."

"Sign there. You all will be our guests tonight; tomorrow, you will be taken to court, where your cases will be decided."

He did not confirm my background, and I had a night to get to know these extraordinary women. Later, I saw the new group of arriving protesters; one was a young woman who did not wear any scarf, wore long leather boots, and shouted at the police officers, "We will take back our country from you, Khamenei mercenaries." I realized that not all woman protesters are from the lower class. She was a wealthy woman protesting the mandatory hijab in the middle of the protests in January.

Being admitted to the Iranian police detention center held a different meaning from being admitted elsewhere, especially if you are a woman and on the second day of your period as I was. We were held in a dark, damp, and dimly lit basement with cement floors and walls. On one side of the corridor was the administration room of the detention center, and on the other were small rooms with toilets and three six-square-meter windowless cells. We had to strip naked in front of the officers and sit down and get up to make sure we had not hidden anything in our anuses or vaginas.

At about 4:00 a.m., a group of young women arrived. They had been arrested at a party and were mostly drunk, scared, and crying.

"Do not admit that you drank alcohol in front of the judge tomorrow; otherwise, you will be lashed," I told them.

A couple of hours later, we were handcuffed two at a time. Every move was problematic; my body and hand were meant to move harmoniously with the other person's body and hand. The prison car was smaller than a van, with cubic iron cabin. We all fit tightly in the back.

After about thirty minutes, we arrived at Evin Court and Prison in the foothills north of Tehran.

We walked two by two into the crowded corridor of Evin Court, where there were also many injured and beaten young male protesters. Their feet were bound with iron fetters. This was the first time in thirty-three years that my gender brought me an advantage in the Islamic Republic. They do not bind women's feet. The officers released our hands, and we went to the court individually. The court was an office room with two desks and some chairs; the judge was a middle-aged cleric.

"Why did you attend the protest?" he asked.

"Misplaced curiosity," I said.

"How old are you?"

"Thirty-one, Haj Aghah," I responded.

"It is too late. If you get married, you will get busy with life and giving birth, and you will not have time for misplaced curiosity," he said.

"Sure, Haj Aghah," I replied.

My trial took less than five minutes. They held our cell phones and ID cards. When I arrived home, the first thing I did was email Nilo.

Four years later, after I had been to London and back, Mr. Masjedi, one of my interrogators from the Ministry of Intelligence, asked me about my 2017 arrest in the protest. I started to laugh nervously.

"It was super funny, let me tell you. When I got arrested, I was so happy because I had a night to get to know protesters from the streets," I said.

Mr. Masjedi was shocked. He realized I was not afraid of being arrested and saw it as an opportunity to better know the regime's opposition. "We will never take you to prison with this attitude," he said.

When I told him that at 4:00 a.m. a group of young women had been transferred there after having been arrested at a party, he responded in a humiliating tone: "They fought against the Islamic Republic too."

At the time, I could not answer him, but in a way he was right. They *had* fought against the regime. We try to live our everyday lives every moment—every time we laugh, dance, or drink. In the Islamic Republic, everyday life is a struggle for the most basic human rights.

. . .

On November 15, 2019, a snowy Friday night, the regime announced that fuel prices would increase by 50 percent. This was not legal, according to the law of the Islamic Republic. Fuel price increases had to be approved by the Parliament in the budget bill of that year before being implemented, but instead the regime passed this measure in the middle of the night, perhaps hoping that our outrage would be quelled if they oppressed us while we were asleep. The next day, nationwide protests broke out against this unfair decision. In the following days, twenty-one cities experienced unrest. All the protesters wanted was to demonstrate against the economic situation and force the regime to retreat.

But the establishment had no tolerance for dissent. Instead, predictably, it responded to the protests with excessive force. Instead of rubber pellets, they fired at people with real bullets. Everything was real: bullets, corpses, bloodshed, wrath. One thing was obvious: Riot police had been authorized to target the heads and faces of protesters. In an interview on the regime's TV channel, one anchor asked Rahmani Fazli, the interior minister, "Mr. Minister, why are the security forces and riot police targeting the heads of the protesters?"

"They shoot their legs too," he calmly replied, seemingly making light of the harsh repression tactics.

The regime shut down internet access in the whole country. Those days were like living in a black hole. We had no means of communication. The interruption of the internet meant we were not able to have access to social media and messaging apps to correct or produce uncensored news; ninety million of us got trapped in the Islamic Republic's jail.

Such a widespread internet blackout was unprecedented, and we hoped it would be over within a few days, but access was restored piecemeal. On November 17, we started to get access to nonthreatening platforms, like bank and taxi apps and domestic Iranian news websites. The headlines didn't surprise me. The supreme leader, Ali Khamenei, expressed his support for the price hike and warned against rolling it back. Though he distanced himself from the decision, in reality he was behind it.

Understanding the political costs associated with the price increase, Khamenei acted very cunningly, kicking the can to the Supreme Council of Economic Coordination, which he created with the express purpose of increasing fuel prices. The council included the president, the head of the judiciary system, and the chairman of the Parliament. "I am not an expert on these issues," Khamenei said in a speech made to a gathering of clerics, "but it, the Supreme Council of Economic Coordination, has my backing if they make any decision." His maneuvering delegitimized the Parliament and moved the state further into dictatorial rule.

On November 19, messaging apps and social media like Instagram and all international websites were still blocked, but I managed to get online using a proxy server. On Twitter, I read a post by the journalist Javad Heydarian confirming the death of his twenty-seven-year-old cousin Farzad Ansarifar. "My dear cousin was shot dead in the head by security forces. His head had been shattered in such a way his mother couldn't identify him. He was an unemployed youth killed by the Islamic Republic," Heydarian wrote.

I wrote a short tweet saying, "There is no impartiality here. We are beside our people or against them." My tweet got hundreds of likes in minutes, and in less than half an hour my phone rang. It was Mahdi Rahmanian, a manager at *Shargh*, my previous workplace. "Fatemeh, Mr. Ghotbi, the judge of Press Court, called me and said he issued a warrant for your arrest. I told him that Fatemeh was a good woman and would listen to me. Delete your tweet and do not do any activities on your social media," he told me. I said thank you and told him I would. I deleted my tweet while crying, feeling suffocated.

I looked at the news online. President Trump was pardoning a Thanksgiving turkey. My Instagram was flooded with my American classmates' eye-catching photos of cooked Thanksgiving turkeys alongside low-quality footage of bloody bodies of Iranian victims. It was that moment when I realized I was living in a parallel world. I saw that an Iranian reporter for Al Jazeera had shared a cooking video on Twitter. They had no idea what we were going through. In the midst of this, I had been receiving messages from Nilo. But I was hesitant to even read them due to anger and fear. I asked myself if she was genuinely worried or cared. Eventually, I read her messages and wrote back:

> It's as if we're dead.
> The internet crackdown and horror are terrible.
> We don't matter to the world. We don't matter to anyone.
> I feel like I can't breathe.
> I've never experienced this kind of censorship.
> Write these down if you care about us.

Then, shaking with rage and frustration while I wept, I added, "Please delete these chats."

Nilo suggested writing together about the protest. We had dreamed of working together for two years, ever since I started sharing my experiences on the ground in Iran. Her offer was like fresh blood in my veins, a new soul. I started writing notes, hoping the internet would work long enough for Nilo to receive them. I wrote to Nilo, "No one can foresee when the next protests will happen: one week, month, or maybe one year from now. But we will never feel the same way we used to, and nothing can undo this. We have experienced unprecedented brutal repression and frustration beyond our capacity to endure quietly. We have learned important lessons too. Iranians are bracing for darker days and mastering more strategies to survive and communicate during internet blackouts. I'm installing apps with offline services. You never know if the internet will be available from one moment to the next."

Nilo created a two-factor authorization email and gave me access. I never actually sent her anything. I put my notes in a draft, and she retrieved them from there. There was no trace. When Nilo sent me the link to our report in *n+1*, I read it in disbelief. I realized the joy of writing without censorship. I started to write anonymously for the *Los Angeles Times* as a correspondent based in Tehran. The headline of my first story was " 'Death to the Dictator': What Is Iran's Future?" It was about the protests in response to the IRGC's killing 176 passengers by firing at a Ukraine International Airlines plane in Tehran.

NILO

GRIEF IS THE BITTER FRUIT THEY SET

Shortly after Fatemeh and I published our joint story in *n+1*, a series of tragedies devastated the Iranian community once again, this time hitting closer to home. In January 2020, the United States targeted and killed the high-ranking IRGC commander Qasem Soleimani in an air strike. The night it happened, my maman texted me, "What will happen to our beautiful country?" My cousins from Tehran asked me over WhatsApp if a war was about to break out. Fatemeh and I were also in communication during that time, sharing our feelings of disbelief and anxieties about how each country might retaliate. "Sometimes I think we are living in a dark nightmare. This can't be real. I hope [Trump] just Tweets and they won't attack. God help us, I am going to take pills to sleep and forget. Praying not to receive an attack until morning," she wrote to me shortly after midnight.

Iranians everywhere were bracing for what unknown was about to unfold that would inevitably make everything much worse. Five days after Soleimani was killed, Iran launched missiles at bases in Iraq that housed American troops to retaliate for Soleimani's death. And then, as Iran and the entire region were on high alert, two missiles launched from an Iranian military site hit Ukraine International Airlines Flight 752, which was en route to Kyiv. The plane was hit just as it was leaving Tehran's international airport, killing all 176 passengers and crew. This flight was one of nineteen that took off from Tehran mere hours after the missile strike on the Iraqi base. That civilian airspace remained open at all during such a tense standoff shows the Islamic Republic's complete disregard for civilian lives.

As the newsroom mobilized to cover this breaking story, I was put in touch with residents near the crash site, because I was one of the only Persian-speaking reporters. One of our sources described to me in disbelief the thundering noise and screeches of the crash and the aftermath that he witnessed. He sent me photos of the crash site, and my camera roll became full of gore: I saw clothing torn and scattered on the ground, suitcases split open, a stuffed animal lying in a pile of other clothes, what might have been body parts (I've blocked out the specificity of this image), and a tattered Canadian passport. Among the plane's passengers were fifty-five Canadian citizens and thirty permanent residents.

The Iranian Canadian community is small, and as the days passed and victims were identified, I learned that I knew people on that plane. A cousin of my close friend. The daughter and wife of the man who owned Amir Bakery, a Persian bakery in my hometown that I go to all the time. We were only a few links away from each other. It could've affected any of us, and in the end the pain seeped out and rooted within. None of my editors asked me how I was doing with the news. My colleagues checked in on me, but I can't remember how honest I was being with them or myself. I was afraid that if I said I was having a hard time with this story, I wouldn't be allowed to cover it, or Iran at all. If I admitted I had feelings about this, there was a fear that my editors wouldn't consider me an objective journalist and I wouldn't be allowed to report on my home country.

A lot of the work that we do as journalists centers on human tragedy. We have no choice but to build resiliency that allows us to move through these horrible and graphic events and provide a public service, informing people about the context, the realities, and the hardships in each story. While I'm a sensitive person, I've developed a process that allows me to recognize what part of this pain is mine and what doesn't belong to me. But with the Ukrainian airliner tragedy, this stocktaking of my feelings felt impossible. The trauma felt as if it were mine. It was too close. I kept returning to the idea of what those passengers were thinking in their final moments. They were flying during the highest point of tension between the United States and Iran since the revolution. Perhaps while they were in Iran, they heard the fiery statements by leaders in the country vowing to seek revenge on the United States for the assassination of Soleimani that were circulating nonstop over state broadcasters and social media. Did they die thinking that the war we've all long feared between Iran and the United States was under way? My friend Cyrus Moussavi summed up perfectly the feelings that many of us dual nationals had at this time. I return to his words whenever I feel in the middle of this push and pull:

> *For the people of Iran, and the 176 people on Flight 752 and their families across the world. My greatest admiration for the people of multinations, who risk their lives to travel back and forth across imaginary borders, driven by family and love and a sense of home or longing. They cross these borders at great expense and with warm hearts, laden with gifts for loved ones on the other side. They move despite the terror and madness and greed of the small-minded leaders who run the world and determine that people can't go from one place to another, let alone call two places home.*

I slipped away quietly from covering Iran after the Ukraine International Airlines missile strike. I didn't have a conversation with my editors, and no one really asked me why. I just stopped pitching story ideas, because I couldn't separate myself from what those in the country were going through. I knew it would be irresponsible of me to report on Iran in this mindset. I didn't want to make any factual errors because I couldn't think clearly, and most of all I didn't know how to not let it overtake my emotions. And again, there was a real fear that if I voiced what was going on to my higher-ups, I couldn't work on Iran-related news in the future. It took a lot for me to cover my own country. As I looked to see how other news organizations were covering Iran, misreporting facts and missing the historical context or nuances, I felt that I had something valuable to add. I knew I could cover my homeland thoughtfully if I could just get out of my own way. But after the Ukraine International Airlines crash, I stumbled backward.

FATEMEH

FOR NOT BEING ASHAMED OF POVERTY

*It's wrong to write about people without living through
at least a little of what they are living through.*

THIS IS ONE of the first lines in *Nothing to Lose but Your Life: An 18-Hour Journey with Murad* by the Palestinian writer and journalist Suad Amiry, who accompanied migrant workers hoping to earn a better living on a harrowing journey across the Israeli border. I deeply identified with Amiry's perspective as a journalist. Like her, I rejected the distant impartiality that many in the media espouse. And when I arrived in London to join the *BBC Persian* newsroom in 2020, I expected to use my expertise on and experience with the Islamic Republic to produce impactful reporting. I expected to have more freedom to report on the Islamic Republic's repression and its impact on the country. But I ended up trading authoritarianism for bureaucracy, with different but equally frustrating roadblocks.

It had not been my intention to leave Iran. I left the country hurriedly after a brush with security forces. In November 2020, I was summoned by the IRGC Intelligence Organization after signing, along with seventeen other woman journalists, including Niloofar Hamedi and Elnaz and Elaheh Mohammadi, a letter naming a well-known editor, Maziar Khosravi, as an abuser. Khosravi was an editor for the politics desk at the newspaper *Shargh* during my time there who had gone on to work as the editor in chief at *Faraz Daily*. In the letter, we testified that he was a sexual abuser who used his power to prey on us young reporters. The IRGC's intelligence wing began summoning all of us, ordering us to come meet with their interrogators. It was then that we found out that Maziar cooperated with members of IRGC's intelligence. The day I was summoned, I quickly bought a ticket from Tehran to Istanbul. When I decided to leave, I did not have time to say goodbye to my family and friends. Shortly after, I landed a job at the BBC.

In Iran in 2017, I won an award for a video report for which I spent an entire snowy night in Tehran with homeless people who were drug addicts. None of my colleagues expected me to say anything at the award ceremony, but I used the occasion to protest the government's censorship of journalism. "Let us independent journalists do our job," I said. *BBC Persian* broadcast my speech. A few years later, I had to repeat the same words to my boss at *BBC Persian* in London— *let me do my job*. I was regularly blocked from telling stories I felt were important.

The refrain of my begging authority figures to *let me do journalism* was repeated over and over. I said this to government censors and interrogators in Iran, and now to my editors in London. When I got there, I realized the work I was assigned was a complete departure from what I expected.

"I didn't leave my life in Iran, my family, and friends to book satellite TV feeds here. Let me do my job, which is to do actual journalism and file reports," I said to the head of *BBC Persian* at BBC World Service. I had been hired to do my own reporting, yet my time was spent organizing the satellite connections of other correspondents reporting on the ground.

"You were hired to fill these shifts," she answered calmly, in words which to me felt devoid of any emotion. I couldn't believe this was happening. I had just stood up for myself against one of the most powerful people in the newsroom and been completely shut down.

Around this time, Niloofar Hamedi sent me a picture of her, our friend Somayeh, and me at my home on 30 Tir Street. In the photo, she and Somayeh are seated on my purple velvet sofa, while I stand behind them, smiling. Along with the photograph, she sent a letter filled with bright, uplifting words, which I drank in like a parched, desperate soul, sip by sip.

"I know these days are hard for you. I know being far from your loved ones is tormenting you. I know you're homesick," she wrote. "But I also know you'll get better. You'll make it through these days. You'll move beyond this. I, and so many others, are waiting for you to shine. I have faith in you. Please have faith in yourself, and don't give up. Don't let go of life and your dreams, Fat."

Nilo and my close friends call me Fat. I wrote back to her: "My dear Nilo, you are my whole life. Even from thousands of kilometers away, you splash color into the gray moments of my life here in London. Your words warmed my heart." This is how we encourage and empower each other—by writing letters and poems to each other.

Despite not being released from my shifts, I produced twenty TV packages and several investigative reports on my days off. Most of these reports garnered more than two million views on *BBC Persian*'s Instagram accounts and went viral. Once again, my reports raised red flags for the regime, sparking controversy. One of my earliest reports exposed the regime's massive budget spent on propaganda tied to the military operations of Qasem Soleimani, the commander of the Islamic Revolutionary Guard Corps, outside Iran. Soleimani was assassinated by order of the then-U.S. president, Trump. Following his death, the regime's officials launched a nationwide campaign to honor him, including renaming streets, highways, airports, and stadiums, publishing more than three hundred books, documentaries, and video games, organizing events like poetry and theater festivals, and establishing a foundation in his name with significant funding. Critics questioned the government's motives, suggesting that the campaign was meant to create a national hero and divert attention from internal issues. This report infuriated IRGC officials and regime authorities.

Another investigative report I worked on exposed the Supreme National Security Council's repression of media and journalists after the IRGC downed the Ukrainian airplane. For three days, Iranian newspapers followed security forces' orders, denying any missile strike possibility. Headlines were deemed "shameful" by the Tehran Journalists' Association, which lamented the loss of public trust. Families of the victims are still seeking justice and accountability, and the Iranian regime's attempts to cover up the truth have only added to their pain and suffering. Hamed Esmaeilion, the spokesman for the families of the Ukrainian plane crash victims, a Canada-based writer and dentist who lost his wife and seven-year-old daughter in the tragedy, shared his thoughts with me: "The plane incident was a test of Iranian media's integrity, which they failed by knowingly spreading lies. Their silence and complicity are seen as equally culpable as the officials' actions. Although I acknowledge that there are honest journalists in Iran who wish to write the truth but cannot do so." The families of the victims of Flight 752 have a slogan that says, "We will neither forgive nor forget."

Two of my notable reports included one on Iranian women's fight against compulsory hijab, published two years before the Jina movement gained momentum. Another report explored the growing popularity of dating apps among Iranian women. Most of my stories highlight the regime's rigid control over our bodies and our agencies. I also produced two stories on the #MeToo movement, focusing on the importance of transitional justice and the significance of genuine apologies from abusers.

Once, I pitched a story about the goods that impoverished people sold on a website called Divar—a bidding website of classifieds, somewhat similar to eBay and Craigslist. My assignment editors and colleagues in London didn't even know what Divar was and did not think it was worth a story. "Here in England, people buy and sell secondhand items. It's good for the environment," my manager said as he rejected my pitch. It gave me insight into how my colleagues saw Iran, with eyes that lived in a developed country for many years. It seemed that their distance from present-day Iran and our realities made it impossible to feel and relate to our struggles. This was a time of high inflation, dwindling job opportunities, and lack of hope for Iranians in the country. As everything shifted to remote learning during the coronavirus pandemic, mothers in Iran sold their hair on Divar to buy smartphones for their children to stop them from dropping out of school. But here I was, listening to *BBC Persian* editors tell me that this was an environmentally friendly practice, rather than an act of desperation that was becoming a normalized feature of life for poorer Iranians. They seemed to have completely lost their empathy for Iranian people.

My last story for the BBC was published in November 2021. The story was about malnutrition in prisons. I interviewed thirty political prisoners in twenty prisons across Iran. According to the World Food Programme, every human being needs at least eighteen hundred calories of energy from food per day. However, the daily caloric intake of Iranian prisoners is about half of this amount. Thus, the Iranian regime is pushing political opponents toward death by imprisoning and systematically starving them. I interviewed Narges Mohammadi, an inspiring and brave human rights activist in Iran who was sentenced to sixteen years' imprisonment for establishing a human rights campaign to abolish the death penalty. In October 2023, while behind bars, she won the Nobel Peace Prize for her role in the Woman, Life, Freedom movement. "Lunch is usually rice and soybeans. Three times a week," she told me in an interview. "It is the worst, smelliest, and most tasteless food in the world." I asked a senior correspondent to watch my report and give me feedback. "What are soybeans?" he asked me. I was surprised that a journalist at his level working at a publication that covers Iran had no idea what Narges was talking about. Cheap and full of protein, soybeans are a main food source for many Iranians. Over the years, because more and more people couldn't afford the price of meat and chicken, we increasingly began eating soybeans. These days, regardless of socioeconomic class, all Iranians experience poverty with our flesh, skin, and bones, and twenty-eight million live under the poverty threshold like me.

I know well what poverty is. Poverty is eating only one meal a day. I always double-check prices, because I live in constant fear that I won't have enough money to buy any given item, and inflation means prices change day by day. Sometimes I return the things I bought because my bank account balance was not enough.

"Take back the milk, please. Thank you. I'll only take the toast and cheese," I find myself often saying to the cashier. My cheeks don't even turn warm with embarrassment anymore. It's fascinating how small traumas become normal. Poverty means that I can no longer afford simple quality sanitary pads because they are expensive, so I have to buy cheap and low-quality ones and have a more painful and annoying period. These cheaper pads itch my skin and leave me with blisters.

Poverty means using Vaseline instead of hand cream. When I go to the pharmacy and hand over my prescription for my ADHD medicine, I repeat this phrase as if it were the chorus of a song: "I don't have money for all my drugs. Just give me one sheet of each, please." I no longer have money for psychotherapy, delicately navigating the wounds of my soul myself. Poverty means forgetting the taste of coffee, forgetting travel, the sea, and the forest. Poverty eats us. Poverty imprisons us. It is about daily humiliation. When I was a child, I was ashamed that when my family members sent me to the supermarket, I had to say that my mother would bring the money for the purchases at the end of the month when my parents received their salary. But I am not ashamed of my poverty anymore, because I understand it was not a choice. And now, choosing to bear the poverty has become its own form of protest. The interrogators told me that if I cooperated with them, I would "be in a great economic situation." I refused. I did not want to dip my bread in people's blood before eating it. There was no way that I would share any information with the regime in exchange for stability. Being in this economic situation is the price I pay for being independent.

One day while at the BBC newsroom in London, I was sitting quietly. It was normal for me to be withdrawn and solitary. My colleague approached me. "You look sad," she said. "What's going on? Do you want to go back to that destroyed country?" That's how she and many of my colleagues saw Iran.

"I love that destroyed country," I replied.

She told me she could not imagine going back there, because she would be forced to wear a hijab. "There is freedom here," she said. But, for me, walking without a hijab in Tehran's streets is part of the fight for liberation. A collective liberation.

On December 17, 2021, when I landed back in Tehran after a year of living in London—taking the risk because my father was suffering with cancer—I knew that there was a chance that I would be arrested. Still, I felt obligated out of love and duty to go back to save my father. I was determined to do everything in my power so that he might suffer less from the common mistakes of the convoluted medical system in Iran. I risked detention and my mental health to take on this responsibility. I swore to myself that I would take care of my father no matter what. I have journalist friends whose parents died while they were in forced exile or while they were locked away in prison. This was the shared nightmare of all Iranian journalists both at home and abroad: not having the chance, and frankly the basic right, to say goodbye to our loved ones. It does not matter whether you are in prison or forced exile. My friend Raha Askarizadeh, a women's rights activist and photographer, was in Evin Prison when her father passed away. Another one of my friends, Bozorgmehr, a journalist at Reuters, lost his father due to cancer when he was in forced exile. And my dear sister Nilo lost her grandmother whom she was so close with, unable to return for her funeral and other religious mourning services. We have a proverb in Farsi: "Dead soil is cold and brings forgiveness." It means that when the burial of your loved ones is carried out, it helps you come to terms with the loss and grief. But when you are not there to feel the soil's coldness with your own hands, this loss will always be fresh.

The day before my flight to Tehran, I rushed to get rid of my devices. I sold my laptop on Facebook Marketplace. An Arab father came to buy it for his high-school-age daughter. I bought a second-hand cell phone in our neighbor's store without any information on it. I took an Uber two hours outside London to buy a new laptop. I wanted it to be wiped clean, just like the phone I bought. When I got to the suburb, I discovered that the person who sold me the laptop was the landlord of the apartment building. That night, he was throwing his tenants a Christmas party. He invited me and my friend "Noor," who had come with me, to join them. There I was, rushing around to get electronics that couldn't be searched by Iran's intelligence agents while Christmas parties were starting. The lives of ordinary people continued around me.

That night, after our long day of errands, Noor came to help me pack and weigh my luggage. After I had lived in London for exactly one year and one month, she was the only friend I had. I left without saying goodbye to other acquaintances or my co-workers. There was no possibility of resignation, a farewell email, hugs, and goodbye photos. I left Iran cloaked and hurried. And I left London the same way.

I wrote emails to my friends abroad, telling them that I was returning to Iran, and it would not be safe to communicate with them. If the regime tried to use me as a tool to connect with them, they would be aware of any possible scenario, including if the regime took me to prison. I did not imagine it would be my last communication with Nilo for nine months. I gave my old phone with all of my data to Noor so that if I got arrested, they would not have access to my contacts.

"Are you sure you don't want me to come with you to the airport, as you don't have a SIM card and internet?" Noor offered as I prepared to head to the airport.

"No, it's okay," I said. But it wasn't okay. I wasn't okay. Outside, the rain started falling harder and harder. She helped me drag the luggage to the street under a downpour. I held on to her and hugged her tight. I knew I might never see her again. After all the ups and downs, of leaving everything I'd known behind multiple times, I knew the routine of solitude well. I looked at her from the back window of the Uber. I drew the final image of her in my heart—a young woman, my sister, standing alone, looking back at me in the middle of a dark street at midnight in rainy London. I returned to the world without her. She stayed in the world without me. None of it was fair. We shouldn't have to break ourselves into pieces under the weight of this regime.

Once again, I had only two large suitcases, a carry-on, a backpack, and a clean phone without any photos, texts, contacts, or memories.

I was sitting in the back of the Uber with everything I owned. After spending two days at airports in London and Doha to get multiple negative COVID tests, I finally arrived in Tehran. I could see the snowy peaks of Mount Damavand from my oval, scratched window. I couldn't hold back my tears anymore.

After getting my passport stamped by the passport control officer at the airport, I heard a voice on my right-hand side. "Miss Jamalpour?" I turned around to see two men, officers from the Ministry of Intelligence. One of them introduced himself as Mr. Vahid, which of course was not his real name. These officials always use fake names when interrogating people like me. He looked about my age and was a thin, scruffy man with dirty blond hair. His shirt was untucked.

"Our colleagues have been waiting for you for two days," he said.

Having seen my friends get arrested over the years, I had heard of this familiar pattern. A Ministry of Intelligence official "greeting" you at the airport and whisking you into mandatory interrogations. No lawyers. No oversight. This is the life of a journalist in the fascistic Islamic Republic.

I was taken to a hotel in Tehran by Mr. Vahid and many other officers. They interrogated me, threatening and attempting to intimidate me. By then, I hadn't slept or eaten for forty-eight hours. The intelligence regime is incredibly smart in Iran. They pick us up at the airport when we're weary after long trips and most vulnerable. Some officers were in different rooms in the suite, and I did not see them; a soldier brought their notes and handed them to the man who would be leading my interrogation.

"Welcome to the country, by the way," the man said. He reminded me of my aunt's husband—a round, middle-aged man, with straight black hair that stood up. He had a fleshy nose and dark eyes and eyebrows and wore rectangular, frameless glasses.

"Thank you," I replied slowly, trying to show that I wasn't intimidated. "Can I ask your name, so I know who I'm talking to?"

"I am Mr. Behzadi," he replied quickly and moved on just as fast. He asked how I came to be hired by the BBC and whether I was in

Iran when I applied. Throughout the conversation, he never broke eye contact.

Mr. Behzadi brought me a new mobile phone and handed it to me. "Sign in with your Apple ID."

Knowing that, if I was detained, my interrogators would want access to any Iranian source or reporter that I had in my contacts list, I had deliberately gotten rid of my U.K. sim card so that I could not complete the two-factor authorization required to sign in. "Sir, look, I won't give names and information. You won't hear any names from my mouth. It is my moral responsibility. I promised this to myself before returning," I responded.

"In our opinion, anyone who works in Farsi-language media abroad is a mercenary," he said sternly.

"Well, then you should be happy. I'm now one less mercenary working for mercenary media."

As my interrogation continued, I could see Mr. Vahid watching intently and taking notes. His light brown eyes moved from looking at Mr. Behzadi and me to his notepad. Out of the corner of my eye, I could see his dirty blond head of hair bobbing up and down while he was taking notes. A woman in a black veil looked on, sitting calmly with her hands folded on her lap, looking right at me. Later, I learned her name was Maryam Sedaghat, also certainly a fake name.

"Go back to London!" Mr. Behzadi screamed at me as I sat in silence, looking down at my hands.

I started to laugh nervously. "This is our country too, sir. And by the way, I am not going anywhere until my father is cured of cancer."

"We will take you to prison because you do not cooperate with us, saying it is your 'moral responsibility,'" he said, using my words against me. "You will be in jail soon."

"If you send me to prison, I will commit suicide. It will be your fault!" I shouted back.

"You do not have enough courage to commit suicide," he continued.

"So, send me to prison; then you will see. And no one would believe that I committed suicide. All will say you killed me."

They went to pray because it was evening *adhan*. After eight hours, I was released, but the Ministry of Intelligence officers informed me that I would have to continue attending interrogation sessions when called. If I did not, they would take me to jail.

Finally, I arrived at home. As I walked into my old living room, I first saw my dad's face. Sitting on a small chair facing the doorway, he was bonier than I had ever seen him. I have my father's face, his elongated black eyes and eyebrows, protruding cheekbones that sit on top of round cheeks, and a pronounced chin. He was wearing a urinary catheter. Each tube that poked out from his body was a painful signpost of his cancer.

My father was unable to get cancer treatment due to all the hospitals being overwhelmed by coronavirus patients. Iran was one of the first countries outside China affected by the coronavirus. Nearly two years after the onset of the pandemic, there were still huge delays in vaccine importation, with many doses not arriving until the summer of 2021, partly due to sanctions, but even more so due to the regime's refusal to work with Western countries. The supreme leader made a speech declaring that Iran would not work with the West. This delay meant not only that more people died from COVID but also that many of our loved ones who were getting treatment for other diseases experienced delays in medical care. Lawyers and plaintiffs who accused the Islamic Republic's supreme leader of intentionally delaying access to the vaccine were sentenced to prison. It was a time when many rich Iranian people, typically insulated from the regime's abuses, realized that it matters who runs the country and that their fate is tied to the working and the middle class's fate too. After Jîna's death, many upper-class neighborhoods experienced protests and demonstrations for the first time.

Mr. Masjedi replaced Mr. Behzadi as chief interrogator starting from my second interrogation. They changed the bad cop for a good cop. My lawyer said it was a good sign; it showed that the officials realized they could not scare me. Both Mr. Vahid and Ms. Sedaghat were also present in all of the first twelve sessions.

At the beginning of one session, Mr. Vahid asked if I had been sexually harassed by any of the officers. I was shocked. I stared at Ms. Sedaghat, who had also been assigned to my case.

"Except for the first day, you treated me like a human. Thank you very much for your kindness," I replied, before adding, "But have you read the letter of Niloufar Bayani, an environmental activist from Evin Prison, about the sexual harassment of IRGC agents?"

None of them had read it. I said, "Niloufar wrote in a public letter about being sexually assaulted and tortured. Seven male agents of the IRGC took Niloufar from a cell to a swimming pool; then the interrogator and the rest of them jumped naked into the water, forced her to watch them, and asked her to get into the water with ridiculous language. They threatened to rape her and described the painful scene of her being raped or executed. It's your job, you should read it," I finished.

Niloufar Bayani, an environmental activist, was convicted in 2019 of espionage by Iranian authorities in a closed-door trial in Iran and received a ten-year prison sentence. The year before, in January 2018, the IRGC Intelligence Organization had arrested environmental activists including Niloufar and seven of her colleagues and imprisoned them with the same charge. The Ministry of Intelligence announced that they were innocent. Still, the Revolutionary Court of the Islamic Republic sentenced them to a combined sixty years in prison. Bayani and three of the other activists were released in April 2024, after more than six years in prison.

In another interrogation session, Mr. Masjedi, the second main interrogator, told me that I was banned from producing any kind of content. I responded, "You cannot shut down my mind." Later, he said, "We believe there is some mismanagement in our country, but we are on the right path. Do you?"

I did not think so, but I did not want to express my disagreement, so I said, "I think I can still build something good and valuable here."

Amir, my lawyer, had advised me to kill time during the interrogation sessions, so I talked about the books I was reading or shared benign family stories. The more I spoke, the less they asked. The goal was not to give them any helpful information. I asked those who were holding me if they had read the book *Istanbul* by Orhan Pamuk. None had.

I explained what the book was about and told them that in the last and brilliant chapter of the book, called "A Conversation with My Mother," Pamuk writes, "His mother, like most mothers in this confounded and crazy geography, believes that no one could be boosted up here, and immigrating to the West means becoming someone." I stopped and looked at the ground.

"But despite all the troubles that I have been dealing with, I think that I still can build something here," I said to the interrogators. "Do you know what Pamuk says to his mother at the end of that chapter?"

"No," replied Mr. Masjedi in his clipped monotone.

"He said that he decided to become a writer. I am writing too," I said. In 2006, Pamuk won the Nobel Prize in Literature, becoming the first Turkish laureate and proving to his mom that he could stay in his homeland and succeed.

"Are you writing about us too?" Ms. Sedaghat asked, perhaps shocked at my boldness.

"Yes," I said. I saw the fear in their eyes at the end. I left the hotel, took my headscarf off, and took a deep breath. I gambled again and won. I did not lie!

After months of being interrogated primarily by men, I began to meet one-on-one with Maryam Sedaghat. She made all kinds of proposals for how I could cooperate with the Islamic Republic—names I could give up, information I could share, even offering to give me a work permit for foreign media and letting me make a documentary with their sponsorship. I continued to refuse.

One day, I was sitting in the lobby of the Espinas Palace Hotel waiting for Ms. Sedaghat. The interrogators were never on time, always arriving late by at least an hour. I was reading a poem by Hushang Ebtehaj and cried, feeling hopeless and tired of the uncertainty.

> *Would you think,*
> *Is the sail broken, and has the lifeboat sunk?*
> *In this ruined land which happiness and joy have escaped from,*

Do you think life has reached a dead end?
Be a river,
It leaves behind all the stones,
keep going,
No miracle is expected from the dead,
  stay alive.

And how I needed a miracle. The miracle of freedom and not going to prison. I cleaned my tears with my scarf. Engrossed as I was in the poem, I did not see Ms. Sedaghat arrive and did not realize that she was watching me. "What are you reading?" she asked.

"The life poem by Hushang Ebtehaj," I told her. She recited it from memory while we walked toward the elevator. She led me to the third floor and into the last room in the corner. " 'No miracle is expected from the dead, stay alive.' This poetry is my favorite too. God will help you," she said.

I realized that hotels in Tehran were working with the Ministry of Intelligence by providing spaces for them to interrogate people like me. She said, "Sorry for being late. A female child rights activist was talking to me about her problems." This meant that she was interrogating children's rights activists too. This regime sees any NGO or collective as a danger; they never let NGO activists work freely.

During a May 2022 interrogation, Ms. Sedaghat asked me about feminism. Previously, in the presence of Mr. Vahid and Mr. Masjedi, I had said that I believed in the equal rights of men and women as outlined in sharia law and the constitution. I had lied, of course. As I sat in my interrogation with Ms. Sedaghat, things were different. "Why are you a feminist?" she asked me. It was just the two of us. At this moment, I realized that my interrogators had assigned Ms. Sedaghat to me because they knew a woman could open me up. Perhaps they understood that I'd feel more comfortable in the presence of a woman. And they were right. I felt that I could be myself. I didn't have to play the role of a blushing, subordinate "good" Muslim girl as I had in the other interrogations. It was not easy to do, but I had to buy time. I figured the longer these sessions dragged on, the less likely I would end up in prison. With Ms. Sedaghat, I dropped the charade and began to talk from the bottom of my heart.

"Do you think we fall asleep at night, wake up in the morning, and say, 'Let's become a feminist. It's classy?' No. I was raped when I was nine years old by my uncle Bijan, my father's youngest brother, who is your colleague and worked at Herasat. I have never talked about that trauma even in front of my therapist."

I continued, "I've always asked myself why during all family gatherings and ceremonies women are doing all the work: cooking, washing dishes, setting the table, and clearing it away while the men are sitting and playing cards," I said. "I was beaten by my father when I was fourteen for not wearing socks. And when I was eighteen years old, I was almost killed. My oldest brother was going through my wallet and other personal items. I grabbed a photo of my boyfriend, ran away from my brother, and ate it to get rid of it in order to survive."

Ms. Sedaghat's eyes became glassy and a crease formed between her eyebrows as she began to cry. "I've always asked myself why we have to eat after the men," she said. It seemed to me that she was deep in thought. She wasn't looking directly into my eyes, but somewhere slightly above them. It almost felt as if she were plowing through her childhood memories. Flipping past them one by one, becoming aware of the times that she too felt smaller in the presence of men. Was she always aware of this dynamic, or did she only become aware of it at that moment? It was hard to know for sure if Ms. Sedaghat cried real tears or if she was just a trained actress. She told me she was the only female agent walking the Ministry of Intelligence corridors during workdays.

I finished the session by saying, "I returned to Iran because I want my niece to suffer less than me as a woman in this country."

On another occasion, Ms. Sedaghat arranged an interrogation session with me in the park. It was a technique to build intimacy and to try to get me to open up. I knew that this was part of her job and that playing out this theater of friendship wasn't any act of genuine kindness.

"This place reminds me of my engagement. My fiancé and I used to come here a lot," she said. We were sitting in Jamshidieh Park in the northernmost point of Tehran, bordered by mountains. The park benches were forest green, and we were under a giant gazebo with terra-cotta tiles on the roof. As we sat on benches across from each other, the physical space heavy between us, several cats approached us. Many cats roamed freely all over Tehran.

"What are they doing here?" Ms. Sedaghat shouted. She began to yelp and shriek, her black veil moving around with every jerky movement. Seeing that she was afraid, I stood and started to move them away with my hands. "It's fine. The cats are hungry and just looking for food," I said. As soon as I got close, the cats began to scatter. Imagine, trying to shoo cats away from your interrogator.

I told her I would not attend any more sessions, that my mental health would not tolerate it anymore. When my father's health got stable after six months dealing with cancer, Amir, my lawyer, told me it was safe to stop attending more sessions.

Among those I know who have been interrogated by the Ministry of Intelligence, I am one of the few who has been appointed a woman expert to their case. When I told Noshin, my photojournalist friend, who was in Evin Prison for three years, that I had a female interrogator who asked me about my childhood in detail, Noshin said, "You should tell her, 'Are you my therapist to ask about my childhood?'"

Fatemeh Sepehri, a woman political prisoner, published an open letter revealing that she had been interrogated by a female interrogator who had asked probing questions about her childhood. Sepehri told the media that the person with whom she'd had a virtual meeting introduced herself as a psychologist of the judiciary system. "You are a psychologist interrogator," Sepehri had told her. I recalled all my interrogation sessions with Ms. Sedaghat like a movie on fast speed: her questions about my childhood and my family, her proficiency in English, and her observant look from our very first session. I finished Ms. Sedaghat's character puzzle too late. None of our conversations had been casual. She was a psychoanalyst interrogator at the Ministry of Intelligence, trained to get into and mess with my head.

NILO

WHAT CAN THEY KNOW OF OUR DISTRESS WHO WATCH US FROM THE SHORE?

A FTER I STEPPED AWAY from covering Iran, the next major news moment took place during the summer of 2020, when we saw the defining nationwide civil rights protest movement of the decade. The Black Lives Matter movement peaked with half a million people turning out on June 6, 2020, to protest in nearly 550 places across the United States against police brutality and systemic racism that overwhelmingly affected the Black community. Heated conversations were happening in the newsroom centered on what it was like for Black journalists to cover this moment. I found myself questioning how editors in positions of power defined the concept of objectivity; Black reporters were called to unstitch themselves from their community both to be allowed to cover this moment and to avoid being labeled biased. I didn't see how this was possible. How could we ignore what was happening and walk into the newsroom as figureless and formless? To me, this conversation made it seem as if only reporters of color—and at this time, specifically Black reporters—were assumed to have implicit bias.

Objectivity has always been placed on a pedestal as the defining framework in my industry. In journalism school and in the various newsrooms where I've worked, mentors and professors would stress that to be a journalist meant that you had to be separate from the subject matter in order to be truly objective. Our industry has debated the notion of objectivity and the line between activism and journalism for years. When *The New York Times* came under scrutiny for its coverage of transgender people, this strain again came to the forefront. Speaking to *Vanity Fair* about discussions in the newsroom, my *New York Times* colleague Astead Herndon explained more about this tension. "I don't believe the journalist-activist binary is useful. Every good journalist I've known has been an activist for values like truth and clarity and transparency," he said. "Plus, as a Black journalist, I've seen how charges of activism can be used to discredit journalists of underrepresented backgrounds who may come to the work of reporting with a different lens." Likewise, I know that my experience informs rather than harms my work. Even when the stories I report aren't about me, my experiences have shaped me and pushed me into this path of journalism. I want to share the stories and voices of people who have been affected by systems of oppression and to investigate the roots of human rights abuses and misuse of force by policing and intelligence systems. But it feels distinctly different to be from the community that I'm covering rather than outside it. How could I separate myself from my own people? The stakes are higher. It's deeply personal.

It wasn't until I read a conversation with the Vietnamese filmmaker, writer, and multidisciplinary artist Trinh T. Minh-ha that I began to see that for me there is no neat way to pull myself apart as perhaps Western journalism might idealize. Trinh talks about the concept of "speaking nearby," a way to explore and speak about a topic in a manner that doesn't objectify it but reflects upon itself. "The tendency is always to relate to a situation or to an object as if it is only outside of oneself," said Trinh, speaking about the type of education she received in Western institutions about filmmaking. "Whereas elsewhere, in Vietnam, or in other Asian and African cultures for example, one often learns to 'know the world inwardly,' so that the deeper we go into ourselves, the wider we go into society."

This was also my instinctive approach to journalism. Inadvertently, I've been going against the Western traditions of storytelling that have been championed in all of the American institutions that have formed my reporting foundation. In every story on Iran that I do, I offer a part of myself to the people I interview. In part, this is how I build trust: I am transparent about where I come from so that people can feel comfortable opening up to me, knowing that I'm not linked to the Islamic Republic or will give the regime information about them. But perhaps at its core, it's a cultural condition. I offer a part of myself so that the people I interview can feel safe offering a part of themselves as well. Doing so also gives me the gift of learning more about Iran and my people, who are from every part of the country, not just Tehran or Tabriz, the places I know best. And while this work is difficult, it's an absolute privilege to be relatively safe in the United States, to connect with my fellow Iranians, and to understand even more about myself through each interview.

I'm aware that in these conversations the power is heavily tipped toward me, the reporter, so I feel the weight and responsibility to portray people and events accurately. There is no room for error, and being so far above or removed from the subject matter feels, in many ways, disingenuous. Trinh characterizes "speaking nearby" as "a speaking that does not objectify, does not point to an object as if it is distant from the speaking subject or absent from the speaking place." Rather, it's a form of approaching the truth by coming right up to it without seizing or claiming it. This indirect approach also speaks to the Iranian cultural mode of communication. Many of the people I have interviewed would speak in parables or reference lines of poetry mixed in with their eyewitness accounts. While "speaking nearby" is often referred to in the worlds of art and literature, I guess I've been "speaking nearby" this entire time—sideways walking like a crab into subject matter, opening up about my personal investment in the story, and then finding the bonus of connecting and learning more about a homeland that I'm unable to return to.

Trinh views "speaking nearby" as an attitude in life, an intentional positioning of oneself in relation to the world. I am not separate from the stories I cover, whether about Iran or not. The idea of pointing at a story with a long stick and giving the reader my retelling of events feels classist at best and an act of colonialism at worst. Maybe it's a humanistic approach, maybe it's the approach of someone deeply ingrained in a non-Western world but implanted here, but sharing myself and being realistic about my closeness to a subject matter only make my reporting better. Or, in the words of Trinh: "Truth can only be approached indirectly if one does not want to lose it and find oneself hanging on to a dead, empty skin."

NILO AND FATEMEH

OUTSIDE THE CONFINES OF MY BODY

WHILE WE HAVE HAD a handful of important figures throughout our history, the Iranian women's rights movement has never had a singular woman taking charge. Each of us is a link on a chain, building upon the movements and actions of those who came before us to create something that would finally empower and benefit us. When we look back at women like Bibi Maryam Bakhtiari, a revolutionary and activist in the Constitutional Revolution, and Sedigeh Dolatabadi, a pioneering figure of Iran's women's rights movement, we see how Iranians have learned to grow and take root under authoritarian pressure, long before that of the ayatollahs and their nascent Islamic Republic. We learned from Bibi Maryam, whose vital role became lost in the patriarchal retelling of Iran's history, that we must take what is owed to us. The leaderless movement of Woman, Life, Freedom, which bloomed out of necessity, is preceded by a century of activism.

"The Iranian women's movement from the constitution to today is not 'mine'; it is 'us.' There was no leader; it was the *women* who led," wrote Farzaneh Ebrahimzade, a historian and writer based in Tehran, on an Instagram story as the Woman, Life, Freedom protests were taking hold across the country and gaining international attention. Ebrahimzade invoked the collective nature of Iran's feminist activism to remind us why it still operates without a singular leader. "This movement is our movement. No one has the right to confiscate it. If someone says that 'I am a leader,' know that they will suppress your objections," she continued.

The sixth generation of Iranian feminists are individualistic and rebellious. They understood that they could not achieve their demands through the regime's legislation or by reforming the current system. Now millions of women in Iran who belong to this sixth generation of feminists are fighting against discrimination laws in their daily lives and every time they walk in public. Their message is clear: Do not be misled by photos shared by state news agencies that show joyous women wearing beautiful silk headscarves. These images do not represent women who can exist openly in their own society. The fabric that hides their hair is dripping with the blood of Jîna and Nika. We will not be suppressed in the name of religion anymore.

The future is unclear. But we are optimistic about these young girls whose only weapon is their hair. They are ready to sacrifice their lives for a free future. We're all ready to pay the price of freedom.

PART III

AZADÎ/AZADI, FREEDOM

For the hair of revolutionary girls,
For my people, for our choice,
Do not be afraid and shout,
For women's rights,
A bright tomorrow awaits us,
The legend of the past is on the lips of children,
The echo of laughter is loud and in unison,
The 'Life and Freedom' chant is our generation's message.

— revolutionary song during 2022 Woman, Life,
Freedom movement by anonymous artists

FATEMEH

FOR KIAN AND HIS RAINBOW

On Enghelab Street, during a protest in the last days of autumn, a young lady without a hijab and in a brown raincoat slipped a pink piece of cardboard with a drawing of a rainbow into my hand. "There is no God of rainbows; we have to make our own rainbow," she had written. The rainbow had become a code of survival and shared pain.

"Dad, trust the police this time." These were the last words of Kian Pir Falak, a nine-year-old child from my province, Khuzestan, in southwest Iran. Kian and his father were returning to their home on November 16, 2022, in the middle of a protest in Izeh. Many in Izeh are members of the Bakhtiari minority, just like me. They are my people. His father listened to Kian and went in the direction the police told them. But they did not make it far when, suddenly, plainclothes security forces started shooting a barrage of bullets into their car from four directions. Kian was killed. His father survived but sustained significant injuries that left him disabled. He lost the ability to use his lower body entirely, unable to stand, walk, or move his legs due to a bullet hitting him in the spinal cord.

Kian's mother, Mah Monir, didn't take Kian's body to the morgue, because she knew that if she did, security forces would steal his body and force them to change their story to get the body back. This is what the regime does: It forces families to change their narrative from the truth to something state approved to explain the deaths of their loved ones, like saying that terrorists killed Kian and not the state forces themselves. Instead, she left Kian's body in her home. She got several large blocks of ice from her neighbors and placed them beside his body until his funeral, both to prevent his body from decomposing and to create a barrier that would stop security forces from stealing his body. Now even pieces of ice are a new layer of collective trauma.

Thousands attended Kian's funeral. In front of the crowd of mourners, Mah Monir bravely told the truth: "They shouldn't say it was terrorists [who killed Kian]. They're lying. The plainclothes forces themselves shot my child." Then she read a poem about the supreme leader:

> *What is a supreme leader?*
> *He has a beard that reaches his chest.*
> *His chest is full of hate.*
> *His heart is like a piece of stone.*
> *All of his words are bullshit.*

State security forces at the funeral tried to silence her. But she pushed forward and continued reading the poem. Mah Monir shouted the last verse, screaming, "Let me sing!" to the forces that tried to stop her.

> *We are a great nation,*
> *We will take Iran back.*

In Islam, we always had to be careful about our sins in the presence of Allah. But Kian's generation is not afraid of Allah. "My son hated the Quran," Mah Monir shouted. "No one has the right to read the Quran at his funeral." Thousands of people at his funeral reaffirmed his mother's words, chanting, "Bakhtiaris do not have a tradition of praying." In Iran, Muslims pray over the dead body before it's put into the ground, but this angry crowd had no respect for Islam. Most of the Bakhtiari people never totally converted to Islam, and we do not practice many of its customs like praying and fasting. More than that, we have kept our dances and music, local outfits, and many other traditions that were against Islamic principles, like shaking hands, hugging relatives, and kissing each other's faces as a greeting.

One video Mah Monir uploaded online ignited a backlash against the regime. In the video, Kian wanted to try the small wood boat that he made. Kian said, "In the name of the God of rainbows, I made this boat for competition and now I want to try it." He put the wood boat in a small container of water, and it floated across the surface. "We conclude that it works," Kian said.

In the days after Kian's death, many universities and schools became full of paper boats that were drawn with splotches of red, a symbol of blood. It reached as far as Babol Noshirvani University of Technology in the north of Iran, where security forces banned paper boats at the school. Imagine. They're afraid of pieces of paper. They're afraid of Kian. They're afraid of us.

Mah Monir posted to her Instagram account a photo of Kian beside a refrigerator in the supermarket. The fridge was full of expensive tropical fruits. Mah Monir wrote that Kian used to take selfies with things that caught his attention. "Kian wanted to taste dragon fruit. It was expensive, and I did not have enough money to buy dragon fruit for him." He was killed at nine years old, having never tasted it.

Mah Monir used to be an art teacher, but after Kian's death, the state fired her and banned her from entering the school, so instead she would hold painting classes for her teenage students beside Kian's grave.

She told people not to bow down to the Islamic Republic. She wrote about how she would sing Kian lullabies. She posted a video of Kian as a baby, where she put him on her feet, rocked him slowly back and forth, and sang this lullaby to him:

> *I broke for you.*
> *I sat down to mourn you.*
> *I cried from star to star.*
> *I cried forever and again.*

Each day, before they shut down her social media accounts, I joined Mah Monir live on Instagram. A girl behind the camera was constantly crying. The tiny speaker's lights turned on and off, and painful traditional Bakhtiari music came out of it. Mah Monir covered Kian's tombstone with rose petals.

The photo on Kian's tombstone was taken on his last birthday. He wore a gray coat with a white dress shirt and jeans, his right hand holding the corner of the left collar as models often do. It was not enough for the regime that the protests stalled after his death; they knew our resistance had not ended. On April 6, 2022, Mah Monir published a photo of Kian's grave showing how security officers had written slogans supporting Khamenei on his grave in red. Mah Monir wrote, "My innocent child, they are scared of your name, they are even scared of your tombstone."

On Mah Monir's Instagram account are many photos of Kian and her family in traditional Bakhtiari clothes, riding horses and aiming guns. These photos represent the thing that the current and former regimes have tried to take from us—our identity.

Bakhtiari people call Mah Monir another Bibi Maryam. On Kian's next birthday, in his absence, Mah Monir's twenty-one-year-old cousin Pooya Moulai-Rad was shot with six bullets and killed by security forces. They want to suffocate Mah Monir and stop her from seeking justice. Ashkan Amini, Jîna's brother, wrote on his Instagram after the death of Moulai-Rad, "It was Kian's birthday. Everyone brought gifts. The killers were not invited, but they brought death as a gift." The security forces did not give the cousin's body to the family for ten days and conditioned the handing over of the body to Mah Monir on her silence. On June 18, Mah Mounir was summoned to the Izeh Intelligence Department. Afterward, her Instagram page, where she campaigned for justice, was shut down. She hasn't been heard from since. The family is thought to be under house arrest.

Now, wherever we are in the world, rainbows and ice cubes remind us of nine-year-old Kian, who was robbed of his life by the Islamic Republic and of his dream of becoming a robotics engineer. A protester wrote on the wall of a building on Tehran Street, "Who should we complain to when the police are murderers?"

NILO

MY PALATE'S BITTER WITH GRIEF'S AFTERTASTE

For months I had been thinking of a video that went viral on September 25, 2022, just days after Jîna was killed. It was a video showing a funeral for Javad Heydari, who was killed while protesting on September 22, 2022, in Qazvin, a historic city that was once the capital of the Safavid dynasty, which ruled Iran from 1501 to 1736. Many Iranians associate Qazvin with that dynasty's architectural achievements and for the period known as the Golden Age, a time when our culture blossomed and grew. But during the uprising, it became known as the city where Javad was shot at close range by police officers and died due to blood loss. Javad was thirty-six when he was killed. He was close with his family, who said that he received an award as a top agricultural producer in Qazvin. In the video of his funeral, there is a crowd of mourners dressed in black surrounding his casket that's buried under a sea of flowers. His sister Fatemeh Heydari is weeping and sobbing out loud as she cuts off her long, highlighted hair and throws it on the casket, sitting there without hijab and with a jaggedly cut bob that hangs unevenly a few inches below her ears.

Iran's security apparatus often goes after families whose loved ones were killed by the state while protesting and has long intimidated them to bury their dead quietly, threatening them with not releasing the body if they're vocal about state involvement in the death. Many family members didn't hold public funerals due to this pressure, but the Heydari family stood defiant.

"The Iranian revolution succeeded because of killings and mourning rituals that came with the killings. Grief translating to rage is super important in Iranian history," said Narges Bajoghli, an assistant professor of Middle East studies at Johns Hopkins University. "Families have been pressured to not make a big deal [of the funerals]. But now people have phones and families are publicly grieving. This is very new."

The Iranian Shiite funerary tradition creates a few opportunities for mourners to gather. There's the funeral itself, then gatherings on the third and seventh days after the death, and then a *chehellom* on the fortieth day. After a protester is killed by security forces, this creates an existing framework for perpetuating at least a forty-day protest cycle from one death. "These memorials become a space for contention for the grieving families, for the broader group of protesters in the country, and then of course [for] the regime security forces that often resort to violence to suppress dissent in these venues," said Reza H. Akbari of the Institute for War and Peace Reporting. "Protesters killed by the state are also elevated to martyrs by the movement."

Iran's clerical leaders understand the power and danger of public grief. They seized on the kinetic energy of how grief can turn into rage and action in antigovernment movements for their own gain. In July 1978, religious leaders—who were then a part of the opposition to the ruling Pahlavi monarchy—organized mass protests around the death of a popular opposition figure, Sheikh Ahmad Kafi. "He died in a car accident, but it was widely known that the car accident was planned and executed by security forces. Mourners in large funeral processions in Mashhad and other cities raised anti-regime slogans; they clashed with the police, who back then fired into the crowd and supposedly killed around forty individuals, according to the protesters," said

Akbari. Seven months after this incident, the revolution would overthrow the shah.

To get an understanding of how funerals and mourning ceremonies had become a new arena for protests, we analyzed eighteen cases of state violence at *The Washington Post,* focusing on three in which security forces used fatal force. A majority of the cases were from the predominantly Kurdish region in the northwest, fitting a pattern of disproportionate use of state force against ethnic minorities. The videos and images that we reviewed showed national police units and the IRGC using live fire and less lethal weapons on mourners. "They want to scare the population, and they want to convey the message that 'we won't let you rest even if you're dead,' " said Shahin Milani, the executive director of the Iran Human Rights Documentation Center, which has worked to verify state attacks on mourning events.

The first case we looked at was the *chehellom* for Hadis Najafi, a twenty-two-year-old woman killed while protesting in Karaj, Iran's fourth-largest city, which is close to the capital. Najafi's death gained attention because she was the same age as Jîna and was killed by the state just five days after her on September 21, 2022. She had a large following on TikTok and Instagram, where followers saw themselves in Najafi—a young, modern, urbanized woman who posted selfie videos of herself dancing and lip-synching. Najafi's last message to her family was a voice note where she talked about the protests: "I really like that now I'm going to protest. Finally, after a few years, I'll be happy that I went to the demonstrations, and everything [will] change."

On the day of her *chehellom* on November 3, 2022, thousands of people planned to go to Beheshte Sakineh cemetery on the outskirts of town. Anticipating large crowds, government forces blocked the highway exit that led to the cemetery. In response, people fanned out across the city, marching in a handful of directions all over Karaj. Security officers also spread out to try to contain them. In the Khorramdasht neighborhood, there was a standoff between protesters and security forces captured on video; on one side were protesters throwing rocks, and members of Iran's riot police wearing black body armor stood on the other. Then we see seventeen-year-old Mehdi Hazrati walk toward the police as a gunshot rings out. Hazrati's body slumps to the ground.

"The shooter, without hesitation or making a mistake, took aim at close range and aimed exactly at the head and shot [Hazrati]," said a Karaj resident whose mother recorded the video. This video later made its way to citizen journalists and activists on Telegram who shared it with me. This source and I spoke about the video in detail on an encrypted messaging app. There has been no formal state inquiry into Hazrati's death, his last moments captured on video and hanging unresolved. In mid-December, mourners gathered at the Beheshte Sakineh cemetery, this time for Hazrati's *chehellom*. The citizen journalist Telegram channel Mamlekate shared footage of a family member who claims that Hazrati's parents were put under house arrest and prevented from visiting his grave.

Unfortunately, there were plenty of other incidents to choose from that were based in the Kurdish region of Iran. The sheer number and overrepresentation of cases in Kurdistan demonstrated the Islamic Republic's well-established pattern of targeting ethnic minorities in times of national upheaval. Most of the estimated twelve million Kurds who live in Iran, making up roughly 12 percent of the population, are in the provinces of West Azerbaijan, Kurdistan, Kermanshah, and Ilam in the west and southwest of Iran. There is also a Kurdish community in North Khorasan province in the northeast. In 1946, the oldest Kurdish opposition group, the Kurdish Democratic Party of Iran (KDPI), established the Republic of Kurdistan, a short-lived autonomous government on Iranian territory that was under Soviet occupation at the time. It lasted for eleven months, after which its leadership was arrested and tried, with many being executed. An estimated twenty of its leaders, including its founder, Qazi Mohammad, were publicly hanged in Mahabad, the republic's capital, and in Boukan and Saqqez. In Kurdish towns, power resided in town councils called *shoura*, which were led by the KDPI. These were instrumental in taking over the shah's police and army barracks in Kurdish areas. But not long after the revolution, an armed conflict broke out between the

Islamic Republic's newly formed IRGC and armed Kurdish groups, particularly the KDPI and Komala, a Marxist-Leninist group. It lasted from March 1979, a month after the revolution, until early 1983. And even when the revolutionary government seized power, it continued its repression against KDPI and Komala until today with its systemic repression and arrests of the group's members.

During the early days of the revolution Ayatollah Ruhollah Khomeini, who was known for his views on ethnic minorities as being contrary to Islam, demanded that the Kurdish opposition be dealt with swiftly and punitively. Following the KDPI's success against the shah's forces in the revolutionary period, there was a wave of Kurdish nationalism that the Islamic Republic was keen to crush. Many Kurdish villages and towns were destroyed, ten thousand Kurds were killed, and thousands more were sentenced to death after illegitimate trials. To this day, the discrimination continues. Kurdish regions experience economic neglect; parents are banned from registering their children with certain Kurdish names; and many Kurdish human rights activists face arbitrary arrests, prosecution, and abuse and disproportionately get handed death sentences for dubious offenses. There's a term, *kolber* in Kurdish or *kolbar* in Persian, to describe Kurdish people in border provinces who at night cross the steep, jagged mountains that line the borders, moving goods between Iran and Iraq to make a living due to the lack of job opportunities in their region. Many of these people have master's and PhD degrees; some are old men who are at retirement age or children who've dropped out of school because they have no choice but to contribute to their family with labor. Some are women whose husbands were killed after the revolution, leaving them to be the sole breadwinners. *Kolbers* cross snowy, frozen mountains where their balance is the only thing saving them from death. They also have to survive being shot at by border guards. All of this is to bring home an income that is far below minimum wage. Kurdpa, a Kurdish news agency, reported that in 2022, 259 *kolbers* were killed and wounded, and three were minors under eighteen years old. In the context of the Woman, Life, Freedom movement, the Islamic Republic has resorted to an intensified, lethal crackdown on antigovernment protesters, even going so far as to blame "separatists" in Kurdish areas for the uprising. The state justified using militaristic force against Kurdish people by labeling them "terrorist separatist groups."

On December 31, 2022, hundreds gathered for a *chehellom* to honor seven protesters killed by security forces in Javanrud, a Kurdish city in Kermanshah province on the west side of the country bordering Iraq. As the crowd reached the Haji Ibrahim cemetery, they were met by a large contingent of government forces. One Javanrud resident told me that roughly three thousand people were there that day, but only a handful of the relatives of those who had been killed were able to make it into the cemetery.

"A policeman from the special police forces used a speaker attached to one of their vehicles to tell people to go home," said a twenty-nine-year-old Javanrud resident. "He said, 'This is a holy place. Don't let there be any blood spilled here.' In a way he was making both a request and a threat."

The video we verified of the cemetery shows more than twenty officers in dark uniforms and body armor, tan-fatigue-dressed officers, and others in what appeared to be civilian clothing. I showed this to Mark Pyruz, an expert on Iran's security units, who told me that the dark-uniformed officers were a part of the FARAJA's Special Unit, FARAJA being the Persian acronym for the national police. Those in tan fatigues were members of the IRGC, and those in civilian clothing seemed to be plainclothes officers working in tandem with these two units.

"[The security forces] were clearly outnumbered by multiples," Pyruz said after he reviewed our collection of visual evidence. "This is typically where one observes the application of lethal force—when police or IRGC/Basij are at an overwhelming numerical disadvantage in confronting a resisting force of protesters." Afshon Ostovar, the associate professor at the Naval Postgraduate School who focuses on Iranian national security, also reviewed footage for this story and added that when the IRGC gets involved, it's a signal that the protests have become a national security concern given the escalation of deploying a militarized unit. "Typically, that means the military is authorized to use a greater degree of violence than the police, including lethal violence to put down the protests."

Pyruz's and Ostovar's analyses lined up with the visuals we collected and with eyewitness testimonies. "The security forces said that we weren't even Muslim, that we were infidels, things like this. And they began to advance on people and start shooting," said another Javanrud resident who was at the cemetery that day. "The Revolutionary Guard started to shoot at us, and we didn't even make a single move. We were just standing in the same place chanting protest slogans." Videos showed a chaotic scene of clouds of what seemed to be tear gas. People are heard coughing loudly as they try to flee. Borhan Elyasi, twenty-two, was killed during this crackdown at the cemetery. Hengaw, a Kurdish human rights group, identified him at the scene and shared graphic footage online that showed Elyasi's bloody body on a hospital stretcher. Other locals I interviewed confirmed his death that day. A lawyer for the IHRDC who researched what happened to Elyasi told me that they couldn't understand why security forces opened fire on mourners that day. The presence of tear gas indicates that security forces did have access to less lethal methods to disperse the crowd, but in the end they used live ammunition and killed Elyasi.

Opening fire on civilians mourning is not just cruel and stomach twisting; it also perpetuates this violent loop. Two spheres are created alongside each other: the mourning rituals that provide opportunities for protests, and the crackdowns by security forces that cement more violence and open a path for new threads of grief. "Each time an individual is killed by regime forces, the movement itself has a martyr. It actually solidifies the cause of protesters, and it kind of increases the price and the cost for all sides—for the protesters' side to continue chanting their demands, and for the regime to actually perhaps increase its violent means to suppress," said Akbari. "Finding an easy off-ramp becomes a big challenge, and that's kind of the moment that we are in in Iran right now. Especially when you have kind of the more peaceful mechanism of dialogue between state and society dismantled by regime officials over time, you don't have that many peaceful methods for communication and negotiation. So, you're stuck in this perpetual cycle of violence and protests without a clear off-ramp ahead."

On November 15, Foad Mohammadi was killed while protesting in Kamyaran, roughly forty miles east of Javanrud, in Kurdistan province, which also borders Iraq. Sources told me that people in town were outraged at Mohammadi's death, and they gathered outside his family's home to pay their respects. When they got there, they were met by various security officers. "We saw that we were surrounded by security forces in uniforms, civilian clothing. Basijis, intelligence agents, they were all over the area. People were chanting protest slogans like 'Woman, Life, Freedom,' and 'Martyrs don't die,'" a Kamyaran resident told me.

We verified a video filmed outside Mohammadi's family home that shows the moment that Borhan Karami, thirty-two, was shot and killed during this gathering of mourners that turned into a demonstration. In the video, we can hear four loud gunshots. Just before he's hit, Karami appears to point in the direction of gunfire. He collapses to the ground after the third shot. From the video alone, we couldn't tell who shot Karami. But the same Kamyaran resident told me that he was right there and saw riot police open fire. "Maybe about five or ten meters away from me, I saw that all of a sudden a young person fell to the ground. He hit the asphalt with his head. People ran away," he said to me on a call over an encrypted app. "We ran over and saw that the shooters were still standing right there on the street. They martyred poor Borhan." This eyewitness also saw when Mohammadi was killed the evening prior, and now he saw Karami's death as well.

Days after Karami was killed, the chief justice of Kurdistan province spoke to a local news site. He confirmed that Karami was fatally shot in the head but said that "no officer was present when this person was shot." A lawyer from the IHRDC told me that the government showed no interest in investigating Karami's case, and as of this writing no one has been held accountable for his murder.

FATEMEH

FOR HANGED HEADS

IN ADDITION to terrorizing mourners, the regime started systematically executing captured protesters. They had lost their primary means of wielding power—controlling women's bodies and imposing Islamic rules on Iranian society—so they were forced to resort to their second, more brutal method of suppression.

The first person executed by the state was Mohsen Shekari. The twenty-two-year-old gamer was killed on December 8. He used to work in a café in east Tehran. After he was arrested for allegedly assaulting an officer, he did not have anyone to meet him in prison and follow his case, no family members, no friends. There were no photos of him, and it took some days until we saw who it was that had been executed by the Islamic Republic.

My friend, who was in the same ward as Shekari in Evin Prison at the time, said, "They would call his name almost every day: 'Mohsen Shekari, get up and put your blindfold on.'" He became hopeless, was under interrogation, and was tortured for half of each day. He usually did not talk with anyone. A few months after his execution, my friend said, "Do you know why they chose him to execute so quickly? Because Mohsen had no one in the world. No one would care about him: no friends or family."

A few days after his execution, a video of him singing a pop song while his friend played the guitar went viral. His voice was ethereal, singing, "Again, I missed seeing your eyes, / Again, my crazy heart is missing you!"

Some people saw the terrorization of the youth, especially those gamers who had a big role in the protests, as a symbolic act by the Islamic Republic. Gen Z used to play strategic online games, but now they were playing those same strategy games in the real world against the Islamic Republic's security forces. On one occasion, a group of young men and women arrived on Enghelab Street near College Bridge riding motorcycles and spread oil across the road so that the riot police, also riding motorcycles, would fall. The young people ran toward the officers, and the police ran away. In less than a minute, the group of protesters managed to open the tanks of the police motorbikes, set them on fire, and block the street, before getting back on their motorbikes and leaving. One of my friends, who witnessed it, said she felt as if she were watching a real-live action movie. The Islamic Republic could not suppress the protests within a few months as they had done with the previous protests. They were afraid to confront Gen Z, who are fearless in facing them down and know how to battle them in the streets.

This generation represents a lifestyle that the Islamic Republic has censored for a lifetime: with lion and sun and equality tattoos, all kinds of piercings, colorful hair, and pets. Yes, here, even having a pet is a legal charge; they can take your pet away anytime they want. Young people try to live normal lives similar to those of other members of Gen Z all over the world, but in Iran their actions represent a "fuck you" to the Islamic Republic.

When the Islamic Republic faced Gen Z for the first time, it exerted extreme violence to suppress them. Yet they brought Mohsen out on national TV to confess to being corrupted by online games! Innocent Mohsen, when they issued his death sentence, was still optimistic about the possibility of the Supreme Court overruling the sentence. He would ask the other prisoners, in disbelief, "They will not execute me, will they? The officer I hit didn't even need medical treatment!" But they did execute him, most likely to send a message to Gen Z.

Mohammad Mehdi "Kian" Karami, a twenty-one-year-old Kurdish man, was another protester executed by the Islamic Republic, in his case due to participation in the funeral of Hadis Najafi, the twenty-three-year-old female TikToker who had been shot dead on the streets while participating in the protests. On November 3, 2022, in Beheshte Sakineh cemetery in Karaj, chaos erupted at Hadis's funeral. The security forces shot a plastic bullet at Hadis's sister's face, fired many tear gas and sound bombs, closed roads, and broke the windows of cars parked along the roads. In one of his last conversations with his father, Karami told him, "Dad, they announced our punishment. Mine is the death penalty, but don't tell Mom anything."

Kian, a karate champion and a member of the Iranian national youth team who had won the national championships, was arrested after being identified on video that day. His dream was to stand on the podium at the world championship. On his father's previous birthday, Kian had promised his father that he would become a world champion. He had a tattoo of the Olympic rings on his arm, but the Islamic Republic did not let his dream come true.

Kian was one of two sentenced to death in the case of Hadis Najafi's funeral. The other person was Seyyed Mohammad "Kumar" Hosseini, thirty-nine, a laborer in the poultry industry in Qazvin. He went from Karaj to Qazvin every morning and returned every night, which took about six hours a day. He had no parents or relatives. He had no one to come meet him in prison. There was no one to take his body. He has only one photo, taken on a trip to Ramsar, a city in the north of Iran, on his Instagram page. The other post is about a bracelet that he had ordered from an online shop that was never sent to him. He followed a car dealership on Instagram that sells reasonably priced used Kia Pride cars that he was never able to afford.

Kian was purposefully targeted for execution for much the same reason that Mohsen Shekari had been: Both were young men from families (or lack thereof) with little means to hire lawyers or fight back against the ruling. There was a deliberate attempt on the part of the regime to make an example of the poorest in society. Several hours before Kian's execution, the prison officials told him and Kumar that they had pardoned them. The prisoners in the same cell said Kumar prayed after hearing this; he was so happy. The others were also led to believe that the officials had canceled the execution order. Then, suddenly, the officials cut off the prison phones and televisions and executed them both.

Mr. Mashallah, Kian's father, was an old peddler. He and his wife, Manijeh, had only one son, whom they had dreamed of raising despite their poverty. Even religious people who supported the regime were shocked by the executions. A friend's mother, who was deeply devout, said she stopped praying the moment the men were killed.

After the executions of Kian and Kumar, Mr. Mashallah and his wife began washing both of their graves every day, as if they were both their sons. Mr. Mashallah used to say he had two sons now and that whatever he did in Kian's memory, he did the same for Kumar. He climbed the mountains in their memory. Once a week, the family would cook thirty portions of food and distribute it among needy people in the name of Kian and Kumar.

Thousands of people in Iran, motivated by their story, also started to distribute food among the needy. The following year, in September 2023, IRGC forces stormed Mr. Mashallah's house. They arrested him and stole Kian's medals one week before the anniversary of Jîna's death. He performed the most peaceful forms of protest to seek justice for his lost sons—climbing, planting trees, and distributing food—but he would become a current version of Kaveh, an ancient Iranian hero who is a symbol of resistance in Iran that has persisted since the tenth century. He was a blacksmith in Kaveh who gathered the people in rebellion against King Zahhak after losing two of his children. After his son was executed, Mr. Mashallah tattooed Kian's last words on his arm. "Dad, they announced our punishment. Mine is the death penalty, but don't tell Mom anything."

Mr. Mashallah has been held in a solitary cell since his arrest. The judiciary system asked for 7 billion *toman*, about $140,000, as bail to release him temporarily until his trial is held. No one could afford it, let alone a peddler, so Manijeh began to go to Kian's and Kumar's graves alone. If loneliness had a picture, it would be her. The regime kills people's innocent children, then kidnaps them to prevent them from seeking justice. Ashkan Amini, Jîna's brother, wrote, "Write for history that they execute us with the morning *adhan* and shoot us at night. Those whose God is merciful, their Prophet was kind, and their imam was oppressed." A group made up of the children of people executed in the 1988 massacre, in which the regime executed thousands of leftist educated students and young political prisoners without holding courts for them, wrote a public letter that read, in part, "Remembering is fighting, and trying not to forget is resistance."

Just a few days after the execution of another three young protesters in Isfahan, Gholam Hossein Mohseni Ajei, the head of the judiciary, declared, "Those who should be executed will be executed." One of them was Mohammad Ghobadlou, a young man who laughed with his feet. In a video on his Instagram account, he sings a poem: "A candle burns, and a worried butterfly circles around the candle. I am burning, but I have no butterfly." Mohammad laughs as he jumps up and down with joy. His friend's voice can be heard saying, "Why are you laughing with your feet?" Mohammad proceeds to laugh even more with his feet.

Mohammad was always joking good-naturedly with everyone in his Instagram videos. All the videos were recorded in the barbershop where he used to work. He had a critical sense of humor. Mohammad says, "Blue-blooded men are not noble. Gentlemen, we are noble. We are the ones who work hard from morning to night to be independent and keep our hands in our own pockets." Mohammad's death sentence was confirmed in the Supreme Court. His father is a veteran and was wounded in the Iran-Iraq War while fighting for the Islamic Republic. Despite his service, the regime showed no mercy to his son. Amir Raisian, Mohammad Ghobadlou's lawyer, tweeted the defects of the case. The key irregularity is that though Mohammad had an altercation with the riot forces, no one was seriously injured, but he was later blamed for the murder of an agent who was killed somewhere else.

Amir is my lawyer too, my lifesaver. Some time ago, when I went to his office, he said with certainty that he would change all these death orders in the Supreme Court. When I came out of his office, the family of Toomaj Salehi, a popular rapper being held in solitary confinement who had been convicted of corruption, was waiting for an appointment with Amir. Confused and desperate, they had come all the way from Isfahan. I thought again of Amir. When Mohammad Ghobadlou's death sentence had been confirmed by the Supreme Court, I was thinking of Amir and his hope to reverse all these death sentences in court. Amir is the lawyer of many activists, filmmakers, laborers, feminists, and political prisoners. His office is always open to us. He never charges us any money.

As I worked on this book, I sent my notes to Amir. He answered, "When did I say that I would change all death sentences? Only a foolish hopeful would say this sentence. I might have said it *should* change. The execution is carried out in the same way. I have not backed down, but they carry out their death sentences without informing anyone or even going through legal procedures. My hands are tied." He added, "After the confirmation of Ghobadlou's verdict, I have raised the case twice in court from the beginning. I didn't give up, but I ran into a wall. The head of the Supreme Court announced that he was against his execution. But even the head of the Supreme Court could not change this decision. Who should I tell this to?" For years, judges in Iran's courts have approved the sentences and punishments given to them by the interrogators of the Intelligence Organization of the IRGC and the Ministry of Intelligence. The power of security agents is even more significant than that of the head of the Supreme Court. Habib Daneshvar, a social activist and journalist who spent several days in jail with Mohammad Ghobadlou, wrote a letter to him:

> *You were young, very young. You had a passion for life, you had it, and you still have it. You were and still are. At least until this moment, no*

one has heard the news of your death! I wish the next sun will shine later, and no one hears the sound of the morning adhan *and your head will never go on the gallows.*

You were among the few arrested in the first days. The interrogator promised to get a lesser sentence from the judge if you cooperated. Instead, providing you with the opportunity to escape the country. He even promised to take care of your asylum case in the destination country. It was enough that you would tell them a few names.

You had no associate and no intention to cooperate with the interrogators. You said to the interrogator, "The blood of my father's friend was spilled on this soil. My father fought for this land for many years, shielding it with his body. Where would I go? I prefer that my blood be spilled on this land rather than escape it."

You have a red card exempting you from compulsory military service because of bipolar disorder. We were sure that no danger would threaten you. Also, a mentally ill person would not be tried in any judicial system.

We were wrong, dear. The judicial system here is different from everywhere else. The shadow of political Islam is darker than all the sinister shadows of the world. Dire shadows lurk in the corners of our courts.

In another post on his Instagram account, Mohammad said, "Do you know exactly when God is with you? When you can say, I got lucky, and I survived."

But sorry, Mohammad, even God cannot help an innocent mentally unwell person like yourself in front of these murderers.

Political prisoners are usually not told in advance that they will be executed. But the officials told Majidreza Rahnavard, another young protester sentenced to execution in Mashhad, as he was on his way to the execution ward in handcuffs, blindfolds, slippers, and striped prison clothes. A reporter stood with a camera and a microphone in front of him, asking for Majid's last words. Majid said with a loud voice that did not shake, "At my grave, don't pray or read the Quran. Just listen to happy music." These executed young men are the proud fighters of our society, the humble seekers of liveliness and happiness. My Instagram feed is full of photos of young people blinded by tear gas and of dead and executed protesters. It looks like a cemetery that stretches from the northern city of Nowshahr on the banks of the Caspian Sea to Zahedan by the Pakistan border in the east. I haven't visited the graves, but I know each one from social media: the flowers, the pictures, and the heart-shaped frames.

But as a protester wrote on a wall in Tehran, "You can execute a revolutionary but not a revolution."

NILO

HOW SWEET THOSE DAYS WHEN WE WERE STILL

A S THE PROTESTS were going on, I started to talk to Milad again. We found each other through Instagram in 2016 and periodically talked over the years, always talking more when some big news event, crisis, or unrest was happening in the country. The first thing he sent me in 2016 was a photo of us from that summer in Tehran. There's a line of young kids sitting on the pool deck. I'm the only girl sitting in a pink bikini while the others are more covered up, wearing denim overalls, soccer jerseys of the local Iranian football clubs, or baggy T-shirts and shorts. I smile at the memory and also cringe at the photo when I look at it. I was just so blindingly *Western* in a neon-pink floral two-piece bathing suit, marching around and not caring what the other girls were wearing. Milad's arm is around my shoulders, and my legs are outstretched, with my ankles crossed over each other, skimming the water of the pool. I remember feeling embarrassed, shy, and delighted to be getting this kind of attention from him. Milad messaged me when he was at my cousin Shirin's wedding in the summer of 2017. I was unable to go because I had just started reporting on Iran, covering the dying stage of the nuclear deal and looming sanctions on Iranians for *The New York Times*, but he video called me from the reception as he danced with my maman, who went to both Tehran and Kurdistan to celebrate the different ceremonies for my cousin, who married into a Kurdish family.

"Jat khaliye koli. Wish U were here," he texted me the night of the wedding. "Jat khaliye" is a phrase we use when we wish someone were with us. The direct translation is "your spot is empty," conveying a longing and a dream of something unfulfilled.

"Me too," I responded first in English, then switching to typing out Persian as I labored over using an alphabet that I had only recently begun learning. "Unfortunately, it's not a good time for me because I'm a reporter."

"Wow ... you've learned Farsi," he wrote back immediately, using the Persian too. "Remember how you used to say my name? You could never say 'Milad' properly and we all laughed about it. But you're so good at reading and speaking now! Okay I'm going to take you around. Who else do you want to see?"

He held me in his hand, my face on the screen, as he toured me around Shirin's wedding. After our video call, he started to send me photos of my cousins and family members whom I hadn't seen for a decade or more. I sent him a string of crying emojis. I so badly wished I was there. "Don't ... your aims are something else. Follow your dreams. Vel kon Irano," he wrote to me, telling me to let Iran go. "Everyone is escape from here and you.... There is nothing special about Iran. I understand u.... I was in your place. I didn't come to Iran for 10 years and now after 5 years of living back in Iran, I wish keh hich vakht bar nemigashtam." We were switching between Persian and English easily. Without even thinking, he wrote to me in Persian to tell me, "I wish that I had never come back." He used our language to punctuate his emotions in the same way that I do.

I hesitated to reach out to Milad when the protests started in September 2022. He's not a journalist like Fatemeh. I knew that of course he wasn't supportive of the Islamic Republic, but I wasn't sure if he was protesting and would accept the risk of speaking with me. I first sent him a message on Instagram asking if he was okay. He responded that he was taking part in the demonstrations.

"Daram barat abo jaroo mikonam biai Tehran.... Age namiram albate," he wrote to me, using a phrase that translates to someone who is getting the house ready for guests, but in this situation Milad meant that he was out protesting to make his country a free place that I could one day visit if he didn't die in the process. "Put this on your Instagram story but erase my name. See you soon," he wrote again in English.

We started communicating on encrypted messaging apps, the ones that he said protest organizers use to make digital channels that were password protected to evade Iran's intelligence apparatuses. I had no idea that he was an organizer too. Milad was in his mid-thirties, and for work he began opening a few different restaurants, cafés, and bakeries across the country. Sometimes he would post photos on Instagram from a visit to a bakery, smiling as he was baking bread with one of their chefs. One of the cafés he owns is near Tehran University in the heart of the city. Universities and schools had become sites of protest organization during this uprising. These centers have always been places for antigovernment activities. My maman was a first-year student in Tehran University at the start of the 1979 Iranian revolution. There, she said, various student groups would gather in the courtyard, debating politics and the ousting of the shah. "Everyone was there, the communists, Marxists, Islamists, monarchists. This is where it started when I was in my late teens," my maman once told me. She remembers the day when the shah's security forces attacked student organizers on November 4, 1978, killing scores of young people. Maman told me that she narrowly escaped being beaten with a baton by an officer who was hitting any young person he could get his hands on. As the Islamic Republic has dismantled civil society over the past few decades that it has been in power, most NGOs and associations that are critical of the government no longer exist. Schools and universities remain some of the only places where a natural gathering of dissent can still happen. From Milad's café near Tehran University and Amir Kabir University, he could see how students were gathering. As the protests began, he became involved as an organizer—spreading the word on dates and times to call on his fellow people to come and take back their streets.

"The protests were not in one place this time like it used to be in [previous demonstrations in] Tehran. It wasn't clear in advance where protests would be. Every neighborhood, every street, every square, was a place of protest. Tehran had turned into many small cities and neighborhoods where people protested, that's why it was hard [for security forces] to stop them," Milad told me. He was in a Telegram group called Youth of the Neighborhoods of Tehran that organized protests on Saturdays and Wednesdays. Street activity in the capital started to slow around December in response to violent state crackdowns.

"In the beginning, people were not afraid. People always thought that there are too many of us in the streets and that a revolution was near. Because of this, people dared to come, thinking that everyone is behind them," Milad said. "When the protests became quieter, the number of arrests increased. [Security forces] caught many people and harassed them. Many [protesters] were blinded [during the crackdowns]. It was very scary."

Over the course of our communications, he kept me informed of what Iranians were talking about. Milad messaged me daily, sending me videos of police violence that I should investigate, flagging what citizen journalist channels were highlighting. He even put me in touch with eyewitnesses for my ambulance investigation. We spoke a lot in December 2022, when the Islamic Republic publicly hanged two twenty-three-year-old protesters, Mohsen Shekari and Majidreza Rahnavard. These executions were carried out just days apart from each other. Human rights groups decried their short, few-weeks-long sham trials and highlighted that one of them likely confessed under torture. The mood was exceptionally bleak, and we turned to each other to try to process even an ounce of this pain. "We're all depressed. Truly, these days are not good for us. If only we could return to that time when we had crushes on each other and could stay there," he wrote to me. These executions were intended to terrify people like Milad, and they did. It sent him into a state of shock, not knowing what he would do next or if protesting was even worthwhile.

I sent Milad a message in October 2023, letting him know that I wanted to write about him. When I asked him to choose a pseudonym, he told me I could use his real name, because he had made the choice to leave the country and start again elsewhere. Milad had left Iran when he was fifteen years old and lived abroad in Dubai, Germany, and Georgia before returning in 2012. He said that he saw Rouhani winning the presidency in 2013 as a blip of hope, because the candidate ran on a platform of diplomacy and engagement with the West. The nuclear deal that was negotiated and signed by Rouhani's government in 2015 made Milad think that he could live the life he wanted in his country. But when Trump unilaterally withdrew from the deal in 2018, Milad, like every other ordinary Iranian citizen, was affected by the severe sanctions and a national currency that decreased in value day by day. He told me that he saw the value of his money fade away right in front of his eyes. Still, I never imagined that he would leave. Many of his friends and family are still in Iran. Milad told me about dealing with a police unit called Amaken, which is tasked with monitoring mandatory hijab and any illegal alcohol in businesses. His café has been affected by this and has been closed for some time, though he added that bribes can be paid to get around this. Everything has come to a head in such a way that Milad doesn't feel as if there were any space for him to live freely in Iran. Aside from the economic downward spiral he has been experiencing, he can't even find pockets of joy in daily life anymore.

"I like off-roading and camping in nature. But now they attack, beat, and arrest hikers. Some time ago, near Mount Damavand, there was a place called Opert. Plainclothes police attacked a hiker there, beating him with an electric baton. One person was paralyzed. In another incident in the Jawahar Dasht of Gilan [province], Basijis attacked the camp of hikers and had severely beaten them." He ended our conversation by telling me that anyone who can emigrate is leaving these days, including many of his friends. And again, he asked me to delete our chats. Before I did, I asked Milad to bring my yo-yo to Canada in case we see each other again.

FATEMEH

FOR THE WOMEN WHO NEVER EXPRESS REGRET

NILOOFAR'S AND ELAHEH'S TRIALS were held in the infamous Revolutionary Court headquarters on Shariati Street—the same place where Sahar Khodayari, known to many as the Blue Girl, was sentenced to prison for attempting to enter Azadi Stadium to watch a match of her favorite soccer team and who tragically lost her life by self-immolation there.

Mohamad Hosein, Niloofar's husband, ran on the morning of Niloofar's trial day. He was inspired by Niloofar's words. One day, Niloofar said to him, "Enduring prison is like training for a marathon. The pain every day, the consistency for a long period. It seems that no matter how much you practice, it's still not enough. But the image of the joy of reaching the finish line erases all pains." *Keep running, keep running, a little more to go.* It's a verse Niloofar sings to herself during long hikes and heavy mountaineering to alleviate the pain of the journey. She wrote this sentence on paper for Mohamad Hosein and sent it from prison:

I'm waiting for you at the finish line of the prison marathon Niloo.

One day, my friend Hoda, who is editor in chief of the online and video sections of *Shargh*, texted me asking to come to my place after work. I said yes, of course. We messaged each other in an encrypted setting; all of our chats were set to automatically disappear after fifteen minutes so that if we were arrested, no one could read them. We never talked on the phone when we got close to our meeting place. We would put our phones on airplane mode or turn them off so security officials couldn't monitor our whereabouts. When we arrived, we would put all our phones into a pot, then placed the pot in the bathroom and kept music playing beside it. We kept a glass of water beside our beds, but not for drinking. It is there so that if we are attacked or arrested at home during the night, we can put the phone in the water to destroy it, or if we have time, we can throw it into the toilet.

When she arrived, Hoda said she wanted to talk to me about a story idea. We have a Journalists' Day in our national calendar; it commemorates the day that the Taliban killed an IRNA journalist in Afghanistan. Hoda said her reporter wanted to work on a story about the harassment of female journalists to publish on that day. I said the only story to cover about journalism in Iran should be about Elaheh and Niloofar. Hoda brought her notebook, and we started brainstorming. I said it should be about their absences, away from their loved ones and their places of work. I said to Hoda that I knew it was risky and mentally draining to cover, but that there was no one but her who could do it. We wrote the whole scenario together. Hoda did her best, and the report went viral. Its title was "Your Absence, Your Empty Places," as I had suggested.

The segment featured Elaheh and her family. Elaheh called from prison. Elnaz, Elaheh's sister, put the phone on speaker and filmed their talk. "I have never regretted writing any report in any field. I have been a journalist for fifteen years. I have done nothing except being my people's voice," Elaheh said, adding, "Prison is hard. The period of detention is hard, being away from family is hard. And there are pressures, interrogations, but when I go back and think about the past, I have no regrets about doing my job." Elaheh's husband, Saeed, said, "My biggest loss is not hearing Elaheh's voice at our home. Our joy was nightly poetry reading by Elaheh. Each night, she randomly chooses one of Forough Farrokhzad's poems and reads." Elnaz said, "Our families and I will never be the normal people that we used to be, our lives have changed since Elaheh's imprisonment, and it will never be the same again." I have never seen Elnaz's eyes so wounded and heartbroken. She wears grief, longing, loss, and desperation on her face. When I watched the recording of Elaheh's call from prison and saw Elnaz's eyes, I cried the whole day and for days afterward. The Japanese TV station NHK broadcast it, and now millions in Japan also know about our imprisoned birds.

The trials of Niloofar and Elaheh were set to be held starting on May 30, 2023. Niloofar's trial would be on the first day; Elaheh's on the second. Everyone demanded their trials be public, but both were held behind closed doors. Shahrzad, the social desk editor at *Shargh*, texted me saying that their trials would be nothing new, that it's all regime propaganda. I knew this to be true. I had hope, but in reality both women were facing sentences of up to sixteen years—ten years for collaborating with the hostile government of America, five years for collusion against national security, and one year for propaganda against the regime.

On July 26, 2023, the 251st day of her temporary detention, Niloofar rejected all the charges against her. Her lawyer requested a fair trial, but the judge didn't allow the lawyers to speak. They didn't let Niloofar's husband and mother see her for even a few seconds. When they took Niloofar from prison to court, they passed by the *Shargh*'s bureau, Niloofar's former workplace. After that, Mohamad Hosein, Niloofar's husband, asked her in a phone call what she felt. Niloofar responded, "Excitement, regret, hope, failure, longing, sorrow, loneliness, pride."

Around this time, Louise, my friend at *The Sunday Times*, messaged me and said that Angelina Jolie's PR team had reached out to her and asked for information about Toomaj, the popular Iranian rapper and singer imprisoned by the regime. As I read Louise's email, something sparked in my eyes. I wrote short bios for Toomaj, Niloofar, and Elaheh and sent them to Louise. On July 25, 2023, Angelina Jolie posted a message on her Instagram to her millions of followers. "Respect and solidarity to Iranian women and men for their courage in defending basic rights and freedoms, and thinking of those imprisoned or facing prosecution—as in other situations where freedom of expression is restricted or denied—including Elaheh Mohammadi, Niloofar Hamedi, Narges Mohammadi, Toomaj Salehi."

Elaheh read this text in front of Abolqasem Salavati, a judge notorious for issuing unjust sentences, including countless death sentences. Elaheh not only defended herself but also defended journalism:

In the Name of the Pen

I am Elaheh Mohammadi. I have been a journalist for fifteen years, and throughout my professional career I have not done anything other than speak for people and take a step toward improving their lives. I have had no connection with any foreign government, and I am proud to stay with the people to be their voice.

I believe that instead of arresting journalists, the security institutions, the judiciary, the government, and the Parliament should listen to people's words and not arrest journalists who have done their work and keep them in temporary detention for many months.

Niloofar Hamedi and I are being tried as representatives of the noble and suffering body of the Iranian press while the authority of the media has been transferred abroad due to security encounters with honest and committed journalists, and these severe encounters with journalists have caused people's annoyance.

The authorities, especially the judicial authorities, should hear the voices of the people, especially the women and journalists who speak their language, and should not respond violently to their rightful demands.

After fourteen months of imprisonment, on October 22, Niloofar and Elaheh were issued thirteen- and twelve-year sentences, respectively. I read the news in disbelief. We expected these sentences, but they still hit us like a slap to the face. I started crying; I drowned in my tears. That day was Niloofar's birthday. She turned thirty-one. She heard the news on the way to the prison meeting hall. What a birthday they made for her. The regime will not be in power that much longer, I told myself, trying to keep calm. I thought of the sad eyes of Elnaz, Elaheh's twin sister. And of Elaheh's taxi driver father, both her and Niloofar's husbands, and Shahrzad, Niloofar's editor, who has lived with a guilty conscience for fourteen months. People called Elaheh and Niloofar little captive birds.

In her call from prison to her husband, Elaheh recited an excerpt of a poem by Hushang Ebtehaj. He recorded her voice and published it on his Instagram account:

> *I see that blossoming of joy,*
> *the loud cry of humanity,*
> *That great celebration of Freedom Day.*

NILO

THE ROSES HAVE ALL GONE

Somehow days stretched out into months. My last investigation about the uprising published in late April 2023. I looked into state violence at funerals that disproportionately targeted Kurds. By this point, most of the street protests had petered out. I was continuing to monitor if there was anything else to investigate, but videos weren't coming out at the same volume anymore.

In February 2023, Khamenei reportedly ordered wide-ranging amnesty for people arrested during the uprising, with the aim of releasing, pardoning, or lessening sentences for "tens of thousands" of people. But this wouldn't hold for long. The Islamic Republic began another wave of repression over the summer, seemingly trying to get ahead of any more protest activity for the anniversary of Jîna's death. In June, Iranian media and international human rights organizations began reporting that authorities were summoning, arresting, and sentencing several activists and protesters whom they had just recently released. On August 16, 2023, authorities arrested at least a dozen women's rights activists, and around the same time they also increased their crackdown on the Baha'i religious community, reportedly arresting eleven Baha'i citizens, including a ninety-year-old former Baha'i leader. The Islamic Republic was resorting to another feature of its playbook of suppressing antigovernment activity—threatening and arresting people without due process who were directly involved in actions against the state, and even those on the periphery. Then, on September 5, 2023, Kurdistan Human Rights Network reported that Jîna's uncle Safa Aeli was arrested in their hometown, Saqqez, sharing that "Aeli was arrested without a court warrant at 13:00 local time as he was returning home when security forces raided his house." He was reportedly warned not to put out any calls or public statements to encourage a gathering for Jîna's death anniversary on September 16, 2023. Days later, security forces summoned Jîna's father as well, and similarly intimidated him to not commemorate his daughter's anniversary. The family's lawyer and journalists who have been covering the case have been harassed. Jîna's grave was also reportedly desecrated, preventing family members from mourning her.

As we got closer to the anniversary, I spoke with Tara Sepehri Far, the senior researcher on Iran and Kuwait for Human Rights Watch, about what these mounting arrests and acts of intimidation meant for the movement. "I think if there is no major public event at the time of the anniversary, it should not be understood as people forgetting it," she said to me in an interview. "I think the conversation is very much alive. People are talking about it in social media, but the authorities are doing everything in their power to make sure that organized events around the anniversary are not happening."

As I was trying to figure out what story I could cover for Jîna's September 16 anniversary, I thought back to Fatemeh Heydari, the sister of the slain protester Javad Heydari, who cut her hair over her brother's casket. I interviewed her for my investigation into the lethal crackdowns on funerals and mourning ceremonies, but I didn't end up including it in the piece, in favor of focusing more on cases where we had visual evidence of security officers using deadly force on mourners. Heydari had become a kind of symbol for families who lost their loved ones. Since her brother was killed, she had become more vocal online, demanding justice for Javad's death. I knew that there were potentially hundreds of Heydaris out there—family members who've been intimidated by the regime to stop drawing attention to how the state killed one of their own. As I began to interview grieving family members and human rights researchers, I learned how these testimonies revealed that Iranian authorities were systematically surveilling and detaining these family members, pressuring them into silence and to stay out of any demonstrations.

"The pressures come in the form of phone calls, summoning families, asking them to keep quiet," Sepehri Far told me. "Families draw a lot of sympathy from the public given that they are basically the lived experience of the injustice that happened to them."

Just like those protesters who were released and rearrested, these family members were experiencing increased pressure and intimidation as September 16 inched closer. I went back and spoke with Heydari, telling her I wanted to do a story focusing on the regime's extending web of methodical intimidation of family members. She told me more details of how life had been for her since Javad was cruelly taken from her family. The Heydari family was among the first to go public about the death of their loved one. Javad, who was thirty-six years old, was killed while protesting in the northwestern city of Qazvin. The video of Heydari cutting her hair over Javad's casket was an early viral image of the protest because it was in line with the defining symbol of hair cutting. "Cutting hair is uniquely associated with this cycle of the protests, and it's a very powerful gesture from Iranian women. They're sarcastically and bitterly stating, 'If it's the hair that's bothering you, here you go. Are you willing to let me be free now?'" Reza H. Akbari told me of the significance of Heydari's cutting her hair. Her revolutionary action propelled the Heydari family into the spotlight, attracting the ire and attention of security and intelligence forces.

"A few days after what happened to my brother and the sharing of the videos, I was arrested and I had to go to court because I was summoned for making propaganda against the government," Heydari told me in an interview. "My father was pressured to say that we are supporters of the regime and that his daughter acted emotionally and we made a mistake."

Their family home was surveilled and raided numerous times over the year, forcing them into hiding. Heydari added that arrest warrants were also issued for her father, her older brother, and more than a dozen relatives. Even her two-year-old niece was briefly detained with her father. Four family members lost their jobs, including Heydari and her sister-in-law, who was fired from her nursing job after being asked about Javad's role in the protests. After months of harassment and intimidation, the family was forced to flee and live in hiding. Heydari told me that they now live in Turkey and keep a low profile.

Sepehri Far, the researcher for Human Rights Watch, confirmed to me that this type of repression was again being felt in an outsize manner among the Kurdish community. "We're hearing a lot of reports from the Kurdistan area that has experienced disproportionate crackdown from the beginning. The protests started there, and the momentum that they had played an important role in the duration of the protests." I reached out to Rebin Rahmani of Kurdistan Human Rights Network, who had also helped me connect with sources for our funeral and mourning ceremonies investigation. He put me in touch with Hiwa Hosseinpouri, whose thirty-two-year-old brother, Azad, was killed at a demonstration. My first conversation with Hiwa was a series of voice notes where I explained the story that I was working on, hoping that he would speak with me about what happened to him and his family. He was hesitant at first, saying that he hadn't given any interviews to media organizations, especially Iranian diasporic media groups that were pro-monarchy.

"I only talk to the media that does not discriminate and recognizes my Kurdish identity as I am a Kurdish person. I am sensitive about my Kurdish identity and would not like my rights to be taken and violated in any way," he said to me. "The voice of the people of Kurdistan should be heard by others."

I told Hiwa that he absolutely would have the space for his Kurdish identity; that wasn't even a question or concern of mine. And that in fact I was focusing on the disproportionate suppression of his community. I didn't quite get why he felt that he wouldn't have the space to do so until I was on a panel at a think tank in Washington, D.C., a few weeks later that was about the lessons that civil society had learned through the Woman, Life, Freedom uprising. Joining me on the panel were Siamak Aram, the president of the National Solidarity Group of Iran, a Washington, D.C., grassroots organization that has been holding demonstrations ostensibly in solidarity with the movement in Iran since Jîna's death, and Cameron Khansarinia, the vice president of the National Union for Democracy in Iran (NUFDI), a pro-regime-change organization that has had Reza Pahlavi, the son of the last shah of Iran, speak at its events. NUFDI even cites him as "Prince Reza Pahlavi" in its mission statement—an interesting disconnect from protesters in Iran who weren't publicly calling for the return of the monarchy en masse. In all the videos of the demonstrations that I watched over the year, I didn't hear any pro-monarchy slogans.

Neither the moderator nor my co-panelists mentioned that the Woman, Life, Freedom movement was led by women. It's something that I didn't even realize until after it was over. They also never referred to Jîna by her Kurdish name, the name that her friends and family use. And the question about women's issues was posed just to me, the only woman on a panel that was meant to discuss a national, antigovernment uprising that swelled in response to Jîna's death with "Woman, Life, Freedom" as the rallying cry. It was a surreal experience where I felt tokenized at best. Then the conversation turned to the topic of ethnic minorities, something that I have reported extensively on throughout this year. The moderator asked Khansarinia how ethnic minorities may be a vulnerability for the Islamic Republic's governance going forward.

"The difference between Iran and other countries, Iranians who are Iranian-Baloch, Iranian-Kurd, Iranian-Arab, Iranian-Lur, I mean, you can go on, on and on, have lived as part of one united country for thousands of years. And so, to your question on the Islamic Republic's strategy, one of their main strategies is to play up those differences," said Khansarinia as he explained that to supplant that, the Islamic Republic had tried to create a national identity through the creation of an Islamic nation. "Iranians, you know, don't really ask one another, 'Are you Kurdish? Are you Arab? Are you Baloch? Are you Lor?'"

Now I completely understood Hiwa's fear of his identity being washed away. Khansarinia was right, the Islamic Republic indeed used Shia Islam to build the foundation of the country and its new national identity. But his characterization of minorities, even going so far as to equate their recognition with viewing the country with a Western lens, felt incorrect and misleading. I spoke with dozens of ethnic minorities in Iran who would always vehemently state that they were Baloch or Kurd or Turk. There was never an Iranian hyphen placed before their identity. In some sense, Khansarinia had a point: Iranians don't ask each other about one's ethnic identity, because many of those in minority groups often lead with it. Even in my own family, my baba instilled a pride in me where I could claim being Azeri, despite not even knowing how to speak our language. Hearing how a U.S.-based Iranian opposition group, that I happened to be sharing space with, was mischaracterizing our country's multiethnic makeup was frustrating, especially when I remembered that it is these groups who are in rooms with legislators and policy stakeholders. It was another somber moment in the diaspora, witnessed by my *Washington Post* colleagues who came to support me. Afterward, all remarked to me how bizarre Khansarinia's comment was. One of my co-workers remarked that it was strange to hear these men say "The Iranian people want..." several times with such authority, inherently claiming to represent an entire nation of people.

After I sent Hiwa some links to previous stories that I had covered, he was willing to speak with me. He also said Rebin's recommendation and how he vouched for me made him feel more comfortable. Hiwa was abroad when he learned about the death of his brother Azad. Azad was killed on November 17, 2022, in an antigovernment demonstration in Mahabad, a city in the northwestern West Azerbaijan province, roughly sixty miles from the Iraq border.

"My brother was a dentist and had a simple life. He wanted freedom. He went to the street to defend his right. He was injured several times, and after being treated, he returned to protest again and did humanitarian work. He transported the injured people to a safe place and treated them," Hiwa told me about his brother Azad, whose name means "free" in Kurdish and Persian.

Hiwa left Iran in 2014 because he was involved in political activities related to Kurdish liberation, and after being arrested and harassed by Iran's authorities, he had no choice but to flee. I withheld where Hiwa has resettled because he told me that since he left, he's received death threats from anonymous sources that he suspects are related to the Islamic Republic. Watching from afar, Hiwa learned about the death of his brother from his friends inside the country. "All my hair has turned white from grief and pressure in these past few months," Hiwa said. "I have had many panic attacks. I am far away, and I feel desperate."

Like his brother, Azad had been active in previous antigovernment movements, but Hiwa said that Azad seemed more determined this time—stating that Azad told him he was willing to die for his freedom. After Azad was killed, his family in Mahabad was under constant state surveillance. "Three of my sisters, my brother, and my brother-in-law were summoned by intelligence officials," Hiwa said. "They confiscated their mobile phones and passports. They threatened them with prison and death. They banned them from any activity on social media. They can't even visit my brother's grave."

The stress had an unimaginable impact on his family. His eighty-year-old father was summoned; his mother suffered two heart attacks in the months during this whole ordeal; and his sisters have fallen into a deep depression. "When you are outside of Iran and cannot be with your family and relatives and be present, your pain and suffering multiply," Hiwa added.

Rebin also connected me with Ramtin Fatehi, a twenty-five-year-old nursing student who now lives in Germany. Ramtin's father, uncle, and aunt had been missing for ten days when he joined a demonstration in Berlin in October 2022 that was held in solidarity with the uprising. His family members had been arrested for protesting in Sanandaj, the capital of Iran's northwestern Kurdistan province, and he hadn't been able to reach them.

"I participated in the protest to be [their] voice," Ramtin told me in an interview. He spoke with the media that day at the rally, hoping to raise awareness of his family's disappearance. But his father, Ramin, was already dead. A friend called that night to tell him the news. "I felt like the world was falling down on me," Ramtin told me as he recalled that day. Hengaw, a local Kurdish human rights organization, reported that Ramin was tortured to death. Like clockwork, the authorities began to intimidate and harass Ramtin's family back in Iran. He told me that each week the Ministry of Intelligence summons one of his family members and threatens them not to participate in protests. "The threats and harassment have increased closer to the anniversary," Ramtin said, referring to the one-year anniversary of Jîna's death on September 16, 2023.

Both Ramtin and Hiwa would love to return home but to a free Iran that has equal rights for them as Kurdish people. "We, the people of Kurdistan and Baluchestan, will get our occupied land back and live freely," Hiwa told me. "I hope all of the people of Iran, and in the world, will live freely and will not be captive to a regime like the Islamic Republic."

In Germany, Ramtin works at hospitals and nursing homes and takes special pride in looking after the elderly. "One of my dreams was to take care of my father in his old age and to be beside him, but the Islamic Republic prevented this dream," said Ramtin, his voice starting to break as he told me that his father was his best friend.

While pressuring victims' families may quash protests and gatherings in the short term, the human rights researcher Sepehri Far said, it could have unintended consequences for the regime. "We have seen the families of the 2019 protest joining forces with those who have been killed, we have seen the families all the way back to the '80s finding this space to speak up," she said. "Every round of protests just brings more people together."

FATEMEH

GOODBYE, MY BELOVED HOMELAND

> *What do I want from my homeland?*
> *Except for a piece of bread and a comfortable mind,*
> *What do I want?*
> *Except a patch of sunlight, and a rain that falls gently*
> *except the window that*
> *opens to love and freedom.*
> *What did I want from the homeland?*
> *Which they have taken from me.*
> *Ah, my beloved homeland, brought to its knees*
> *Goodbye*
> *Goodbye.*
>
> —a poem by Sherko Bekas,
> a Kurdish poet

As soon as Nilo told me we had finalized the contract for this book, I messaged Amir, my lawyer, on Signal, asking him if he had time to meet. He responded to me immediately. I went there without a phone, but this time I took the risk of bringing my laptop. Whenever I meet with him, it means I am up to something—banned reporting, filming, or being interrogated.

Amir was on the phone when I arrived. As I waited, a female lawyer was facing me and very slowly asked me if I was a political or national security case. I laughed bitterly and said that I am a journalist, which from the Islamic Republic's perspective made me both. She answered that I was quite right!

When Amir was done, I entered his office and told him about the book. He asked me to read it to him. I read the first three pages of the first chapter. He said that that was enough and that this book would bring me the charges of blaspheming against Islam and corruption on the earth. I asked him what he thought would happen to me if I were to be in Iran when the book is published. He asked me if I wanted to spend the rest of my life in prison like Saad Salman, an eleventh-century Persian poet, known as the prisoner poet. I told him that I wasn't much interested in literature and did not want to spend my life in prison reading and writing. Amir urged me to leave Iran as soon as possible, before the anniversary of Jîna's death, because the regime would be coming for all of us.

I loved living in Iran, and I did not want to go. But Amir urged me to leave. He said that this may be the last chance to get out before the anniversary. "This regime will change, and you are more impactful outside, we need you outside to be our voice," he said. Amir knew the possibility of my being imprisoned for a long time was very high. He pleaded with me, "Be rational for once, Fatemeh." I said okay, I will be logical. He suggested that I go to the airport without a phone and SIM card and, when the plane takes off, send him a message from another number and write "the plane wheels turn around" to indicate that I had made it out.

I packed my whole life into one twenty-kilogram suitcase and one ten-kilogram carry-on. I never thought this would be the most challenging time I left Iran. I did not have a student visa, a scholarship, a work permit, or a job offer. More than that, I did not have a certain future. I just had my words and a book contract. Since I left Iran for Istanbul in July 2023, I have moved fourteen times. Sometimes I just had an address and the time that I could stay there; sometimes I stayed with a stranger who never talked to me or whom I never met. It was like living like a guerrilla. For nine months, I could not open a bank account because of the U.S. sanctions on Iran and, by extension, Iranians. It's the reality of our lives as Iranians, suppressed by the regime and sanctioned by the rest of the world, squeezed by both.

I walk alone in the darkness. It is my fate, my destiny. It does not matter whether I am in Brooklyn, New York, or Queen's Park, London; if I am going for a walk at 5:00 a.m. out of anxiety or at 11:00 p.m. to release my anger. I walk out my loneliness in the darkness. But I believe that this dark tunnel will lead to the light.

We ourselves are unheard parts of stories. I will not see how Farham, my five-year-old nephew, grows up. I will not be there to read him books. I will not be there when my fifteen-year-old niece falls in love. I will not be there to take my parents to the doctor. I lost my family. I lost my people and my mother language. I lost my friends. My worst nightmare came true. I lost my country.

One day, my friend Taraneh, the actress who had been arrested in front of her home, texted me. "Do not be scared to return; we will not let them imprison you. I will be in front of Evin's door until they release you," she said.

"I will return," I responded. "Let me finish this book. No one can take our homeland from us."

We didn't know that during Taraneh's detention, she was given drugs and pills that would later cause an unknown autoimmune disease that damaged her skin tissue. The cocktails of medications given to prisoners are often linked with subsequent and suspicious diseases. At the time of writing, Taraneh has been in the hospital for more than six months, dealing with an unknown disease. We didn't know they could be so evil as to try to take a mother's life from her daughter. But I believe that Taraneh will overcome this disease and return to the front lines. We need her.

The Ministry of Culture and Islamic Guidance and its associated Cinema Organization have announced that twenty female actors who removed their hijab during the Woman, Life, Freedom movement and published pictures of themselves without a hijab on their social media or participated in ceremonies such as the funerals of their colleagues without wearing a hijab are hereafter banned from acting or taking part in any artistic project. In response to the Ministry of Culture and Islamic Guidance banning her from acting, Taraneh wrote on her Instagram, "I will not wear the fabric that killed my sisters. Blood is still dripping from that mandatory scarf that you hold on to our heads in the bathroom and bedroom in your movies." I sent her a picture of my writing about the hijab for this book, in which I also refer to the hijab as dripping with blood. Taraneh sent me black and red hearts in response.

A political prisoner has nothing to lose except her body and life. Her body is the last card she can play, so in times of protest she uses it even at the risk of damaging it. Shortly after I left the country, my friend Bahareh started a hunger strike in response to the suspicious death of a protester at Evin Prison on September 1, 2023. Bahareh lost about seventeen pounds in the strike's first ten days. Having a friend on hunger strike is like being told your friend has cancer and you have seven days to find a rare drug for her to survive. When we hear about it, we know that we have a week without access to her outside the prison's walls to find a way to persuade her to end her hunger strike to save her own life. In a hunger strike, the body consumes itself. It uses its muscles and vital organs for energy. The kidneys and the liver are seriously damaged or fail. When their roommate is on hunger strike, instead of "good night," prisoners will say, "Goodbye until tomorrow, our comrade fighter," each night.

Bahareh was imprisoned during the Green Movement in 2009 and was detained for nine and a half years. Her crime was asking for the right to pursue her graduate studies, because she was among the student activists who were banned from universities. Bahareh was released early after seven and a half years, and free for a few years. But then, in January 2020, the IRGC shot down the Ukraine International Airlines flight, killing 176 innocent passengers. Bahareh could not stay silent; she wrote a tweet and asked all to attend protests.

Bahareh and I made plans to meet so I could interview her about her call to protest for the *Los Angeles Times*. I waited for her for half an hour. When she did not show, I called a mutual friend. "Ali, please do not panic, but tell me, Is Bahareh usually a punctual person or not?" I asked. He answered that she was usually on time. I found out later that Bahareh had been arrested. The judiciary system sentenced her to another four and a half years of imprisonment for calling for protest.

A year into her new prison sentence, Bahareh once again answered the call to protest, this time for the lives of prisoners. On the thirteenth day of her hunger strike, she was transferred from Evin to the hospital. Nahid, a mutual friend, cried nonstop to me on the phone, saying, "Bahareh will die; she is melting like a candle. She is determined and stubborn. She wants to kill herself in revenge for this year of her young life spent in prison and her continued imprisonment." Her life was her last weapon, but it should not be, we need her for the future of free Iran, we need all of them.

Mina, our friend and colleague, also called me crying. I told her not to cry, that we should find a solution, and think about whom she would listen to if they asked her to stop her hunger strike. I answered myself, "Jîna's family. Find them and ask them." Mina and my friends reached out to them through their lawyer, Saleh Nikbakht.

Mojgan Eftekhari, Jîna's mother, published a story on her Instagram account, asking Bahareh to end her hunger strike. "I strongly request you to end your hunger strike because the people of Iran need your life and health." It worked, Bahareh ended her strike after thirteen days and published a public letter, giving her respect to Jîna's family and others who reached out to her. "I will break my hunger strike, but not my promise. My promise is with myself and with you, the suffering people of my homeland. We stand and fight until the day when we erase any trace of the Islamic Republic, this anti-freedom regime, from the soil of Iran."

Mina sent news of her letter to our group chat on Telegram, saying, "Congratulations to all of us. We saved Bahareh's life while being separated in different countries. The sisterhood made it."

NILO

WE WAIT FOR LIGHT AND DARKNESS REIGNS

A YEAR AFTER THE PROTESTS, Iran's Parliament approved a new draconian enforcement of the hijab and women's dress code, the "Protection of the Family Through Promoting the Culture of Hijab and Chastity" law. The bill passed overwhelmingly in September 2023: 152 to 34 votes with 7 abstentions. Once again, the regime responded to its people's calls for freedom by suffocating them. This law contains seventy-one articles that not only give more government control over women's lives and bodies but also threaten private businesses that fail to report women violating the dress code. It's as if they were asking us all to spy on one another. Repeat offenders, and even those who mock these new rules, could face heavier fines, longer prison sentences of up to fifteen years, and a ban on leaving the country. Even worse, other punishments for noncompliance include lashes, loss of employment, exclusion from higher education, restricted access to government services, and even the death penalty, if the offense includes spreading "corruption and prostitution" on a large scale; notably, anti-hijab activists have been prosecuted under prostitution charges in the past.

Its Orwellian arm extends into the digital space by using technology systems like traffic monitoring cameras and artificial intelligence to identify offenders. One article of the law seems to encourage vigilante violence by protecting those who "enforce" this law by stating that people cannot be "held accountable for carrying out an obligation under Sharia." Iran's president, Masoud Pezeshkian, publicly opposed the enforcement of this law both during his campaign and even days before it was due to roll out in December 2024. Iranian law requires the president to carry out parliamentary resolutions, and as of this writing in June 2025 its daily application has not yet crystallized. With the level of rage steadily increasing over the issue of hijab, the Islamic Republic finds itself in a stalemate: The repressive system is afraid of our people taking back the streets again; it fears another nationwide movement that could make international headlines.

As Iranians waited to see what the regime's next move would be, women continued to boldly protest. In November 2024, at a university in Tehran, a young Iranian woman was recorded arguing with security forces while stripped down to her underwear. The video of her confrontation went viral and was memed and shared all over social media. I verified the videos of the young woman, whose identity I could not independently confirm, and spoke with an eyewitness to understand what happened. The first video showed the woman with her arms crossed and surrounded by a crowd of bystanders walking down the sidewalk alone after arguing with security. "This is not just a momentary solitary act of defiance," said Khosro Isfahani, an open-source investigator with the Atlantic Council who tracked the spread of the video online. "She's rebelling against the whole system of oppression that women face in Iran."

An eyewitness I spoke with was a university student who saw everything unfold. He said that he saw a member of the Basij grab her arm with both hands as he dragged her toward him. Seeing that the woman was not wearing a hijab, the eyewitness watched as two security officers started beating her and tried to force her inside a security post near the university's entrance. And because they were "pulling her by [grabbing] her clothing," her top was ripped off in the struggle. The girl began screaming *bi-sharaf*, or "shameless," a frequent insult lodged against those aligned with the regime. "You've turned the university into a whorehouse, and now you're worried about what I'm wearing?" she said, referring to the officers tearing off her blouse, according to the witness. The security officers didn't react, he added, and instead started making calls on their cell phones. As the woman walked "proudly, without fear and without paying any mind to how cold it was," according to the witness, a car with four male security officers approached her. They attacked her and smashed her head onto the body of the car, he said, before throwing her in the back seat in broad daylight and driving away.

Immediately, the propaganda machine began to whir. The university's public relations director said that the woman suffered from a "mental disorder." A government spokesperson told the newspaper *Ham-Mihan* that she was taken from the police station to a "center for treatment." Nahid Naghshbandi, an Iran researcher at Human Rights Watch, told me that these claims are part of the government's playbook for suppressing hijab-related incidents—falsely reframing the situation as a mental health crisis. "They want to say that these people are not in their right mind," she said, noting that this is a tactic used to humiliate women who resist wearing the hijab. Naghshbandi added that there was little to no information about her case despite its getting so much attention online.

In December 2024, just days before the rumored enactment of the hijab law, Parastoo Ahmadi sang live on YouTube. The twenty-seven-year-old artist defied the Islamic Republic's more than forty-year ban on women singing in public. Performing outdoors in an ancient caravansary, an old roadside inn historically built along the Silk Road that provided a space for merchants to rest, Parastoo sang proudly in a floor-length black dress, her willful long brown hair hanging below her shoulders, her lips and fingers painted a bright raspberry. She started her performance by introducing the members of her all-male band. The image invoked the long history of our beautiful homeland;

Parastoo sang on a raised platform covered with a Persian carpet, and behind her were centuries-old brick archways that have been here long before, and will undoubtedly outlive, the Islamic Republic. Her video received more than two million views within a week. Unsurprisingly, she was arrested and charged with conducting an "illegal concert." Her case is still pending, but she was released from jail just a day later—a move that her lawyer viewed as reflecting the regime's growing fear of public dissent. Parastoo sang well-known songs, including protest anthems that spoke to the struggles of her fellow Iranians. "From the blood of the young people of the homeland, tulips have bloomed," she declared in verse full of emotion. The caption of her YouTube video serves as her public statement. It seems fitting to let Parastoo speak to you directly about why she risked certain arrest and harassment with her artistic statement:

> *I am Parastoo, a girl who wants to sing for the people I love. This is a right I could not ignore: singing for the land I love passionately. Here, in this part of our beloved Iran, where history and our myths intertwine, hear my voice in this imaginary concert and imagine this beautiful homeland. . . . I am grateful to all those who have supported me in these difficult and special circumstances.*

FATEMEH AND NILO

FOR RESISTANCE AND HOPE

IN EVIN PRISON'S WARD for woman political prisoners, fifty-nine of our sisters live together. They do yoga each morning, and three times a week they play volleyball.* The women's ward is made up of three rooms, two are forty square feet and one is roughly fifty square feet, connected by a narrow corridor. All the openings and windows are covered with thin blinds. Only one window is cracked open to the foothills of the Alborz Mountains that surround Tehran, jagged peaks dotted with snow. There are bunk beds in all the rooms, and some of the newer prisoners have to sleep side by side on the floor in the middle of the hall due to a lack of space—a symptom of the Islamic Republic's campaign of mass arrests.

Niloofar Hamedi, who was transferred back to Evin after being sentenced to thirteen years in prison, is a marathon runner. Wearing flimsy rubber prisoner slippers with a thick band that covers the top of her feet, she runs in the prison's small yard. Accustomed to end-

---

* All the sources written about here come from Fatemeh's interviews with recent female political prisoners. Their words serve as an oral history.

less distances and wide horizons, she paces back and forth in a small, rectangular outdoor space that's less than two thousand square feet. Putting one foot in front of the other, slipper by slipper, she uses up all of the twenty to thirty minutes she is allowed to be outside, her only opportunity to feel fresh air.

Niloufar Bayani tends to her small gardens. Narges Mohammadi does the same. Elaheh Mohammadi sits on a bench with her back to the walls where she can see some trees from afar. She loves trees. There weren't any windows in Qarchak Prison, so when Elaheh was transferred from Qarchak to Evin, she was happy to finally see the sky, the moon from behind Tehran's often lingering smog, and the trees that had grown to greet her.

For many years, the women's ward of Evin has turned from a typical prison ward to the front line of protests, reactions to national unrest, and the union of different political groups. Even behind bars, we find a way to come together. After Jîna was killed, the women in Evin set their headscarves on fire in the prison's yard while chanting, "Woman, Life, Freedom." They are the inheritors of a nation's decades-long collective fight for freedom and have collectively been sentenced, unjustifiably, to more than a century of prison time. Woman political prisoners in Evin do not remain silent in the face of the regime's repression. They use every opportunity to protest and react to human rights violations by the regime, gathering and chanting in the prison yard or, like Bahareh, dedicating themselves to hunger strikes.

In one of the last fights of woman political prisoners against mandatory hijab, Narges Mohammadi, imprisoned for her human rights activism, refused to wear hijab to be taken to the hospital. The judiciary system eventually had to give in after she and several female prisoners went on a hunger strike for three days. Only then did she go to the hospital to have heart surgery. Many former prisoners went to the hospital to visit her there but were not allowed in. One of them was Nooshin Jafari, who later wrote on her Instagram page, "Yesterday I saw one of the most magnificent pictures in the hospital, Narges Mohammadi, the most beautiful woman, in a coat and skirt and without a hijab, escorted by an army of veiled women and men and security agents who wore masks."

Each of these actions carries a heavy price; the imprisoned women are denied the right to use phones and attend weekly cabinet-style meetings with family. They may be sent to solitary confinement for punishment, and the judicial system will open new cases for them without any semblance of due process, which ends up in more years of prison time being tacked onto their sentences. Still, the women refuse to back down, growing closer rather than further apart. The diversity of woman prisoners in Evin has made them understand each other's suffering better. Our sisters in Evin are human rights activists, documentary filmmakers, and journalists who are imprisoned alongside Baha'i, Kurdish, Sunni Arab, Baloch, leftist, and pro-Pahlavi prisoners who got arrested for their political activism and organizing. If only the regime knew that instead of putting out the flame of our movement, being together in prison reinforces us; we roar into an electric storm as we more intimately learn about one another's suffering, particularly that of our sisters belonging to minority groups.

Elnaz, Elaheh Mohammadi's twin sister, was taken to Evin Prison for two hours. Like her twin, Elnaz was charged and convicted on fraudulent charges in retaliation for her journalism. She is currently released on a suspended sentence of four years, but if she commits another supposed crime, she will be imprisoned. According to Iranian law, however, she must still serve one-fortieth of her sentence inside prison. That is how she ended up jailed with her sister for a couple of hours. The day she was taken to prison, everyone was worried that she would be held and not released. But Elnaz was just happy to be able to see her twin sister up close, not from behind the dirty glass that separated them during visits. This allowed her a small moment of joy; she got the chance to hug her twin, her other half, for two hours.

Elnaz reflected on the experience in a post on her Instagram page. "Those wonderful women had prepared handmade gifts for me. Golrokh made me beautiful dark brown slippers and Sepideh Qalian gave me a leather wallet. Sepideh Kashani's gifts were two leather bookmarks. Sarvnaz gave a beautiful wooden necklace; Niloufar Bayani gave me a bag of fresh mint that she had planted herself in the prison's yard and picked from her small garden for me." The women also prepared a meal for Elnaz. "Today I had the most delicious lunch of my life around a white plastic table: rice with vegetables and fish," she wrote. "Niloufar Bayani, this special person, cooked a special soup for me, and the beautiful and resilient Niloofar Hamedi made a delicious dessert with the jam she had made."

The entire time that they were reunited, Elnaz and Elaheh's hands remained entwined, holding each other with the tightness of twins, two sisters and best friends who know this moment of physical closeness may be fleeting. Elnaz ended her day in prison on October 28, 2023. According to Elnaz, "When saying goodbye, Narges said softly, 'Don't forget that we will come out one day and build a beautiful world together.'" Elnaz responded, "For sure, with women like you, we will make it." Elnaz told Niloofar Hamedi that everyone outside the prison loves them and that everyone knows them and prays for their freedom.

On January 14, 2024, after seventeen months in temporary detention across multiple prisons, Niloofar Hamedi and Elaheh Mohammadi were released from Evin Prison. They were released on bail at 100 billion Iranian rials (approximately $200,000) but remain banned from leaving the country. They were greeted by hundreds outside the prison gates, walking without hijabs and flashing victory signs. They were embraced by loved ones who had eagerly awaited their release. Less than twenty-four hours later, the Iranian judiciary announced a new case against them, accusing the journalists of violating dress codes for appearing in public without proper head coverings immediately after their release.

During limited in-person meetings with visitors, the political prisoners wear their own clothes, brought to them by their families or husbands. They wear makeup and do their hair. It's as if they were dating. In the morning, they start getting ready. One takes the other's clothes. Another borrows a red lipstick. Everyone helps each other look beautiful and strong. Women earn their living expenses by working in prison workshops, and they bring the items they make as gifts for friends and family—gifts from the small and gloomy workshops of Evin. These handmade gifts are signs of life and resistance: leather bags with fine stitching, wooden necklaces with carved signs of the Woman, Life, Freedom movement, and bracelets with the tricolor design of the Iranian flag without Allah in the middle—all from the fingers of our captive birds. Former woman political prisoners run an Instagram page selling handmade art products produced by current female political prisoners.

They are the heroes of society, and their memory is honored in different ways. On days when newspapers publish their photos, even as the media and newspapers suffer low sales and diminishing influence, all copies of that newspaper sell out. Athletes run in marathons in memory of them. Climbers ascend to the peaks of mountains in their name. People paint graffiti of their photos on walls around the city. These are all new and symbolic methods of protesting against the Islamic Republic. We have paralyzed the Islamic Republic with our civil disobedience, without the violence of the 1979 revolutionaries.

Narges Mohammadi published a letter on her Instagram account telling the story of an unbelievable day in the women's ward in Evin where her fellow sisters staged a demonstration against judges who visited them. Narges's words and her sisters' actions represent us, our power, our solidarity, and our sisterhood. There's no better way for you to experience this than by reading what happened that day in Evin Prison in Narges's own intoxicating words:

> *On Wednesday, December 27, 2023, the judges of the Revolutionary Court and judicial authorities came to Evin Prison, but they faced a trial organized by the woman prisoners and had to escape from their ward. Imagine the moment when justice arrives, a day when you will have to face the crimes you have committed. The visit of authorities to Evin Prison unfolded in memorable scenes. The name Mohsen Shekari, the first protester executed in connection with the Woman, Life, Freedom movement, echoed dozens of times in the women's ward.*
>
> *The judges who had issued death sentences, including Mohammad-Reza Amouzad, who had issued the death sentence for twenty-two-year-old Shekari, were hidden among the security forces inside the*

room, and the slightest sound from them could not be heard. The prisoners in front of the doors declared, "Our presence here is not to pursue our own cases but to protest against the repressive policies of the judicial authority." The voices of protesters grew louder in all corners of the building. "Stop issuing death sentences. Halt the death machine, executions, and torture. Do not execute Reza Rezaei and Mojahed Kourkour. Executions are government murders and must be stopped." It was a day when judges from the Revolutionary Court and judicial authorities entered the women's ward, encountering the resilience and resistance of women against oppression, torture, imprisonment, and execution. What unfolded was a powerful image of a people's "trial" and "people's justice" for judicial figures involved in the committing of heinous crimes, and the issuing and executing of inhumane sentences.

Courageous women stood firm inside the prison, facing the judges who had handed them down their sentences. Their sole demand was the cessation of oppression and violence against the people of Iran. They shouted, urging the authorities to stop executions and torture. Judges and officials amid numerous security forces lacked the courage to step out of their room or accept our entry into the chamber. At this moment, it was as if the language of the perpetrators were paralyzed in the face of justice. It was a powerful scene.

We, the woman prisoners, stood in front of the door without flinching. Security forces and prison guards pulled us back and forth. We fell to the ground a couple of times, but we rose again and stood firm. We interlocked our hands like a chain and chanted and sang. There was a moment in the corridor where there was nothing but the echoing of women shouting, "Mohsen Shekari." The image of [the judicial official Mohammad-Reza] Amouzad, gradually lowering his head beneath the iron bars of the window as if he were attempting to hide, became a particularly memorable scene.

The prisoners on both sides of the door were shouting, "Death to the dictator," "Death to the Islamic Republic," "Woman, Life, Freedom," and sang "Bella Ciao" without stopping. Sepideh Gholian lifted her head above the iron bars of the window and addressed Amouzad, demanding, "Why did you kill Mohsen Shekari? Why did you kill Mohammad Mehdi Karami?" She wanted answers for two more young men, also executed in connection with their participation in the Woman, Life, Freedom uprising. The number of guards and security forces increased moment by moment. Prison officials asked the prisoners to leave, but the prisoners insisted, saying, "We won't go, and we demand accountability for their crimes."

Security forces pushed back on them, saying that they could only request information about their own cases, and the prisoners insisted that they were here to declare that the judicial authority must stop the death machine. The demand was clear, and the method was resistance and standing against oppression, on the streets and in prison. Then female prisoners found themselves in a narrow passageway and were pushed back by security forces and prison officers. They fell to the ground ... and at that moment the high-ranking judicial authorities and judges left the women's ward while women were shouting, "Shame, shame!" "Murderer, get lost!" and "Woman, Life, Freedom," and the doors were slammed behind them and locked.

Today marks a trial. Right now, the public is convening a trial for you at the core of Evin Prison within the women's political ward.

It signifies a quest for justice: Remember this day. Long live resistance and hope.

ACKNOWLEDGMENTS

FATEMEH

For years, the Islamic Republic has worked to isolate Iran, erecting invisible walls to sever connections between those inside and outside the country. Through this book, Nilo and I, two Iranian journalists on opposite sides of this wall, built a bridge. The higher the regime raises its walls, the bolder we become in leaping over them—until the day they finally collapse. A social worker once told me: "When you interview victims, like sex workers, you reopen their wounds. But like a doctor or social worker, you must also know how to close them." Writing this book felt like reopening my own wounds without knowing how to heal them. Some remain raw. Whenever I revisit these pages—especially my first email to Nilo, filled with the hope of seeing her in Tehran—I find myself overwhelmed by tears.

Nilo once said we unpacked suitcases filled with trauma and pain to write this book. Our unspoken agreement was to carry our own burdens. To lighten the weight for each other, we spoke less and less. Each of us had to face our traumas alone. But as the contemporary poet

Ahmad Shamlou once wrote, "distance is a futile experience." Thank you, Nilo. Together, we found strength. Together, we empowered each other to defy the barriers meant to keep us apart.

In January 2021, I began my notes for this book with a quote from Iranian feminist Touran Mirhadi: "We must turn our great sorrow into great work." Nilo and I tried to channel our deepest sorrows into this book. But we wanted it to end on a note of light, resilience, and gratitude by showing the rich lives that women prisoners have built for themselves despite their confinement. As the first feminist anthem of the women's movement in Iran, says:

> *I sprout,*
> *Upon the wound on my body,*
> *Solely by the decree of my existence,*
> *For I am a woman, a woman, a woman.*

To Concepción, our dear editor, thank you for not giving up on me—even on the days I had given up on myself. Your unwavering belief in me and in this project has meant the world. Thank you for the countless hours you spent listening to my tears. I know that comforting an Iranian journalist in exile was never part of your job description, yet you embraced it without hesitation. Through it all, you stood by me—far beyond what your professional role required.

Concepción, I am deeply grateful for your endless patience, your sensitivity to the nuances of writing in my second language, and your help in bringing the soul of the Persian language—its beauty and intricacy—into my English writing. Thank you for your brilliant edits, which made our texts infinitely more powerful and beautiful.

I want to express my love to my family. To Momo, my youngest brother—I'm so proud of the feminist you've become. To my father and Hossein, my older brother—I've witnessed how your views have evolved toward embracing gender equality. To Ehsan and Masoud, my younger brothers, you've been my anchor and lifeline. Thank you, Dadashis. To my mom, Mina, who let me fly. To Somayeh, my sister; Farham, my nephew; and Fatemeh, my niece, my life wouldn't have meaning without you. I know you may have hoped for a different path, but I'm deeply grateful that you've accepted me for who I am.

From January to September 2022, when I was being interrogated by security forces, I found refuge at VII Bistro in Tehran after each session. Sitting on the last iron chair by the wall, I would rest my face in my hands and cry—sometimes for an hour—before I could write. One day, Shirin, a nineteen-year-old art student and barista at the cafe, brought me a drawing. It showed two abstract figures embracing. At the bottom, she had written:

> *To Fatemeh!*
> *To gently touch the scar on your neck and say,*
> *"The sun always rises from the left."*

Thank you, Shirin. Later I met Mina Akbari, who gave me a safe space to write. Through her I met Taraneh, a voice in the #MeToo movement in Iranian cinema. Soon after the Woman, Life, Freedom movement erupted, and I was there—editing revolutionary videos, writing petitions, and working on the front lines under the regime's watchful eyes. To Nafiseh, my therapist, who held thirty sessions for free. To Shadi, my trainer, who worked with me three times a week—also for free. To Amir Raeisian, my lawyer, who tirelessly defends the voiceless. Thank you.

I know that for every name I mention here, I will have to answer to interrogators if I ever return to Iran. But I have decided not to censor myself anymore. I choose to live in the circle of truth and pay for its expenses. When Amir told me I had to leave Iran, I was utterly desperate. As an Iranian I had no destination, no place to go. I left his office in tears, walking home, wondering where I could turn for help—to save myself, to save us, to save this book. Only one name came to mind: Jason Rezaian. And I was right. Nilo reached out to Jason; he saved my life, just as he has saved many other journalists. Jason and Nilo made it possible for me to safely reach the United States, to write without fear and with security. Thank you, Jason—not just for your support but for the extraordinary and inspiring person you are.

Whenever I fled Iran, I found refuge in Louise Callaghan, my friend and *The Sunday Times* war correspondent in Istanbul. More than a friend—a sister. She was the first to read my notes and told me I was writing better than 90 percent of the people she knew, even though English is not my first language and I did not learn it through formal education. Through Louise I started working with Alexander, my British writing teacher, who charged only twenty pounds per session—almost nothing. To Anna, Claire, Masha, and Banu, who became my sisters in Istanbul. To Nahid and Hoda, who sold their gold jewelry just to buy tickets to see me one last time before I left Istanbul. Thank you.

To Joan Susie: After I spent months living out of suitcases and moving fourteen times, Joan Susie offered me a small, newly built and designed home in her backyard in Silver Spring for four months for free. Her generosity knew no bounds. Curious, I asked Joan why she had chosen to help me, to offer me her space without even knowing me. She told me her mother had been a journalist and had passed away a year ago. When her daughter, Emma, saw Nilo's story on Instagram—shared through friends—about an Iranian journalist in exile searching for a place to stay, she immediately thought of her mother. In her memory, they decided to support me. But Joan's kindness went beyond giving me a home. She bought me a new phone, took me to the Social Security office, and helped me piece my life back together.

Thank you, Tara Sepehri Far, my Iranian friend in exile in D.C. The day I arrived, Tara picked me up from the train station. Having a friend with whom I could speak Farsi and have conversations about Iran was a privilege—a rare comfort in exile. Thank you for making life easier and less lonely.

Thanks to Wallace House, with its bright windows, warm hall, glowing fireplace, welcoming staff, and supportive fellows—my family. One of my deepest thanks goes to Joshua Sharpe. During summer break, when Ann Arbor was empty, only Josh stayed behind to finish his book, *The Man No One Believed: The Untold Story of the Georgia Church Murders*. Through his work Josh has helped secure the release of two innocent people sentenced to life imprisonment. It was an interesting intersection. For days we sat together, each working on our books—his about prisoners in the United States, mine about my friends imprisoned in Iran. Josh became my first source of guidance whenever I faced challenges, whether professional or cultural. He has been my ever-cool English teacher, the one who taught me that "the tables have turned" and that even in exile, in a new and unfamiliar world, I'm that "bad bitch," the one who faced interrogators and walked away stronger.

Finally, thanks to Niloofar and Elaheh. It is a heavy responsibility to write about you and for you. I am sorry I could not be at your trial. I am sorry I could not visit your families. I am sorry I was not there for you. I have been forced into silence, into the shadows to finish this book, to be our voice. I was not there when you were released because I must tell this story. The Islamic Republic robbed me of the chance to witness your face framed in liberation with wind in your hair. Freedom fighting is a marathon, like the Olympic torch relay, where each woman carries the fire forward. A series of runners passing the flame through different cities, classrooms, and educational spaces, each contributing and illuminating the path for the next. Niloo, Elaheh, Shokuh, Nilo, Elnaz, Negin, Nahid, Hoda, Mina, Taraneh, Ghocheh, Marzi, Sarvnaz, Golrokh, Bahareh, Sepideh, Maryam, Nooshin, Somayeh, Manizheh, Sudabeh, Narges, me, and countless others—each carrying our part, passing it forward, ensuring the light never fades. You are my sisters.

> *Your thought is my concern,*
> *Your laughter is my joy.*
> *Don't stop fighting—*
> *The sky is ours,*
> *Even if the cell doors are rigid.**

NILO

My paternal grandfather used to say, "When your *sofreh* is empty, the ones who sit down next to you are the true souls who matter. That is your community." Existing as an Iranian sometimes feels as if the *sofreh*

---

* "Hichkas, "He Was My Brother," hip-hop song, February 3, 2012, posted August 24, 2023, by Rebin Tataloo, YouTube, 1 min., 58 sec., https://www.youtube.com/watch?v=JubbGQaho2w.

were filled with dishes of alienation and heartbreak. I feel so grateful to the incredible people who've sat with me through this book, through all my reporting, as I've tried to find my place in this world. I would be nowhere without my loving, kind, and deeply supportive family. Baba Hossein, Maman Roya, Nargess, and Nazila: I'm so lucky to be a member of our family unit. It's rare that after more than thirty years together, we are still so tightly knit. Each of us is a finger on a hand, as Maman says, always endeavoring to work together. It's because of Baba's fearlessness, Maman's deep pool of kindness, Nargess's steady advice, and Nazila's determination and work ethic that I grew to be this Nilofar. Thank you for loving me and always allowing me to be my whole self.

One million thank-yous aren't enough for my thoughtful and intuitive agent, Julia Eagleton, for taking a chance on me after coming across my Persian poetry essay. Without you, this book would've never been made. Your ideas, passion, and calm guidance are an anchor. Concepción de León, you are a gift to any writer and have made this editing process so seamless. I so appreciate that you deepened your understanding of Iran with such enthusiasm and how you made space for me by encouraging me to stop making myself smaller. I'll carry this with me long after we publish. My Khaleh Neda Toloui-Semnani, your incisive reads, endless support, and multiple tarot cards guided me through the rockiest of seas. To Fatemeh, what a gift to be able to learn so much about each other through this project. I'm inspired by your bravery, and I feel grateful to have finally met in person again after all these years.

A significant portion of this book was written at the home of Margot Paris and Chuck Brook in France. Margot, Chuck, thank you for being my second family. We marched up and introduced ourselves to you as three young Tabrizy sisters when we immigrated in 1994, and you always made your home one where I felt safe enough to step into my creativity. Writing often feels solitary, and I am so lucky that my dearest Maya Tanaka was my writing accountability partner throughout this process. Maya, you were the catalyst that loudly pushed me into free writing the first few pages for Julia that would eventually open the door to this book. You shoved me right out of my self-doubt—lovingly, of course. Walking this creative path is a lot less lonely and indescribably more joyful when we're together. The rest of this book was written at the Capilano Library (the home of my childhood summer reading programs), the Brooklyn Public Library, and many cafés in Brooklyn, Vancouver, London, Marseille, Los Angeles, Ho Chi Minh City, and Madrid.

Haley Willis was perhaps subjected to the most early reads of the proposal, scraps of writing, and the technical journalism passages. Haley joon, you've helped me reframe my impasses and insecurities. You're a gifted reporter and warmhearted sister, and I learn from you constantly. Thank you for reading *Shahnameh* within days of meeting me. Thank you to Arash Azizi, Sarah Cahlan, Stephen Day, Daphnée Denis, Tessa DiPietro, Eric Fernandez, Nkenna Ibeakanma, Ishaan Jhaveri, Emma Julian, Joyce Sohyun Lee, Hooman Majd, Jaclyn Mintzberg, Jason Rezaian, Alexander Samaha, Christiaan Triebert, Martina Veltroni, and Danielle Wolfe for also reading or listening to early drafts. And to Meko, who read far too many words and was very helpful in finding poems that made their way onto these pages.

I somehow was a full-time journalist at *The Washington Post* while writing this book. In fact, the book deal came to fruition during the first three months at my then-new job. Thank you to Micah Gelman, Nadine Ajaka, and Elyse Samuels for their full support right from day one, and for giving me precious time during demanding news cycles to write this book. The entire Visual Forensics team was so uplifting throughout the process, especially Joyce Sohyun Lee. In the final stretch of edits and rewrites, Joyce and I were working on an investigative project on Native American boarding schools. Joyce, thank you for always being understanding of my numerous stresses and encouraging me right to the finish line.

Last, I want to acknowledge the lineage of strong Iranian women in my life: Mamani, Shokat Khanum, Maman Roya, Nargess, Nazila, Khaleh Mastaneh, Khaleh Shahlah, Neda Toloui-Semnani, Porochista Khakpour, Leila Gharagozlou, Katayoun Khosrowyar, Anna Hossnieh, and Parasto Backman. All of you have admirable strength and grace. The world is fiercer and more loving with you in it. And to our sisters in Iran: No one can stop us from finding each other. Fatemeh and I connected on a chance meeting, and my Telegrams and Signal chats are filled with messages from journalists and women in Iran sharing their experiences. No matter how bleak and how heavy our present, soft light blankets our future. My only aim is to be the *khak-e pay-e mardom,* and I hope this book is one part of that.

NOTES

INTRODUCTION

NILO AND FATEMEH

x   On the same day: "Iranian Security Forces Arrested Iranian Journalist Hamed Shafiei on September 24, 2022, in Tehran," Committee to Protect Journalists, cpj.org/data/people/hamed-shafiei/.

x   "I went to Kasra": Saman Movahedi Rad, "No Illegal Action Has Been Taken" (in Persian), *Shargh Daily*, Oct. 22, 2022, هیچ اقدام خلاف قانونی صورت نگرفته است, https://www.sharghdaily.com/.

x   The accompanying image: The Independent Center for Human Rights in Iran (@ICHRI), "Activists are reporting that Jina Amini, 22, has died after being arrested by #Iran's 'anti-vice' police for her alleged improper hijab," Twitter, Sept. 16, 2022, 3:33 p.m., twitter.com/ICHRI/status/1570767899975127040.

x   A police spokesperson told: Movahedi Rad, "No Illegal Action Has Been Taken."

x   Alongside a photo: Niloofar Hamedi (@NiloofarHamedi), Twitter, Sept. 16, 2022, twitter.com/NiloofarHamedi/status/1570751037019148292. Twitter suspended her account; the photo she took can be viewed at Maryam Afshang,

"The Journalists Imprisoned for Reporting the Death That Shook Iran," BBC, May 4, 2023, www.bbc.com/news/world-middle-east-65466887.

xi The image was reminiscent: Elahe Khosravi (@elahekhyegane), "Today, when I arrived at Kasra hospital, some women were standing on the hospital steps and shouting. At first, there were not many security forces," Twitter, Sept. 16, 2022, 7:41 p.m., twitter.com/elahekhyegane/status/1570830369154560003?s=20.

xi "A woman was running": Reza Baraheni, "Daf," www.domino.blogfa.com/post/81.

xi One of the earliest poetic: Nilo Tabrizy, "Between the Lines," *Guernica*, July 16, 2020, www.guernicamag.com/between-the-lines/.

xii In the days and weeks: Omid Khazani and Sarah Parvini, "How 'Baraye,' a Song About Iran's Protests, Became an Anthem for Women, Freedom, and an Ordinary Life," *Los Angeles Times*, Oct. 12, 2022, www.latimes.com/world-nation/story/2022-10-12/la-fg-how-baraye-a-song-about-irans-protests-became-an-anthem.

xii "For dancing in the streets": Ibid.

xii When he posted: "Shervin Hajipour Receives Best Song for Social Change Award for 'Baraye,'" Grammys, Feb. 5, 2023, www.grammy.com/news/shervin-hajipour-baraye-winner-best-song-for-social-change-watch-2023-grammys-65th-grammy-awards-acceptance-speech.

xiii He was barred: "Iran Pardons Grammy Award Winner Whose Song Became an Anthem to the 2022 Protests," Associated Press, Sept. 23, 2024, apnews.com/article/iran-shervin-hajipour-grammy-mahsa-amini-amnesty-ebcd60fa8d8b0e94534c05be103494ba#.

xiii Though his travel ban: "Iranian Grammy Award-Winning Singer Ordered to Start Prison Sentence," Radio Farda, July 30, 2024, www.rferl.org/a/iran-hajipour-song-baraye-prison-sentence/33056822.html.

xiii "For me it's a question": Shervin Hajipour (@shervinine), Instagram, 2022, posted July 30, 2024, www.instagram.com/p/C-DUs3UNNsL/?hl=en.

xiv "Idiot men": Ahmad Shamlou, "Ahmad Shamlou, I am not your enemy, I am your negation" (in Persian), *Echolalia*, July 16, 2017, احمد شاملو/ عدوی تو نیستم من انکارِ توام, www.echolalia.ir.

xiv It went viral: Rosie Swash, "Arrests and TV Confessions as Iran Cracks Down on Women's 'Improper' Clothing," *Guardian*, Aug. 23, 2022, www.theguardian.com/global-development/2022/aug/23/arrests-and-tv-confessions-as-iran-cracks-down-on-women-improper-clothing-hijab.

xiv They beat her: "Resistance Against Compulsory Hijab; Sepideh Reshnu Was Arrested" (in Persian), DW Farsi, July 18, 2022, مقاومت علیه حجاب اجباری؛ سپیده رشنو دستگیر شد, www.dw.com/fa-ir.

xv "A person who fights knows": Sepideh Rashnu (@sepidehrashnu_), "In the disciplinary committee, they gave two blank pages," Instagram, May 13, 2023, www.instagram.com/p/CsLOcS6oUi5/?igsh=cnFyNnV3eW9jcHF0.

PART I

FOR WOMAN, LIFE, FREEDOM

3   Half an hour later: Elaheh Mohammadi, "A Homeland of Sorrow" (in Persian), *Hammihan*, Sept. 18, 2022, گزارش خبرنگار اعزامی هممیهن از سقز محل زندگی و خاکسپاری مهسا امینی, https://hammihanonline.ir/بخش-اندوه-وطن-یک-23/1062-جامعه. یک وطن اندوه.
4   "We will not bow": Ibid.
4   On Jîna's tombstone: Ibid.
5   Öcalan presented: Sahar Karimi and Nahid Molavi, *Roozarooz Media* (@roozarooz_media), "Killing the dominant man," Instagram, video, Aug. 5, 2023, www.instagram.com/p/CvknUfioE-L/?next=%2Flajedet%2F&hl=es.

FOR STUDENTS. FOR THE FUTURE.

7   In Tehran, the country's capital: Shayan Sardarizadeh (@Shayan86), "This clip of #MahsaAmini protests in Tehran is from a few days ago that's only been published today. In it, riot police attempt to detain two protesters," Twitter, Oct. 6, 2022, 5:30 p.m., twitter.com/Shayan86/status/1578038297489612800.
7   even in Mashhad: 1500 Tasvir (@1500tasvir_en), "Nov. 17, Mashhad, Khorasan. 'We don't want the Islamic Republic. Death to the Islamic Republic! You're done!' #MahsaAmini," Twitter, Nov. 17, 2022, 8:22 p.m., twitter.com/1500tasvir_en/status/1593323805203746817.
7   Led by young women: Zeinab Nobowati, "Iran's Woman Life Freedom Movement and the Critique of Mandatory Hijab," American Philosophical Association (blog), Oct. 16, 2023, blog.apaonline.org/2023/10/16/irans-woman-life-freedom-movement-and-the-critique-of-mandatory-hijab/.
7   largest and most widespread: Farnaz Fassihi, "Iran Protests Surge to Dozens of Cities," *New York Times,* last modified Sept. 26, 2022, www.nytimes.com/2022/09/24/world/middleeast/iran-protests.html.
7   The government responded: Catherine Thorbecke, "Iran's Sweeping Internet Blackouts Are a Serious Cause for Concern," CNN Business, Sept. 24, 2022, www.cnn.com/2022/09/24/tech/iran-internet-blackout/index.html.
7   Since 2009, when Iran: Todd R. Weiss, "Iran Blocking Google, YouTube, Gmail to Protest Film: Reports," *eWeek,* Sept. 24, 2012, www.eweek.com/security/iran-blocking-google-youtube-gmail-to-protest-film-reports/.
7   As a result, Iranians: "About 80 Percent of Iranians Use Tools to Circumvent

Restrictions on Internet, MP Says," Radio Farda, July 7, 2022, www.rferl.org/a/iranians-circumvent-internet-restrictions/31933593.html.
8   One video showed: Erin Cunningham and Emily Tamkin, "What Is the Revolutionary Guard? A Look at the Iranian Military Unit Trump Has Deemed Terrorists," *Washington Post*, April 8, 2019, www.washingtonpost.com/world/2019/04/08/who-are-revolutionary-guards-look-iranian-military-unit-trump-has-deemed-terrorists/.
8   As the Basiji: 1500 Tasvir (@1500tasvir), Telegram, Oct. 5, 2022, t.me/Tasvir_1500/6227.
8   In Karaj, a big: 1500 Tasvir (@1500tasvir), Telegram, Oct. 5, 2022, t.me/Tasvir_1500/6174.

FOR NOT BEING AFRAID ANYMORE

13 According to Islam, after we die: Abu Amina Elias, "Hadith on Sirat: Believers Purified by Justice Before Entering Paradise," Daily Hadith Online, Dec. 5, 2021, www.abuaminaelias.com/dailyhadithonline/2021/12/05/purified-by-justice/.
14 I told myself, "Don't let the bastards": Margaret Atwood, *The Handmaid's Tale* (McClelland & Stewart, 2019), 335.
14 With Louise's help: Fatemeh Jamalpour, "'By the Time You Read This, I Might Be in Jail'—the Daily Terror of a Female Protester in Iran," *Sunday Times* (London), Oct. 8, 2022, www.thetimes.com/world/asia/article/by-the-time-you-read-this-i-might-be-in-jail-the-daily-terror-of-a-female-protester-in-iran-6jzgq99th.
14 An artist had added: Ella Feldman, "Tehran's Fountains Turn Blood Red in Anonymous Protest Art," *Smithsonian Magazine*, Oct. 14, 2022, www.smithsonianmag.com/smart-news/tehrans-fountains-turn-blood-red-in-anonymous-protest-art-180980932/.

FOR THE SUN AFTER LONG NIGHTS

16 Thousands would be taken: "Iran: Thousands of Detained Protesters and Activists in Peril," Human Rights Watch, Nov. 3, 2022, www.hrw.org/news/2022/11/03/iran-thousands-detained-protesters-and-activists-peril.
17 The state was killing: Nilo Tabrizy, Atthar Mirza, and Babak Dehghanpisheh, "When Protesters Were Killed in Iran, Their Funerals Became Deadly," *Washington Post*, April 21, 2022, www.washingtonpost.com/world/interactive/2023/iran-protests-funerals-mahsa-amini/.
17 and under the cover of night: Patrick Wintour, "Iran Protests: Family of Boy, 9, Killed in Night of Violence Blame Attack on Security Forces," *Guardian*, Nov. 17, 2022, www.theguardian.com/world/2022/nov/17/iran-protests-young-boy-among-deaths-night-of-turmoil-mahsa-amini.

18 It's clear that Iranians: "Support for Protests in Iran Significant: '81 Percent of Iranians Do Not Want an Islamic Republic,'" Utrecht University, Feb. 6, 2023, www.uu.nl/en/news/support-for-protests-in-iran-significant-81-per-cent-of-iranians-do-not-want-an-islamic-republic.

FOR DANCING IN THE ALLEY

20 Even then, we were: Maryam Hosseinkhah, "March 1979: The Six-Day Protest That Postponed the Mandatory Hijab," Aasoo, Sept. 27, 2018, www.aasoo.org/fa/articles/1767.
20 Called the Girls: Golnaz Esfandiari, "Uncovered 'Girl from Revolution Street' Picks Up Steam in Iran," RadioFree Europe/RadioLiberty, Jan. 30, 2018, www.rferl.org/a/iran-hijab-islamic-dress-women-protests-girl-from-enghelab-street/29007848.html.
20 Forty-five years after: "The Statement of Feminist Collectives and Groups on the Occasion of the First Anniversary of 'Jin, Jian, Azadî' Revolutionary Movement," Feminists for Jîna, feminists4jina.net/archives/1555.
21 Security forces lined: Miriam Berger, "Death of 16-Year-Old Protester Adds New Fuel to Iran Uprising," Washington Post, Oct. 6, 2022, www.washingtonpost.com/world/2022/10/06/iran-protests-nika-shakarami-mahsa/.
22 It was trying to intimidate: Joshua Askew, "Fact-Check: Are UK Weapons Being Used Against Protesters in Iran?," Euronews, April 11, 2023, www.euronews.com/my-europe/2022/10/21/fact-check-are-uk-weapons-being-used-against-protestors-in-iran.
23 "Hand in hand, we become the sea": Unknown artists, SoundCloud, soundcloud.com/zan-zendegi-azadi-jina/pjizwns81gsv.
24 She's right; being queer: United Nations, "Iran: UN Experts Demand Stay of Execution for Two Women, Including LGBT Activist," press release, Sept. 28, 2022, www.ohchr.org/en/press-releases/2022/09/iran-un-experts-demand-stay-execution-two-women-including-lgbt-activist.

FOR CONTINUOUS CRYING

29 Civil society has been: Five female prisoners in Iran and Ghazal Golshiri, "Letters from Five Imprisoned Iranian Women: 'We Are Guilty of a Desire to Live,'" Le Monde, Sept. 12, 2023, www.lemonde.fr/en/international/article/2023/09/12/letters-from-five-imprisoned-iranian-women-we-are-guilty-of-a-desire-to-live_6133148_4.html.
29 Journalists in the country: "With 41 Journalists in Prison, Iran Is Now the World's 3rd Biggest Jailer of Journalists," Reporters Without Borders, Oct. 14, 2022, rsf.org/en/41-journalists-prison-iran-now-world-s-3rd-biggest-jailer-journalists.

264 · Notes

30 It feels like a betrayal: Khosro K Isfahani (@KhosroKalbasi), "A video of #Mahsa_Amini (Jîna) dancing a Kurdish dance, her last dance," Twitter, Sept. 19, 2022, twitter.com/khosrokalbasi/status/1571802829479624705.

30 She danced the Halparke: Samaneh Zohrabi, "Halparke Dance, Born of Kurdish Myths," Taste Iran, May 31, 2021, www.tasteiran.net/stories/12098/halparke-kurdish-dance.

30 I can't tell you: Afshang, "Journalists Imprisoned for Reporting the Death That Shook Iran."

32 I watched my colleagues: Amanda Darrach, "How *The New York Times* Verified the Iran Missile-Strike Footage," *Columbia Journalism Review,* Jan. 15, 2020, www.cjr.org/q_and_a/new-york-times-iran-ukraine-flight.php.

32 Our investigation revealed: Christoph Koettl et al., "How the Philadelphia Police Tear-Gassed a Group of Trapped Protesters," *New York Times,* June 25, 2020, www.nytimes.com/video/us/100000007174941/philadelphia-tear-gas-george-floyd-protests.html.

FOR MY SISTER, YOUR SISTER, OUR SISTERS

34 The two agencies: "A Joint Statement of the Ministry of Intelligence and the IRGC Intelligence Organization About the Recent Riots," Tasnim Agency, Oct. 28, 2022, tn.ai/2795144.

34 ten to fifteen years: "Jailed Journalists Elaheh Mohammadi and Niloofar Hamedi Indicted on Multiple Charges," Human Rights Activist News Agency, April 26, 2023, www.en-hrana.org/jailed-journalists-elaheh-mohammadi-and-niloofar-hamedi-indicted-on-multiple-charges/.

34 or even the death penalty: Mostafa Salem, "Journalists Who Reported on Mahsa Amini's Death Stand Trial in Iran," CNN, May 31, 2023, www.cnn.com/2023/05/31/middleeast/iran-journalists-arrest-mahsa-amini-intl/index.html.

34 With the nation: "Journalist Elaheh Mohammadi Arrested," Human Rights Activist News Agency, Sept. 29, 2022, www.en-hrana.org/journalist-elaheh-mohammadi-arrested/.

34 Like Elaheh: "Jailed Journalists Elaheh Mohammadi and Niloofar Hamedi Indicted on Multiple Charges."

34 On December 19, 2022: "Niloofar Hamadi and Elaheh Mohammadi Taken to Qarchak Prison," IFJ, Dec. 19, 2022, ifj-farsi.org/?p=9089.

35 Niloofar's husband wrote that in Qarchak Prison: "Niloofar Hamedi and Elaheh Mohammadi Were Transferred to Evin" (in Persian), Khabaronline, May 1, 2023, https://www.khabaronline.ir/news/1760856/-نیلوفر-حامدی-و-الهه-محمدی-به-اوین-منتقل-شدند.

35 For months, they were: Elnaz Mohammadi (@elnazmohammadii8), Instagram, May 22, 2023, www.instagram.com/p/CrvZOaMt6Rj/.

35 "If within my poems": Sherko Bekas, "Separation," rihlajourney.wordpress.com/2014/11/01/separation-sherko-bekas-kurdish-poet-1940-2013/.

36 Mohammad, Niloofar's husband: Mohamadhosein Ajorloo (@mohamad hosein_ajorloo), Instagram, Jan. 5, 2023, www.instagram.com/p/CnCfyIotjPt/.

36 The regime picked her up: "Iranian Actor Taraneh Alidoosti Arrested After Criticism of Death Penalty," *Guardian*, Dec. 17, 2022, www.theguardian.com/world/2022/dec/17/iranian-actor-taraneh-alidoosti-arrested-after-criticism-of-death-penalty.

36 Taraneh had also: Taraneh Alidoosti (@taraneh_alidoosti), Instagram, Nov. 9, 2022, www.instagram.com/p/CkwBqrkraMU/.

36 Taraneh was widely: Thomas Erdbink, "Asghar Farhadi, Iran's Master of the Ordinary, Wins a 2nd Oscar," *New York Times*, Feb. 27, 2017, www.nytimes.com/2017/02/27/world/middleeast/asghar-farhadi-oscar-iran.html.

37 For many, the father: Babak Ghafouriazar, "The Generation Trapped by Father in a Patriarchal Manner in *Leila's Brothers*," Radio Farda, May 27, 2022, www.radiofarda.com/a/cannes-festival-2022-leila-brothers/31871761.html.

37 Thirty actresses did: "These Female Actresses Banned from Playing" (in Persian), *Aftabnews*, Oct. 25, 2023, https://www.etemadonline.com/اینفوگرافیک/بخش-اینفوگرافیک-637885/11-بازیگران-زن-ممنوع-التصویر-ممنوع-الکار.

FOR THE WOUNDS OF BALUCHESTAN

41 The nationwide protests: Nilo Tabrizy and Haley Willis, "What Video Footage Reveals About the Protests in Iran," *New York Times*, Oct. 4, 2022, www.nytimes.com/2022/10/04/world/asia/iran-protest-video-analysis.html.

41 The U.S.-based: "The Brutal Government Crackdown of September 30, 2022," Iran Human Rights Documentation Center, Oct. 19, 2022, iranhrdc.org/bloody-friday-in-zahedan/.

41 And the head: "Issuing 45 Indictments for the Accused of the Zahedan Riots" (in Persian), *Ghatreh News*, Nov. 2, 2022, صدور ۴۵ کیفرخواست برای متهمان اغتشاشات زاهدان, www.tasnimnews.com.

41 Baluchis make up: "Iran: Human Rights Abuses Against the Baluchi Minority," Amnesty International, Sept. 2007, 2, www.amnesty.org/en/wp-content/uploads/2021/08/mde131042007en.pdf.

42 *Gozinesh* is an ideological: Ibid., 6.

42 Under *gozinesh* rules: Ibid.

42 a member of the Azeri minority: Ata Mahamad, "Pezeshkian's Ethnicity and Jalili's Campaign Fail to Mobilize Turk Voters," IranWire, June 30, 2024, iranwire.com/en/politics/131251-pezeshkians-ethnicity-and-jalilis-campaign-fail-to-mobilize-turk-voters/.

42 appointed the first Sunni: "President Appoints Iran's First-Ever Sunni Cabi-

42 net Member," Radio Farda, Aug. 27, 2024, www.rferl.org/a/iran-rare-sunni-appointment-government-pezeshkian/33094191.html.
42 In 2005, an armed group: "Iran: Human Rights Abuses Against the Baluchi Minority," 14.
43 The group's leaders: Ibid., 15.
43 The following year, members of the IRGC: Ibid., 7.
43 The aim was to reuse: Ibid., 8.
43 Fuel is cheaper: "Etemad Newspaper's 'Shocking' Report on Fuel Workers in Sistan and Baluchestan," Radio Farda, June 15, 2023, www.radiofarda.com/a/32460616.html.
44 The indiscriminate state-sanctioned: Cora Engelbrecht, Nilo Tabrizy, and Ishaan Jhaveri, "'It Was a Massacre': How Security Forces Cracked Down in Southeastern Iran," *New York Times*, Oct. 14, 2022, www.nytimes.com/2022/10/14/world/middleeast/iran-zahedan-crackdown.html.
44 referring to a violent: "Iran: At Least 82 Baluchi Protesters and Bystanders Killed in Bloody Crackdown," Amnesty International, Oct. 6, 2022, www.amnesty.org/en/latest/news/2022/10/iran-at-least-82-Baluchi-protesters-and-bystanders-killed-in-bloody-crackdown/.
44 The solidarity with Kurdistan: Engelbrecht, Tabrizy, and Jhaveri, "'It Was a Massacre.'"
44 By around 1:00 p.m.: Ibid.
47 He referred to: Farnaz Fassihi and Rick Gladstone, "With Brutal Crackdown, Iran Is Convulsed by Worst Unrest in 40 Years," *New York Times*, Dec. 1, 2019, www.nytimes.com/2019/12/01/world/middleeast/iran-protests-deaths.html.
47 Our "Bloody Friday" story was published: "The New York Times global publication addressed the crime of killing the people of Zahedan on September 30, 2022," Haalvsh, Telegram, Oct. 15, 2022, t.me/haalvsh/5891.

FOR DEFENSELESS BODIES AND LIVES

48 Protesters hacked: Ehsan Mehrabi, "Ten Pieces of News from the Hacked Bulletin of the IRGC Commander" (in Persian), IranWire, Dec. 4, 2022, https://farsi.alarabiya.net/amp/views/2022/12/04/-ده-خبر-از-بولتن-هک-شده-فرمانده-سپاه؛-خامنه-ای-فیلم-عمامه-پرانی-دیده.
49 *20:30* is the name: "'Failed Design'; New Television Confessions in '20:30,'" BBC Persian, Jan. 19, 2019, www.bbc.com/persian/iran-features-46935197.

FOR THE IMPRISONED INTELLECTUALS

53 We started to see: Nilo Tabrizy and Ishaan Jhaveri, "How Iran's Security Forces Use Ambulances to Suppress Protests," *New York Times*, Nov. 23, 2022,

www.nytimes.com/2022/11/23/world/middleeast/iran-protesters-detained-ambulance.html.

53 "People are going to be": Ibid.
54 I was put in touch with a university student: Ibid.
55 One particularly brutal day: Yann Bouchez and Ghazal Golshiri, "In Iran, Students at Prestigious Sharif University Are at the Forefront of the Revolt," *Le Monde,* Jan. 21, 2023, www.lemonde.fr/en/m-le-mag/article/2023/01/21/in-iran-students-from-the-prestigious-sharif-university-are-at-the-forefront-of-the-revolt_6012443_117.html.
55 Eyewitnesses I spoke with: Tabrizy and Jhaveri, "How Iran's Security Forces Use Ambulances to Suppress Protests."
55 One video that we verified shows an ambulance: Ibid.
56 Dressed in scrubs: Ibid.
56 Mashhad is a conservative: Karim Sadjadpour, "The Battle for Iran," *Atlantic,* Dec. 31, 2017, www.theatlantic.com/international/archive/2017/12/the-battle-for-iran/549446/.
57 Along with my colleagues: Nilo Tabrizy, Atthar Mirza, and Babak Dehghanpisheh, "Videos Show Escalating Crackdown on Iranian Protests," *Washington Post,* Feb. 2, 2023, www.washingtonpost.com/world/2023/02/02/iran-protests-government/.
58 In Iran, it's a risk: Roxana Saberi, "Iran Protesters Shot by Police So Afraid to Go to Hospitals They're Asking U.S. Doctors for Help Online," CBS News, Oct. 11, 2022, www.cbsnews.com/news/iran-news-protests-deaths-people-shot-afraid-hospital-arrest-us-doctors-help/.
58 Some Baluchi people: Fred Petrossian, "Iran's Invisible Children," Global Voices, Aug. 1, 2019, globalvoices.org/2019/08/01/irans-invisible-children/.
58 When the state attacks: "Extreme Inequality: The Human Rights Situation of Iran's Baloch Minority," Iran Human Rights Documentation Center, July 10, 2019, iranhrdc.org/extreme-inequality-the-human-rights-situation-of-irans-Baloch-minority/.
58 not having these cards: Payam Rasouli, "Iran Health Care," Iranian Surgery, May 4, 2019, iraniansurgery.com/en/iran-health-care/.
59 More than a hundred Baloch: "At Least 100 Baloch Citizens Arrested by Iran's Security Forces," Iran International, Jan. 5, 2023, www.iranintl.com/en/202301059419.

FOR NIKA AND THE MOON

62 We all sang: Parham Ghobadi, "The Security Forces 'Kidnapped' the Body of Nika Shakarami and Buried It Secretly," *BBC Persian,* Oct. 3, 2022, www.bbc.com/persian/iran-63125642.

62 She took her thermos: @Atashshahkarami, Instagram, May 1, 2022, www.instagram.com/p/Crs4iTQurZs/.

63 She never made it: @AtashShahkarami, Instagram, March 10, 2022, www.instagram.com/p/CpnE4uzt9Dc/?igshid=MzRlODBiNWFlZA%3D%3D.

63 She belonged to: Amanolahi Sekandar, "The Lurs of Iran," *Cultural Survival*, Feb. 17, 2010, www.culturalsurvival.org/publications/cultural-survival-quarterly/lurs-iran.

63 After she disappeared: @Atashshahkarami, Instagram, Sept. 26, 2022, www.instagram.com/p/Ci-yuQONHG8/.

63 They circulated her photo: "After 10 Days of Not Being Informed, Nika Shakarami's Family Encountered Her Dead Body in Kahrizak," *BBC Persian*, Sept. 30, 2022, www.bbc.com/persian/articles/c3gwqw4xk5po.

63 With her beautiful body: "A Classmate of the Teenage Girl Killed in the Protests: Nika Shakarami Was Outgoing and Friendly," VOA News, Oct. 3, 2022, ir.voanews.com/a/nika-shakarami-iran-protests/6773827.html.

63 Nika's final day: @Nasrin_shahkarami1356, Instagram, www.instagram.com/reel/CvU8oNitJYQ/?igshid=MzRlODBiNWFlZA==.

63 Then, according to a CNN: Gianluca Mezzofiore, Katie Polglase, and Adam Pourahmadi, "What Really Happened to Nika Shahkarami? Witnesses to Her Final Hours Cast Doubt on Iran's Story," CNN, Oct. 27, 2022, www.cnn.com/2022/10/27/middleeast/iran-nika-shahkarami-investigation-intl-cmd/index.html.

63 It was later discovered: @Atashshahkarami, Instagram, April 4, 2022, www.instagram.com/p/CqnONKctdhE/.

63 "At around 9:00 a.m.": @Atashshahkarami, Instagram, July 28, 2023, www.instagram.com/p/CvQAQ4ftcbN/.

64 After her family: Ibid.

64 In a video, her mother held: Facebook, Oct. 3, 2022, www.facebook.com/watch/?v=1629536580773643.

64 Nika's aunt Atash was detained: "The Security Forces Kidnapped the Body of Nika Shakarami and Arrested Her Aunt" (in Persian), IranWire, Oct. 3, 2022, https://iranwire.com/fa/news-1/108235-و-ربوده-را-شاهکرمی-نیکا-پیکر-امنیتی-نیروهای-کردند-بازداشت-را-خالهاش.

64 They steal the bodies: Somayeh Malekian and Guy Davies, "Iran Accused of Stealing Bodies of Slain Protesters as Families Rush to Reclaim Loved Ones," ABC News, Dec. 3, 2022, abcnews.go.com/International/iran-accused-stealing-bodies-slain-protesters-families-rush/story?id=94343370.

64 They bury them: "The Islamic Republic of Body Snatchers," IranWire, Nov. 22, 2022, iranwire.com/en/politics/110239-the-islamic-republic-of-body-snatchers/.

64 "I birthed you": Baba Fighani Shirazi, Ganjoor, ganjoor.net/faghani/divan/ghazal/sh21.

64 This phrase is: Kave Meshkat, "Narration of Child Soldiers in the Iran-Iraq War," *BBC Persian*, Sept. 22, 2020, www.bbc.com/persian/iran-54256272.
65 "What do you want": @AtashShahkarami, Instagram, Oct. 13, 2022, www.instagram.com/p/Cjq1ohjtw5Y/?igshid=MzRlODBiNWFlZA==.
65 She wanted to emigrate: @AtashShahkarami, Instagram, Oct. 17, 2022, www.instagram.com/p/Cj1Rl17Nmy2/?igshid=MzRlODBiNWFlZA==.
65 "Our stunning Nika": @AtashShahkarami, Instagram, Oct. 13, 2022, www.instagram.com/p/Cjq1ohjtw5Y/?igshid=MzRlODBiNWFlZA%3D%3D.
65 Aida, Nika's sister: @Aidashkrmi, Instagram, Dec. 25, 2022, www.instagram.com/aidashkrmi/?igshid=MzRlODBiNWFlZA%3D%3D.
65 She loved spiderwebs: @Aidashkrmi, Instagram, July 19, 2023, www.instagram.com/aidashkrmi/.
65 "Discovering the secret": @Aidashkrmi, Instagram, Jan. 31, 2023, www.instagram.com/aidashkrmi/.
66 "Why are you sad": Linda Pastan, "Why Are Your Poems So Dark?," *Poetry*, Aug. 2003, www.poetryfoundation.org/poetrymagazine/poems/41918/why-are-your-poems-so-dark.
66 The year after Nika: "The Café Where Nika Shakarami Worked Became the Social Responsibility Headquarters of Tehran University," Iran International, Dec. 19, 2023, www.iranintl.com/202311208259.
66 In a story about: Hamidreza Khaledi, "Behind the Scenes of Café Closures Around the University: Preventing the Rebirth of Protests Through the Purification of Cafés" (in Persian), *Etemad*, October 7, 2023, https://www.etemadonline.com/-خالص-ها-تاآرامی-اعتراضات-تهران-دانشگاه-کافه-9/634928/سیاسی-بخش.سازی.
66 Nika's workplace: The "Café Where Nika Shakarami Worked Became the Social Responsibility Headquarters of Tehran University."
66 which is used to hold training: "Explaining the Details of Setting Up the Social Responsibility Headquarters of Tehran University," (in Persian) Fars News Agency, Dec. 19, 2023, https://irna.ir/xjPh5c.
67 On the anniversary of Nika's: @AtashShahkarami, Instagram, Sept. 16, 2023, www.instagram.com/p/CxQIa3TNxqL/?igshid=MTc4MmM1YmI2Ng%3D%3D.
67 When her aunt told her: @AtashShahkarami, Instagram, July 26, 2023, www.instagram.com/p/CvKOyjwtUBO/.
67 Atash told Nika's mourners: Ibid.
67 A father of one of these: @hooman_sharifi, Instagram, June 1, 2024, www.instagram.com/p/C7rq5sxtfKF/?igsh=MTJjc21qeHhjZzVtNQ==.

FOR THE ENDLESS AND REPETITIVE

69   The largest and most organized: Nilo Tabrizy, "M.E.K.: The Group John Bolton Wants to Rule Iran," *New York Times,* May 7, 2018, www.nytimes.com /2018/05/07/world/middleeast/john-bolton-regime-change-iran.html.

69   It has a well-established: Lindsey Hilsum, "The Shadowy Cult Trump Advisors Tout as an Alternative to the Iranian Government," Channel 4 News, Sept. 6, 2018, www.channel4.com/news/the-shadowy-cult-trump-advisors-tout-as-an -alternative-to-the-iranian-government.

69   This group enjoys: Tabrizy, "M.E.K."

69   In order to resettle: Office of the Spokesperson, U.S. Department of State, "Delisting of the Mujahedin-e Khalq," U.S. Department of State, September 28, 2012, https://2009-2017.state.gov/r/pa/prs/ps/2012/09/198443.htm.

70   "MEK was still": Tabrizy, "M.E.K."

70   But this group: Ibid.

70   In February 2023, the opening speaker: Akela Lacy and Murtaza Hussein, "Amid Ongoing Iran Protests, Congress Boosts Cultish MEK Exile Group," *Intercept,* Feb. 11, 2023, theintercept.com/2023/02/11/iran-protests-mek-congress -maryam-rajavi/.

70   Sherman, who led: Mostafa Aslani, "Brad Sherman: I Commend Maryam Rajavi for Her Commitment to a Democratic Iran," Iran News Update, July 7, 2016, irannewsupdate.com/news/iranian-opposition/brad-sherman-i -commend-maryam-rajavi-for-her-commitment-to-a-democratic-iran/.

70   While I was still: @iamnazaninnour, "@nytimes What's going on, guys?," Instagram, Oct. 3, 2022, www.instagram.com/reel/CjQIWoPLDqY/?igshid= MzRlODBiNWFlZA==.

70   It stated that most: Vivian Yee and Farnaz Fassihi, "'Out-of-Reach Dreams' in a Sickly Economy Provoke the Rage in Iran," *New York Times,* Oct. 2, 2022, www .nytimes.com/2022/10/02/world/middleeast/iran-protests-economy.html.

70   a failed agreement: Nilo Tabrizy, "Iranians Fear Medicine Shortages as U.S. Tightens Sanctions," *New York Times,* Nov. 11, 2018, www.nytimes.com/2018/11 /11/world/middleeast/iran-sanctions.html.

70   No one was in the streets: Tabrizy and Willis, "What Video Footage Reveals About the Protests in Iran."

72   We were looking into a video: @lawan_shno, Instagram, "Fire in Sepah Bank," Sept. 23, 2022, www.instagram.com/p/Ci3V6WlPd7m/.

PART II

FOR WHAT THEY STOLE FROM US

77 In January 1906: Mark F. Bernstein, "An American Hero in Iran," *Princeton Alumni Weekly*, May 9, 2007, paw.princeton.edu/article/american-hero-iran.

77 as he was headed: Muhammad Sahimi, "Iranian Women and the Struggle for Democracy I," *Frontline*, Tehran Bureau, PBS, April 15, 2010, www.pbs.org/wgbh/pages/frontline/tehranbureau/2010/04/iranian-women-and-the-struggle-for-democracy-i-the-pre-revolution-era.html.

78 Our story stretches: Leila Seradj, "Upsetting the Idea of Centuries: The Origins of the Women's Movement in Iran, 1850–1925" (master's thesis, Tufts University, 2015), dl.tufts.edu/concern/pdfs/og354s08m.

78 The tension here: Ibid.

78 The nation suffered humiliating defeats: Ibid.

79 The Reuter concession: "Foreign Concessions: Reuter," SaedNews, Oct. 10, 2021, old.saednews.com/en/post/foreign-concessions-reuters.

79 He was essentially playing: Ceren Uçan, "A Tale of Two Railways and the Reuter Family," *Middle Eastern Studies* 55, no. 1 (2018): 22–32, doi.org/10.1080/00263206.2018.1485658.

79 It was called "the most extraordinary": "Foreign Concessions: Reuter."

79 Lord Curzon, one of: "Past Foreign Secretaries: George Nathaniel Curzon," Gov.UK, accessed July 12, 2024, www.gov.uk/government/history/past-foreign-secretaries/george-curzon.

79 For a period of seventy years: Alessandro Bausani, *The Persians: From the Earliest Days to the Twentieth Century* (St. Martin's Press, 1971), 168.

79 construct all railways: "Foreign Concessions: Reuter."

79 Then, in 1890: Markus Schlotterbeck, "Iranian Resistance to Tobacco Concession, 1891–1892," Global Nonviolent Action Database, Swarthmore College, July 16, 2009, nvdatabase.swarthmore.edu/content/iranian-resistance-tobacco-concession-1891-1892.

79 a close relative: Eftekhar Blarashk, "Tobacco Sanction," Institute for Iranian Contemporary Historical Studies, Jan. 19, 2016, www.iichs.ir/en/gallery/3618/1/tobacco-sanction.

79 This allowed Talbot's: Schlotterbeck, "Iranian Resistance to Tobacco Concession."

79 The effects roiled Persian society: Ibid.

80 Mirza Hassan Shirazi: Sahimi, "Iranian Women and the Struggle for Democracy I."

80 The movement spread: Schlotterbeck, "Iranian Resistance to Tobacco Concession."

82 In the anti-concession protests: Sahimi, "Iranian Women and the Struggle for Democracy I."
82 Even royal women: Ibid.
82 "Women's perseverance": Ibid.
82 Society during this time: Ervand Abrahamian, *Iran Between Two Revolutions* (Princeton University Press, 1983).
82 European urban societies: Ashkan Rezvani-Naraghi, "A Street-less Revolution: The Production of Public Spaces During Iran's 1905–1906 Constitutional Revolution," *Histoire Urbaine* 55, no. 2 (2019): 91–106, www.cairn.info/revue-histoire-urbaine-2019-2-page-91.htm.
82 These ties were much stronger: Ervand, *Iran Between Two Revolutions*.
82 And the absence: Abrahamian Ervand, "Oriental Despotism: The Case of Qajar Iran," *International Journal of Middle East Studies* 5, no. 1 (1974): 36, www.jstor.org/stable/162341.
83 The first modern women's rights: Behrouz Turani, "The Silent Anniversary of Iran's Audacious Constitutional Revolution," Iran International, Aug. 5, 2022, www.iranintl.com/en/202208058654.
83 Wounded by concessions: "History of Iran: Constitutional Revolution," Iran Chamber Society, accessed Feb. 13, 2024, www.iranchamber.com/history/constitutional_revolution/constitutional_revolution.php.
83 Women took part: Sahimi, "Iranian Women and the Struggle for Democracy I."
83 A journalist and activist: "Iranian Personalities: Sediqeh Dowlatabadi," Iran Chamber Society, accessed Feb. 14, 2024, www.iranchamber.com/personalities/sdowlatabadi/sediqeh_dowlatabadi.php.
83 Mohtaram Eskandari, a member: Shadyar Omrani, "Iranian Influential Women: Mohtaram Eskandiari (1895–1924)," IranWire, July 18, 2023, iranwire.com/en/women/118615-iranian-influential-women-mohtaram-eskandari-1895-1924/.
84 founded the first school: Shadyar Omrani, "Iranian Influential Women: Bibi Khanoom Astarabadi," IranWire, July 4, 2023, iranwire.com/en/influential-women/118159-iranian-influential-women-bibi-khanoom-astarabadi-1859-1921/.
84 But I want to tell: Tahereh Taslimi, "Iranian Women You Should Know: Sardar Maryam Bakhtiari," IranWire, June 15, 2020, iranwire.com/en/special-features/67178/.
84 The Bakhtiari tribe, the most powerful: Ibid.
84 Her father, Hossein: Saghar Sadeghian, "Expressing Selves: A Comparative Study of the Memoirs of Tāj al-Saltana and Bībī Maryam Bakhtiyārī," *International Journal of Persian Literature* 4, no. 1 (2019): 37–67, www.jstor.org/stable/10.5325/intejperslite.4.0037.
84 The Bakhtiaris are a nomadic: Enayat Asadi and Vicky Hallett, "Photos: In This Nomadic Tribe in Iran, Women Persevere Despite Hardships," *Goats and Soda* (blog), NPR, Oct. 7, 2022, www.npr.org/sections/goatsandsoda/2022/10

/07/1092344655/photos-in-this-nomadic-tribe-in-iran-the-women-persevere-despite-hardships.

84 Bibi Maryam was only: Shadyar Omrani, "Iranian Influential Women: Maryam Bakhtiari, 1874–1937," IranWire, June 28, 2023, iranwire.com/en/influential-women/117976-iranian-influential-women-maryam-bakhtiari-1874-1937/.

84 She was made to join: Taslimi, "Iranian Women You Should Know: Sardar Maryam Bakhtiari."

85 Bibi Maryam became a skilled: Omrani, "Iranian Influential Women: Maryam Bakhtiari."

85 In 1906, the Qajar leader: "History of Iran: Constitutional Revolution."

85 After the bombardment: Taslimi, "Iranian Women You Should Know: Sardar Maryam Bakhtiari."

85 After this violent attack: Omrani, "Iranian Influential Women: Maryam Bakhtiari."

85 Her home in Isfahan: Ibid.

85 Early one morning in July: Sadeghian, "Expressing Selves."

86 They stayed underground: Taslimi, "Iranian Women You Should Know: Sardar Maryam Bakhtiari."

86 It had been in place: Nasser Karimi and Jon Gambrell, "As More Women Defy Hijab Laws, Iran's Government Pushes Back," Associated Press, May 10, 2023, apnews.com/article/iran-headscarf-hijab-protests-unrest-7cfce99b8841d6df5e8ad95ec8032b28.

86 When the military commander: Shiva Balaghi, "A Brief History of 20th Century Iran," Grey Art Museum, New York University, 2015, greyartmuseum.nyu.edu/2015/12/a-brief-history-of-20th-century-iran/.

86 and established his dynasty: Michael P. Zirinsky, "Imperial Power and Dictatorship: Britain and the Rise of Reza Shah, 1921–1926," *International Journal of Middle East Studies* 24, no. 4 (1992): 639, www.jstor.org/stable/164440.

86 Then he took the country: Poupak Tafreshi, "The Struggle for Freedom, Justice, and Equality: The History of the Journey of Iranian Women in the Last Century" (master's thesis, Washington University in St. Louis, 2010), 929, openscholarship.wustl.edu/etd/929/.

86 At the same time, a period: Ibid.

86 As such, one significant piece: Sahar Maranlou, "Hijab Law in Iran over the Decades: The Continuing Battle for Reform," University of Essex, *Essex Blogs*, Oct. 12, 2022, www.essex.ac.uk/blog/posts/2022/10/12/hijab-law-in-iran-over-the-decades-the-continuing-battle-for-reform.

87 a Turkish nationalist leader: "Kemal Atatürk (1881–1938)," BBC, 2014, www.bbc.co.uk/history/historic_figures/ataturk_kemal.shtml.

87 Reza Shah tried to force: Ahmed El Amraoui and Faisal Edroos, "Why Ataturk's Legacy Is Debated 80 Years After His Death," Al Jazeera, June 11, 2018, www

.aljazeera.com/features/2018/6/11/why-ataturks-legacy-is-debated-80-years-after-his-death.

87 The reforms in Turkey: Jenny B. White, "State Feminism, Modernization, and the Turkish Republican Woman," *NWSA Journal* 15, no. 3 (2003): 145–59, www.jstor.org/stable/4317014.

87 Modernist intellectuals in Iran: Noushin Ahmadi Khorasani, *Intellectuals and Hijab* (Self-published by author, 2012), 26, ir-women.com/16054.

87 In 1936, Reza Shah: Maryam Sinaee, "Eighty Five Years On, the Shah's Ban on Hijab Still Divides," Iran International, Jan. 7, 2022, www.iranintl.com/en/202201070683.

FOR THE FREEDOM OF CHOICE

89 Three decades of massive: Noushin Ahmadi Khorasani, *One Million Signatures' Movement: A Story from the Inside* (Self-published by author, 2007), 96, noushinahmadi.files.wordpress.com/2010/11/cover_1milion-2zzxx.jpg.

89 Reza Shah was pushed: Khorasani, *Intellectuals and Hijab,* 84.

89 Mohammad Reza Pahlavi was twenty-one: "Mohammad Reza Shah Pahlavi, Biography of the Last King," *BBC Persian,* Jan. 31, 2009, www.bbc.com/persian/iran/2009/01/090131_ir_shah.

90 In October 1949: "Who Was Mohammad Mossadegh?," Northeastern Illinois University, https://www.neiu.edu/academics/college-of-business-and-technology/mossadegh-initiative/who-was-mohammad-mossadegh.

90 He ultimately refused: Khorasani, *One Million Signatures' Movement,* 107.

90 On August 19, 1953: Nasser Karimi and Jon Gambrell, "A CIA-Backed 1953 Coup in Iran," Associated Press, Aug. 25, 2023, apnews.com/article/iran-1953-coup-us-tensions-3d391c0255308a7c13d32d3c88e5f54f.

90 The coup was successful: "Dr. Mohammad Mossadegh from Birth to Death," Rouydad24, June 16, 2021.

91 American companies once: Keyvan Hosseini, "What Happened to Iran's Oil After the August 19 Coup?," Radio Farda, Aug. 12, 2014, www.radiofarda.com/a/fk_downfall_e41/25429849.html.

91 "Iranian people who faced": Mehrdad Darvishpour, "Backgrounds and Consequences of the Iranian Revolution," Radio Farda, Feb. 12, 2018, www.radiofarda.com/a/anniversary-revolution/29034450.html.

91 In March 2000: Darioush Bayandor, "Don't Just Blame Washington for the 1953 Iran Coup," *Foreign Policy,* Nov. 21, 2019, foreignpolicy.com/2019/11/21/dont-blame-washington-1953-iran-coup-mosaddeq/.

91 The coup against Mossadegh: "Mohammad Reza Shah Pahlavi, Biography of the Last King."

91 He tried to make: Ali Afshari, "The White Revolution: A Window to the Why

Notes · 275

and Failure of the 1979 Revolution," Radio Farda, Jan. 27, 2020, www.radiofarda.com/a/iran-white-revolution-after-6-decades/31674038.html.
91   After fifty-five years: Ibid.
92   "Some people think": Khorasani, *Intellectuals and Hijab*, 112.
92   Their goal was to overthrow: Ibid., 126.
92   These activists undermined: Ibid., 112.
92   Islamists were against: Suzanne Maloney and Keian Razipour, "The Iranian Revolution—a Timeline of Events," Brookings Institution, Jan. 24, 2019, www.brookings.edu/articles/the-iranian-revolution-a-timeline-of-events/.
92   Communists, Marxists, Iranian students: Homa Katouzian, "The Iranian Revolution of 1979," Middle East Institute, Jan. 29, 2009, www.mei.edu/publications/iranian-revolution-february-1979.
92   After succeeding, the Islamists: Hossein Bastani, "Rereading Four Decades of 'Removal Literature' in the Islamic Republic of Iran," *BBC Persian*, Feb. 11, 2019, www.bbc.com/persian/iran-features-47186703.
93   He was exiled: "Ayatollah Khomeini (1900–1989)," *BBC News*, www.bbc.co.uk/history/historic_figures/khomeini_ayatollah.shtml.
93   Unlike his father, Mohammad Reza Shah: Darvishpour, "Backgrounds and Consequences of the Iranian Revolution."
93   The number of mosques: Dariush Homayoun, "Mohammad Reza Pahlavi: Confused Between Religion and West," *BBC Persian*, Jan. 27, 2010, www.bbc.com/persian/iran/2010/07/100727_shah_annive30_homayoun_religion.
93   Noureddin Kianouri, one of: Heshmat Hekmat, "The Common Point Between Ayatollah Khomeini and Kianouri Is the Oppressed and the Working Class," *BBC Persian*, Jan. 30, 2012, www.bbc.com/persian/iran/2012/01/120114_l44_tudeh_party_islamic_republic_cooperation.
93   On October 12, 1978: Hamid Zoralnor, "The National Front and Ayatollah Khomeini on the Eve of the Revolution," *BBC Persian*, Aug. 11, 2011, www.bbc.com/persian/iran/2011/08/110811_l78_bakhtiar_20th_anniv_hamid_zolnour.
93   During his exile: Mohammad Heydari, "Velayat al-Faqih, a Theory for Holding Power," *BBC Persian*, Aug. 28, 2016, www.bbc.com/persian/blogs/2016/08/160828_l44_nazeran_velayte_faghih_khomeini.
93   The opposite happened: Mehrdad Farahmand, "Valery d'Estaing and Iran Revolution," *BBC Persian*, Dec. 3, 2020, www.bbc.com/persian/world-55176821.
94   During his stay: "Imam Khomeini's Stay in Paris and Its Domestic and International Consequences," Center of Historical Documents Survey, Oct. 4, 2023, historydocuments.ir/?page=post&id=2172.
94   "We will not close": Kambiz Fattahi, "Ayatollah Khomeini's Promises to the US," *BBC Persian*, June 5, 2016, www.bbc.com/persian/iran/2016/06/160605_kf_khomeini_pledges_us.
94   Ghotbzadeh and Yazdi often: Kambiz Fattahi, "Behind the Scenes of the PBS

Interview with Ayatollah Khomeini," *BBC Persian*, Feb. 5, 2015, www.bbc.com/persian/iran/2015/02/150204_u01-maneil-khomeini.

94 Yazdi wrote in his memoir: "Unsaid Stories About Imam Khomeini Interviews" (in Persian), IRNA, March 23, 2023, https://www.irna.ir/news/85056874/ناگفته‌های-مصاحبه‌های-امام-خمینی-ره-در-نوفل-لوشاتو.

94 "a woman is a man's equal": Mahnaz Matien and Nasser Mohajer, *Iranian Women's Uprising, March 8th 1979*, vol. 1, Renaissance (Noghteh, 2013), 529, en.noghteh.org/iranian-womens-uprising-march-8th-1979-1/.

94 He had delivered a sharp: *CBC News*, YouTube, www.youtube.com/watch?v=n-grR1e6dw8.

94 At the same time, Khomeini: Kambiz Fatahi, "Ayatollah Khomeini's Pledge to America," *BBC Persian*, Jan. 5, 2016, bbc.com/persian/iran/2016/06/160605_kf_khomeini_pledges_us.

94 In January 1979: Kambiz Fatahi, "How Did America Give Up on the Shah?," *BBC Persian*, Jan. 2, 2016, bbc.com/persian/iran/2016/06/160602_u01_iran_shah_us.

95 Khomeini returned to Iran: "Chronology of the Revolution," *BBC Persian*, Feb. 1, 2019, www.bbc.com/persian/iran-47059845.

95 Air France plane paid for: Reza Haghighat Nejad, "Who Paid the Rent of Khomeini's Plane?," Radio Farda, Feb. 2, 2019, www.radiofarda.com/a/iran-history-revolution-khomeini-flight-back-to-country-chartered/29747584.html.

95 On February 10: "Chronology of the Revolution."

95 Mohammad Reza Shah and two: "Iranian Women You Should Know: Farah Pahlavi," IranWire, Aug. 18, 2015, iranwire.com/en/special-features/61285/.

95 Though this was not the case: Farhang Ghavimi, "'1001 Days' and Other Memories in an Interview with Farah Pahlavi," Radio Farda, Nov. 2, 2021, www.radiofarda.com/a/exclusive-iv-with-shahbanou-on-1001-days-memoir/31541706.html.

95 "If a person will be remembered": Saadi, Ode 28, Ganjoor, ganjoor.net/saadi/mavaez/ghasides/sh28.

95 Farah has had a lasting: Ghavimi, "'1001 Days' and Other Memories in an Interview with Farah Pahlavi."

95 Born in 1938: "Iranian Women You Should Know: Farah Pahlavi."

96 She ordered and oversaw: City Theater of Tehran homepage, city.theater.ir/.

96 Farah also opened: "A Conversation with the Former Queen About the Modern Art Works in Museum" (in Persian), DW, Jan. 16, 2017, https://www.dw.com/fa-ir/گفتگو-با-شهبانوی-پیشین-ایران-درباره-گنجینه-آثار-مدرن-هنری-بخش-اول/video-37151991.

96 Roudaki Hall, a multipurpose: "Introduction to Vahdat and Rudaki Halls" (in Persian), *Hamshahri Online*, https://www.hamshahrionline.ir/photo/222429/آشنایی-با-تالارهای-وحدت-و-رودکی.

96 Its design is reminiscent: "Conversation with the Former Queen About the Modern Art Works in Museum."

96 On February 2, 1979, the regime: Eliz Sanasarian, *The Women's Rights Movement in Iran* (Praeger, 1982), 127.

96 There, a mob: Babak Ghafuri Azar, "'It Was Not Clear What Kind of Anger It Was'; Kamran Shirdel Account of the Attack on the 'Castle' During the Days of the 1979 Revolution," Radio Farda, Feb. 2, 2022, www.radiofarda.com/a/kamran-shirdel-account-of-attack-on-shahreno-in-the-days-of-the-revolution/31683209.html.

96 The revolutionaries paraded: "How Did the Shahrno Burn?" (in Persian), Rouydad24, Jan. 30, 2022, https://www.rouydad24.ir/fa/news/202673/شهرنو-تهران-چگونه-در-آتش-سوخت-تصاویر.

97 Thousands of angry women headed to the streets: Hosseinkhah, "March 1979: The Six-Day Protest That Postponed the Mandatory Hijab."

97 Hengameh Golestan was one: Lucy Davies, "Witness to Revolution: The Women of Iran 1979," *Telegraph*, Sept. 10, 2015, www.telegraph.co.uk/photography/what-to-see/hengameh-golestan—witness-1979/.

97 That woman became known: Elaheh Sourooshnia, "Wandering Between Joan of Arc and Meliheh Nikjomand" (in Persian), HarassWatch, July 28, 2021, https://harasswatch.com/news/1815/پرسه-در-فاصله-ژاندارک-و-ملیحه-نیکجومند.

98 "I remember that coat": Ibid.

98 Those six days: Hosseinkhah, "March 1979: The Six-Day Protest That Postponed the Mandatory Hijab."

98 During this time, all universities: Bastani, "Rereading Four Decades of 'Removal Literature' in the Islamic Republic of Iran."

98 It approved lashing: Ehsan Mehrabi, "Morality Police: 40 Years of Compulsory Hijab in Iran," *BBC Persian*, Sept. 17, 2022, www.bbc.com/persian/articles/c728x75gpz0o.

98 Amid an atmosphere: Khorasani, *Intellectuals and Hijab*, 190.

98 women who refused to wear: Bastani, "Rereading Four Decades of 'Removal Literature' in the Islamic Republic of Iran."

98 The Family Protection Law, which defined restrictions: Khorasani, *One Million Signatures' Movement*, 15.

98 The Pahlavi bill: Sanasarian, *Women's Rights Movement in Iran*, 7.

98 In the ten years: Khorasani, *One Million Signatures' Movement*, 8.

FOR MY MOM, YOUR MOM, OUR MOMS

100 It was an issue of *Zan-e rooz*: Liora Hendelman-Baavur, *Creating the Modern Iranian Woman: Popular Culture Between Two Revolutions* (Cambridge University Press, 2019).

105 "I love your hands": Forough Farrokhzad, "Another Birth," https://forughfar rokhzad.org/selectedworks/selectedworks1.php#Another%20Birth.

FOR THE REGRET OF A NORMAL LIFE

112 He's a member: Lionel Beehner, "Iran's Ethnic Groups," Council on Foreign Relations, Nov. 29, 2006, www.cfr.org/backgrounder/irans-ethnic-groups.

115 In September 1980, the then-president: Mark Bucknam and Frank Esquivel, "Saddam Hussein and the Iran-Iraq War," National War College at the National Defense University, 2001, nwc.ndu.edu/Portals/71/Images/Publications/Sad dam%20Hussein%20and%20the%20Iran-Iraq%20War.pdf.

116 In 1980, under pressure: Philip Shehadi, "Economic Sanctions and Iranian Trade," *Middle East Report* 98 (July/Aug. 1981), merip.org/1981/07/economic -sanctions-and-iranian-trade/.

116 European nations announced: Sari Gilbert, "Common Market Limits Curbs on Iran," *Washington Post*, May 19, 1980, www.washingtonpost.com/archive /politics/1980/05/19/common-market-limits-curbs-on-iran/782a5b6e-a15c -40b7-8850-2cc7ab15ff31/.

FOR THE GIRL WHO WISHED TO BE A BOY

117 Between 1981 and 1990: Shabnam Majidi, "A Population of 21 Million Aged 18 to 35, the 1980s Generation, Is Aging Out of Youth" (in Persian), Iranian Students' News Agency, Dec. 26, 2018, https://www.isna.ir/news/1401121309075 /جمعیت-۲۱-میلیونی-۱۸-تا-۳۵-ساله-ها-خروج-دهه-شصتی-ها-از-سنین-جوانی/.

117 Khomeini, the post-revolution: Ruhollah Khomeini, "Sahifeh-ye Imam," *Book of Imam Khomeini*, 4:300, farsi.rouhollah.ir/library/sahifeh-imam-khomeini /vol/6/page/300.

118 Ali Khamenei, the current: "An Overview of the Revolutionary Supreme Leader's Statements About the Irreplaceable Role of Motherhood" (in Persian), Khamenei.ir, Jan. 10, 2023, https://farsi.khamenei.ir/speech-content?id=54907.

118 "We should weep": YouTube, www.youtube.com/watch?v=juWD9qV0a2E.

118 "Khamenei is another Khomeini": YouTube, www.youtube.com/watch?v =WdsAlfThkfw.

119 They chant: VOA News, YouTube, www.youtube.com/watch?v=kPfBfvS_-Jg.

121 But because we were girls: "Ayatollah Khamenei: It Is Forbidden for Women to Ride Bicycles in Public," *BBC Persian*, Sept. 18, 2016, https://www.bbc.com /persian/iran/2016/09/160918_l26_khamenei_cycling_women_forbidden.

FOR A LIFETIME OF LONELINESS

132 A year after his inauguration: Rick Gladstone and Satoshi Sugiyama, "Trump's Travel Ban: How It Works and Who Is Affected," *New York Times*, July 1, 2018,

www.nytimes.com/2018/07/01/world/americas/travel-ban-trump-how-it-works.html.

132 If I landed in Iran: Julian Borger, "Reporter Jason Rezaian on 544 Days in Iranian Jail: 'They Never Touched Me but I Was Tortured,'" *Guardian*, Feb. 18, 2019, www.theguardian.com/media/2019/feb/18/reporter-jason-rezaian-on-544-days-in-iranian-jail-they-never-touched-me-but-i-was-tortured.

FOR CHANGING RUSTED MINDS

135 At the time, we were living: Mehrad Vaezinejad, "Khatami; From the presidency of the Hamburg Islamic Center to the Presidency of the Islamic Republic of Iran," *BBC Persian*, Aug. 1, 2005, www.bbc.com/persian/iran/story/2005/08/050801_pm-mv-khatami-profile.

136 The circulation of reformist: Omid Montazeri, "Criticism of the Spring of Reformist Newspapers," *BBC Persian*, May 21, 2020, www.bbc.com/persian/iran-features-52699068.

136 The circulation of books: Sadegh Zibakalam, Davood Afshari, and Abdollah Aslanzadeh, "The Causes of Coming into Power of Khatami (Reform Government 1997/1376) on the Basis of Samuel Huntington's Theory of Uneven Development," *Political and International Researches Quarterly* 1, no. 3 (2009): 51–76, pir.shahreza.iau.ir/article_559639.html?lang=en.

136 Khatami's presidency recorded: Behrang Tajdin, "Four Presidents, Five Charts; What Did Rafsanjani, Khatami, Ahmadinejad, and Rouhani Do to Iran's Economy?," *BBC Persian*, Aug. 5, 2021, www.bbc.com/persian/business-58094048.

136 The supreme leader ordered: Moein Khazaeli, "Mass Seizing the Newspapers in 2000: The Beginning or the Continuation of the Process of Repression?," Radio Zamaneh, April 30, 2019, www.radiozamaneh.com/443786/.

136 In one of his speeches: "The Head of the Reform Government Has Repeatedly Said, 'I Am a Procurement Officer,'" (in Persian) Borna News Agency, Dec. 5, 2020, https://borna.news/fa/news/1095720/ی-من-بود-گفته-بارها-اصلاحات-دولت-رئیس-دارد-زینتی-اختیاراتی-ایران-در-جمهور-رئیس-هستم-تدارکاتچی-ک.

138 In September 2006: "Police Prevented 71 Women Wearing Improper Hijabs From Flying" (in Persian), *Tabnak*, Jun. 14, 2010, https://www.tabnak.ir/fa/news/104294/پرواز-از-پلیس-زن-71%8C%80%E2کرد-جلوگیری-بدحجاب.

139 According to an investigative: Maryam Lotfi, "Every Four Days, a Woman Has Been Killed" (in Persian), *Shargh Daily*, July 5, 2023, https://www.sharghdaily.com/بخش-روزنامه-100/886696-هر-چهار-روز-یک-زن-کشی.

140 The government began to impose: Bijan Yeganeh, "University Gender Quotas; Another Example of Gender Discrimination," Radio Farda, Feb. 27, 2008, www.radiofarda.com/a/f1_girls_universities/436671.html.

140 According to a Human Rights Watch report: "Criticism of Human Rights

Watch on 'Discrimination' Against Women in Iran's Labor Market," *BBC Persian*, May 25, 2017, www.bbc.com/persian/iran-40054617.

140 The Islamic Republic News Agency: Parsa Piltan, "Chronology of One Hundred Days of Election Protest in Iran," *BBC Persian*, Sept. 22, 2009, www.bbc.com/persian/iran/2009/09/090920_bd_pp_ir88_timeline_election.

140 Then we learned: "Attack on Mir Hossein Mousavi's Headquarters on the Day of Voting in the 2009 Elections" (in Persian), *Eghtesadnews*, April 9, 2022, https://www.eghtesadnews.com/رسانه-سایر-اخبار-بخش-قبل-ما-دستگیری-حکم/487442/61-حمله-به-ستاد-میرحسین-موسوی-در-روز-رای-گیری-در-انتخابات-را-پیروز-اعلام-کرد-ها.-از-انتخابات-صادر-شده-بود-کیهان-احمدی-نژا-د.

140 This became known as: Piltan, "Chronology of One Hundred Days of Election Protest in Iran."

140 The Ministry of Communications: Ibid.

140 In his victory speech: Roozbeh Bolhari, "From 'Dust and Trash' to 'Depressed and Sad Minority,'" Radio Farda, July 8, 2009, www.radiofarda.com/a/f6_Iran_Khamenei_Opponents_Akbareen/1771569.html.

141 Neda Agha-Soltan: "Iranian Authorities Scramble to Negate Neda Soltan 'Martyrdom,'" *Times* (London), June 23, 2009, www.thetimes.com/article/iranian-authorities-scramble-to-negate-neda-soltan-martyrdom-3cdj7jzh728.

141 After thirteen years: Stephen Collinson, "A Rare Moment of Public Self-Criticism by a Former President," CNN, Oct. 18, 2022, edition.cnn.com/2022/10/18/politics/barack-obama-iran-self-reflection-analysis/idex.html.

141 After the suppression of text: Piltan, "Chronology of One Hundred Days of Election Protest in Iran."

141 Many Iranian families: "What Can Be Done When 71% of People Watch Satellite?!" (in Persian), *Tabnak*, Dec. 18, 2013, https://www.tabnak.ir/fa/news/365680/چه-می‌%E2%80%8Cکنند%E2%80%8Cوقتی-71-درصد-مردم-ماهواره-نگاه-می‌-کرد-توان.

141 Later, the police began: "Re-collection of Satellite Dishes by the Police Force in Tehran" (in Persian), DW, Aug. 24, 2014, https://www.dw.com/fa-ir/جمع‌آوری-دو-باره-دیشهای-ماهواره-توسط-نیروی-انتظامی-در-تهران/a-17886553.

141 The police's war: VOA, YouTube, www.youtube.com/watch?v=qYH-GtSPnqo.

143 The next day, all the news: Negin Hemadzadeh, "Liali Qadr; Revival Ceremony of the Twenty-First Night—Imamzadeh Saleh" (in Persian), ISNA, April 12, 2022, https://www.isna.ir/photo/1402012311325/لیالی-قدر-مراسم-احیای-شب-بیست-و-ی-کم-امامزاده-صالح.

145 One of the most important investigative reports: Fatemeh Jamalpour, "'Memorandum of Construction' of the Municipality with the IRGC," *Magiran*, July 8, 2024, www.magiran.com/article/2984079.

146 On April 22, 1979: "A Narrative of How the Islamic Revolutionary Guards Corps

Was Formed" (in Persian), Islamic Revolution Documentation Center, April 21, 2020, https://www.shabestan.news/news/1048602/روایتی-از-نحوه-تشکیل-سپاه-تفرقه-افکنی-موقت-بین-نیروهای.

146 This militia group didn't even: "How the IRGC Was Formed 41 Years Ago" (in Persian), ISNA, April 21, 2020, https://www.isna.ir/news/99020200872/۴۱-سال-پیش-سپاه-چگونه-تشکیل-شد.

146 President Rafsanjani first: "Memoir of Hashemi Rafsanjani, Construction Commander" (in Persian), https://www.iranketab.ir/book/16888-construction-commander.

146 the establishment of Khatam-al-Anbiya: "The IRGC Commercial and Financial Institutions: Khatam-al-Anbiya Construction Headquarters," IranWire, April 9, 2019, iranwire.com/en/features/65741/.

146 On May 11, 2004: Sadegh Saba, "Closing Tehran's New Airport: 'An Action Toward the Political Sovereignty of the IRGC?,'" BBC Persian, May 11, 2014, www.bbc.com/persian/iran/story/2004/05/040511_ssabaairport.

147 The IRGC has benefited: "Islamic Revolutionary Guards Corps: Structure and Missions," IranWire, April 9, 2019, iranwire.com/en/features/65735/.

147 In 2006, *BBC Persian*: "IRGC and Its Presence in Iran's Economic Field," *BBC Persian*, Oct. 14, 2006, www.bbc.co.uk/persian/iran/story/2006/10/061014_an-iran-wsj.shtml.

147 In a Facebook post: Fatemeh Jamalpour, Facebook, www.facebook.com/fatemeh.jml/posts/750150191718396.

148 Despite their efforts: Fatemeh Jamalpour, "'Shargh' Reporter's Two-Day Experience of Retail in Tehran Metro, the Peddler Does Not Get Off" (in Persian), *Shargh Daily*, June 9, 2013, https://www.sharghdaily.com/بخش-اخبار-3/562178/دس-تفروش-پیاده-نمی-شود.

148 I shared a deeply empathetic: Fatemeh Jamalpour, "One Night with Homeless Women in Tehran" (in Persian), *Shargh Daily*, June 17, 2014, https://www.sharghdaily.com/بخش-اخبار-3/586940/یک-شب-تا-صبح-پا-به-پای-زنان-کا.

149 Khadijeh and her daughter: Fatemeh Jamalpour, "Run, Behnoush, Run" (in Persian), *Shargh Daily*, Oct. 10, 2015, https://www.sharghdaily.com/بدو-بهنوش-بدو/بخش-روزنامه-100/75550-.

149 In 2004, women had launched: Masoumeh Naseri, "Women in Stadium; I Was One of the 'White Scarves,'" *BBC Persian*, Oct. 10, 2019, www.bbc.com/persian/sport-49973747.

150 There, I met fifteen: "A Detention Center Instead of a Stadium, a Story by Fatemeh Jamalpour, Shargh Reporter," Radio Zamaneh, June 21, 2014, www.tribunezamaneh.com/archives/51775.

150 Over the next few days: "Iran Bans Women Fans from Volleyball Matches," Al Jazeera, June 22, 2023, www.aljazeera.com/news/2014/6/22/iran-bans-women-fans-from-volleyball-matches.

FOR THE IMAGE OF REPETITION

152 Back then, she was a student: "Fatemeh Jamalpour—Iran," Reham al-Farra Memorial Journalism Fellowship, United Nations, accessed June 26, 2023, www.un.org/en/reham-al-farra-memorial-journalism-fellowship/fatemeh-jamalpour-iran.

155 Many newspapers in Iran: Nilo Tabrizy, "Iranian News Media on Trump: 'He Just Whined,'" *New York Times*, Oct. 17, 2017, www.nytimes.com/video/world/middleeast/100000005498619/trump-iran-reactions-nuclear-deal.html.

155 There are reformist organizations: "Iranian Court Sentences 2 Journalists to Jail on Propaganda Charges," Committee to Protect Journalists, Nov. 12, 2019, cpj.org/2019/11/iranian-court-sentences-2-journalists-to-jail-on-p/.

155 There are hard-line organizations: Ehsan Mehrabi, "Inside the Iranian Regime's Propaganda Machine," IranWire, Nov. 11, 2022, iranwire.com/en/journalism-is-not-a-crime/109692-irib-fars-serajinside-the-iranian-regimes-propaganda-machine/.

156 There's even the newspaper *Kayhan*: "Newspaper Close to Iran's Leader Defends Russia Against Critics," Iran International, July 7, 2022, www.iranintl.com/en/202207073782.

156 and Tasnim News Agency: Mary Louise Kelly, "Political Journalist for Tasnim News Agency in Iran on U.S. Relations," *All Things Considered*, NPR, Jan. 9, 2020, www.npr.org/2020/01/09/795002114/political-journalist-for-tasnim-news-agency-in-iran-on-u-s-relations.

FOR BLOODY ABAN AND ITS FIFTEEN HUNDRED LIVING MARTYRS

158 On December 28, 2017: Jamshid Barzegar, "What Will Happen if the Protests Continue in Iran?," *BBC Persian*, Jan. 5, 2018, www.bbc.com/persian/iran-42580026.

165 The headline of my first: Melissa Etehad, "'Death to the Dictator': What Is Iran's Future?," *Los Angeles Times*, Jan. 14, 2020, www.latimes.com/world-nation/story/2020-01-14/iran-announces-arrests-over-downing-of-ukrainian-plane.

GRIEF IS THE BITTER FRUIT THEY SET

166 In January 2020, the United States targeted: David Botti and Nilo Tabrizy, "Video Shows Aftermath of U.S. Strike That Killed Top Iran Commander," *New York Times*, Jan. 3, 2020, www.nytimes.com/video/world/middleeast/100000006902165/baghdad-airport-strike-reaction-soleimani.html.

167 And then, as Iran: Malachy Browne et al., "New Video Shows Two Iranian Missiles Hit Ukrainian Plane," *New York Times*, Jan. 14, 2020, www.nytimes.com/2020/01/14/world/iran-plane-crash-video.html.

167 The plane was hit: "Canada's Response to Ukraine International Airlines Flight 752 Tragedy," Government of Canada, www.international.gc.ca/world-monde/issues_development-enjeux_developpement/response_conflict-reponse_conflits/crisis-crises/flight-vol-ps752.aspx?lang=eng.
167 That civilian airspace: Browne et al., "New Video Shows Two Iranian Missiles Hit Ukrainian Plane."
167 Among the plane's passengers: "Canada's Response to Ukraine International Airlines Flight 752 Tragedy."
167 The daughter and wife: @ntabrizy, "My hometown bakery in North Vancouver has closed," Twitter, Jan. 12, 2020, 11:52 a.m., twitter.com/ntabrizy/status/1216402564251635713.

FOR NOT BEING ASHAMED OF POVERTY

172 One of my earliest: Fatemeh Jamalpour, "In the Name of Qasem Soleimani; From Books and Computer Games to the Conference of Mothers Who Named Their Children Qasem," *BBC Persian*, Jan. 3, 2021, www.bbc.com/persian/iran-55503336.
173 Another report explored: BBC, YouTube, www.youtube.com/watch?v=upoP3NgwYNg.
173 I also produced two stories: Fatemeh Jamalpour, "Aggrieved Plaintiffs Who Do Not Want the Accused in Rape Case to Be Executed," *BBC Persian*, May 1, 2021, www.bbc.com/persian/iran-features-56845118.
174 Thus, the Iranian regime: Fatemeh Jamalpour, "Working Conditions and Malnutrition in Iranian Prisons," *BBC Persian*, Nov. 4, 2021, www.bbc.com/persian/iran-59163889.
174 I interviewed Narges: "16-Year Prison Sentence for Narges Mohammadi," Amnesty International, June 2, 2016, www.amnesty.org/en/wp-content/uploads/2021/05/MDE1341712016ENGLISH.pdf.
174 These days, regardless of socioeconomic: "Warning of Iranian MP: The Population Below the Poverty Line Has Reached 28 Million People," Radio Farda, July 25, 2023, www.radiofarda.com/a/32517709.html.
185 "You are a psychologist": "Fatemeh Sepehri Was Transferred to the Prison Hospital During a Virtual Meeting with the 'Psychological Interrogator,'" VOA News, April 16, 2024, ir.voanews.com/a/interrogation-session-psychologist-fatemeh-sepehri/7572350.html.

WHAT CAN THEY KNOW OF OUR DISTRESS WHO WATCH US FROM THE SHORE?

186 The Black Lives Matter movement: Larry Buchanan, Quoctrung Bui, and Jugal K. Patel, "Black Lives Matter Movement May Be the Largest Movement in U.S.

History," *New York Times,* July 3, 2020, www.nytimes.com/interactive/2020/07/03/us/george-floyd-protests-crowd-size.html.
187 "I don't believe the journalist-activist": Charlotte Klein, "Inside the *New York Times* Blowup over Transgender Coverage," *Vanity Fair,* Feb. 27, 2023, www.vanityfair.com/news/2023/02/new-york-times-trans-coverage-debate.
187 "The tendency is always": Nancy N. Chen, "'Speaking Nearby': A Conversation with Trinh T. Minh-ha," *Visual Anthropology Review* 8, no. 1 (Spring 1992), www.situatedecologies.net/wp-content/uploads/Trinh-Speaking-Nearby-1983.pdf.
188 Trinh characterizes: Ibid.
189 Trinh views: Ibid.

OUTSIDE THE CONFINES OF MY BODY

190 We learned from Bibi: Taslimi, "Iranian Women You Should Know: Sardar Maryam Bakhtiari."

PART III

193 "For the hair of revolutionary girls": "Woman, Life, Freedom" movement by anonymous artists, YouTube, https://www.youtube.com/watch?v=9Au1pjo8X70.

FOR KIAN AND HIS RAINBOW

195 "Dad, trust the police": "Kian Pir Falak's Mother About the Moment of Shooting at Their Car, Kian Said to Trust the Police This Time" (in Persian), *Hamshahri Online,* Nov. 19, 2022, https://www.hamshahrionline.ir/news/721096/ببینید-ادعاهای-مادر-کیان-پیرفلک-درباره-لحظه-تیراندازی-به-خودرو.
195 His father survived: "Kian Pir Falak's Father Discharged from Hospital After 60 Days," *Etemad Online,* Jan. 16, 2021, www.magiran.com/article/4377764.
196 This is what the regime: Roghayeh Rezaei, "Body Theft; Another Strange Phenomenon in the Islamic Republic" (in Persian), IranWire, Nov. 20, 2020, https://iranwire.com/fa/features/110111/جنازه‌دزدی-یک-پدیده-عجیب-دیگر-در-جمهوری-اسل-امی/.
196 She got several large: "Preservation of the Corpse of Kian Pir Falak with Ice at Home" (in Persian), Rouydad24, https://www.rouydad24.ir/fa/tags/137105/1/کیان-پیرفلک.
196 "They shouldn't say": Babak Dehghanpisheh, "The Killing of a 9-Year-Old Boy Further Ignites Iran's Anti-Government Protests," *Washington Post,* Nov. 18, 2022, www.washingtonpost.com/world/2022/11/18/iran-protests-izeh-kian-pirfalak/.

196 Then she read a poem: YouTube, www.youtube.com/watch?v=bIINR-UIElc.
196 "What is a supreme": IranWire, YouTube, Nov. 18, 2022, www.youtube.com/watch?v=Nt4iYXAn6xo.
196 State security forces: Ibid.
196 "We are a great nation": VOA, Nov. 18, 2022, www.youtube.com/watch?v=430aCAS5wdo.
197 In the days after Kian's death: @RadioFarda_, Twitter, Nov. 23, 2022, 8:55 a.m., x.com/RadioFarda_/status/1595415658174480386.
197 It reached as far: @jokuevara, Twitter, Nov. 22, 2022, 7:27 a.m., twitter.com/jokuevara/status/1595031225819090945?s=46.
197 Mah Monir used to be: "Mah Monir Moulairad, the Mother Who Has the Same Story: They Killed My Son, Kian," *BBC Persian*, June 16, 2023, www.bbc.com/persian/articles/cmjvl5zejg2o.
198 "My innocent child": Ibid.
198 On Kian's next birthday: "Pooya Moulai Rad, the Cousin of Kian Pir Falak's Mother, Was Killed by Direct Fire from Security Officers," Radio Farda, June 11, 2023, www.radiofarda.com/a/kian-pirfalak-s-relative-shot-to-dead-by-iran-s-security-forces/32454443.html.
198 "It was Kian's birthday": Ashkan Amini, Instagram, www.instagram.com/ashkanamini__?igsh=MWc4MHA2ZmI2YzF5dw==.
198 The security forces did not: "Mah Monir Moulairad, the Mother Who Has the Same Story."

MY PALATE'S BITTER WITH GRIEF'S AFTERTASTE

200 Many Iranians associate: Zainab Mahmood, "Iran's Safavid Dynasty," Asia Society, asiasociety.org/education/irans-safavid-dynasty.
200 But during the uprising: Maryam Dehkordi, "Javad Heydari: 40 Days of Confusion, Pressure, and Mourning," IranWire, Oct. 31, 2022, iranwire.com/en/politics/109197-javad-heydari-40-days-of-confusion-pressure-and-mourning/.
200 His sister Fatemeh: Joe Snell, ed., "How *The Post* Reported on Iran's Violence at Protester Funerals," *Washington Post*, video, posted May 24, 2023, YouTube, 2 min., 25 sec., https://www.youtube.com/watch?v=2md8EjMeW5s.
201 Iran's security apparatus: Amnesty International UK, "Iran: Families of Children Killed by Security Forces Facing 'Relentless Intimidation'—Report," press release, Dec. 12, 2022, www.amnesty.org.uk/press-releases/iran-families-children-killed-security-forces-facing-relentless-intimidation-report.
201 There's the funeral: Tabrizy et al., "When Protesters Were Killed in Iran."
202 To get an understanding of how funerals: Ibid.
202 Najafi's last message: Fereshteh Ghazi, "Who Was Hadis Najafi?," Radio Farda, Sept. 28, 2022, www.radiofarda.com/a/iran-protests-victims-hadisnajafi/32055773.html.

203 Telegram channel Mamlekate: @Mamlekate, "Mehdi Hazrati's family house arrest," Telegram, Dec. 15, 2022, t.me/mamlekate/75545.

203 Most of the estimated twelve million: "The Kurdish Population," Fondation-Institut Kurde de Paris, accessed Nov. 4, 2024, www.institutkurde.org/en/info/the-kurdish-population-1232551004.

203 There is also a Kurdish: *Iran: Human Rights Abuses Against the Kurdish Minority* (Amnesty International, 2008), 3, www.refworld.org/pdfid/489174f72.pdf.

203 In 1946, the oldest: Ibid., 4.

203 An estimated twenty: "Body of Historical Iranian Kurdish Leader's Son to Be Buried in Mahabad," Kurdistan24, July 14, 2022, www.kurdistan24.net/en/story/388943.

203 were publicly hanged: *Iran: Human Rights Abuses Against the Kurdish Minority*, 4.

203 These were instrumental: Abrahamian, *Iran Between Two Revolutions*, 257.

204 It lasted from March 1979: Franc Milburn, "Iranian Kurdish Militias: Terrorist-Insurgents, Ethno Freedom Fighters, or Knights on the Regional Chessboard?," *CTC Sentinel* 10, no. 5 (2017), ctc.westpoint.edu/iranian-kurdish-militias-terrorist-insurgents-ethno-freedom-fighters-or-knights-on-the-regional-chessboard/.

204 During the early days: *Iran: Human Rights Abuses Against the Kurdish Minority*, 4.

204 Following the KDPI's success: Milburn, "Iranian Kurdish Militias."

204 Many Kurdish villages: Christopher De Bellaigue, *In the Rose Garden of the Martyrs: A Memoir of Iran* (HarperCollins, 2005), 60.

204 Kurdish regions experience: *Iran: Human Rights Abuses Against the Kurdish Minority*, 2.

204 There's a term: Gordyaen Benyamin Jermayi, "The 'Ungrievable' Lives of Kurdish Women Kolbers," Kurdish Center for Studies, June 25, 2023, nlka.net/eng/the-ungrievable-lives-of-kurdish-women-kolbers/.

204 Many of these people: "259 Kolbers Killed and Injured in 2022," Kurdistan Press Agency, Jan. 3, 2023, kurdpa.net/fa/news/2023/01/5.

204 Some are women whose: Jermayi, "'Ungrievable' Lives of Kurdish Women Kolbers."

204 All of this is to bring: "259 Kolbers Killed and Injured in 2022."

204 Kurdpa, a Kurdish news agency: Ibid.

204 the Islamic Republic has resorted to: "Islamic Republic Steps Up Military Crackdown in Kurdish Cities," Iran International, Nov. 20, 2022, www.iranintl.com/en/202211207781.

206 People are heard: "Hengaw Statistical Report on the Killing of At Least 134 Kurdish Citizens During the Jina Revolution + PDF File," Hengaw Organization for Human Rights, March 11, 2023, hengaw.net/en/news/2023/03/hengaw

-statistical-report-on-the-killing-of-at-least-134-kurdish-citizens-during-the-jina-revolution-pdf-file.
206 Hengaw, a Kurdish human rights: @Hengaw_English, "footage of the moment of Burhan Eliasi's death, who was shot by government forces in Javanroud," Twitter, Dec. 31, 2022, twitter.com/Hengaw_English/status/1609126527618228225.
207 On November 15, Foad Mohammadi: "Iran Forces Kill 15 Civilians; Death Toll Reaches 98 in Kurdistan," Kurdistan Human Rights Network, Nov. 22, 2022, kurdistanhumanrights.org/en/news/2022/11/22/iran-forces-kill-15-civilians-death-toll-reaches-98-in-kurdistan/.
207 We verified a video: Ibid.
207 Days after Karami: "Details of the Killing of Borhan Karami in the Kamyaran Riots" (in Persian), *Hamshahri Online*, Nov. 22, 2022, جزئیات کشته شدن برهان کرمی در درگیری‌های کامیاران ؛ گلوله به سر او شلیک شد | ماموری در محل قتل برهان کرمی حضور داشت؟, www.hamshahrionline.ir.

FOR HANGED HEADS

208 The twenty-two-year-old: "Iran: Horrifying Execution of Young Protester Exposes Authorities' Cruelty and Risk of Further Bloodshed," Amnesty International, Dec. 8, 2022, www.amnesty.org/en/latest/news/2022/12/iran-horrifying-execution-of-young-protester-exposes-authorities-cruelty-and-risk-of-further-bloodshed/.
209 "Again, I missed": YouTube, www.youtube.com/watch?v=zIo9WhQCKLk.
209 Yet they brought: Aparat, www.aparat.com/v/9Qb6m.
210 in his case: "Iran Protests: 15 Minutes to Defend Yourself Against the Death Penalty," *BBC News*, Jan. 18, 2023, www.bbc.com/news/world-middle-east-64302726.
210 the twenty-three-year-old: "'We Want Everyone to Know Her Name': TikToker Hadis Najafi, 23, Shot Dead in Iran Protests," Sky News, Sept. 20, 2022, news.sky.com/story/we-want-everyone-to-know-her-name-hadis-najafi-the-23-year-old-tiktoker-shot-dead-in-iran-protests-12706404.
210 The security forces shot: VOA, YouTube, www.youtube.com/watch?app=desktop&v=9rPXngDlj7Q.
210 Kian, a karate: "Iran Protests: 15 Minutes to Defend Yourself Against the Death Penalty."
210 Seyyed Mohammad "Kumar" Hosseini: "Iran Hangs Two Men Accused of Killing Security Agent During Protests," Reuters, Jan. 7, 2023, www.reuters.com/world/middle-east/iran-hangs-two-men-alleged-crimes-committed-during-protests-judiciary-2023-01-07/.
210 There was no one to take: Pooya Stone, "Horrific Details of Torture and Execution of Detained Protesters in Iran's Prisons," Iran Focus, Aug. 25, 2023, iran

focus.com/life-in-iran/49906-details-of-torture-and-execution-of-detained-protesters-in-irans-last-year-nationwide-protest/.
211 Then, suddenly, the officials: Ibid.
211 He and his wife: Ibid.
211 After the executions: Fatemeh Jamalpour, "One-Year Anniversary of the Uprising and Pressure on the Families of Those Killed; The Government's Constant Fear of Litigation," Iran International, Sept. 17, 2023, www.iranintl.com/202309171181.
211 He performed the most peaceful: Ibid.
211 Kaveh, an ancient Iranian: Ganjoor, ganjoor.net/ferdousi/shahname/zahak/sh7.
211 Mr. Mashallah has: "Detention of Father of Executed Iranian Protester Sparks Concerns," Iran International, Oct. 16, 2023, www.iranintl.com/en/202310165506.
212 judiciary system asked: "5 Security Charges in Mashallah Karami's Indictment" (in Persian), Iran HRS, Dec. 20, 2023, https://iranhrs.org/ماشاالله-کرمی-در-کیفرخواست.
212 "Write for history": Ashkan Amini, Instagram, www.instagram.com/ashkanamini__?utm_source=ig_web_button_share_sheet&igsh=ZDNlZDcoMzIxNw==.
212 A group made up: "Iran: 1988 Mass Executions Evident Crimes Against Humanity," Human Right Watch, June 8, 2022, www.hrw.org/news/2022/06/08/iran-1988-mass-executions-evident-crimes-against-humanity.
212 Just a few days: "Those Who Should Be Executed Will Be Executed," Radio Farda, May 31, 2023, www.radiofarda.com/a/32436550.html.
212 "A candle burns": Instagram, www.instagram.com/mohammadghobadlou.20?utm_source=ig_web_button_share_sheet&igsh=ZDNlZDcoMzIxNw==.
212 "Blue-blooded men": Ibid.
213 "You were young": Instagram, www.instagram.com/p/C2awFf4xSIIS4CBjgBDS3ANodncSNxUWsXXHyso/?utm_source=ig_web_copy_link.
214 "Do you know exactly when": Instagram, www.instagram.com/mohammadghobadlou.20?utm_source=ig_web_button_share_sheet&igsh=ZDNlZDcoMzIxNw==.
214 "At my grave": VOA, YouTube, www.youtube.com/watch?v=nsqqtfoHoXE.

HOW SWEET THOSE DAYS WHEN WE WERE STILL

218 She remembers the day: Muhammad Sahimi, "The Hostage Crisis, 30 Years On," *Frontline*, Tehran Bureau, PBS, Nov. 3, 2009, www.pbs.org/wgbh/pages/frontline/tehranbureau/2009/11/30-years-after-the-hostage-crisis.html.
219 when the Islamic Republic publicly hanged: "Iran: Horrifying Execution of Young Protester Exposes Authorities' Cruelty and Risk of Further Bloodshed."

219 and Majidreza Rahnavard: "Iran: Public Execution of Majidreza Rahnavard Exposes Authorities' Revenge Killings," Amnesty International, Dec. 12, 2022, www.amnesty.org/en/latest/news/2022/12/iran-public-execution-of-majidreza-rahnavard-exposes-authorities-revenge-killings/.

219 These executions: Ghazal Golshiri, "Iran's Public Executions Terrorize Protesters," *Le Monde,* Dec. 18, 2022, www.lemonde.fr/en/international/article/2022/12/18/in-iran-public-executions-to-terrorize-protesters-and-quell-the-revolt_6008162_4.html.

219 sham trials: "Iran: Horrifying Execution of Young Protester Exposes Authorities' Cruelty and Risk of Further Bloodshed."

219 confessed under torture: "Iran: Public Execution of Majidreza Rahnavard Exposes Authorities' Revenge Killings."

FOR THE WOMEN WHO NEVER EXPRESS REGRET

221 "Enduring prison is like": Mohamadhosein Ajorloo, Instagram, www.instagram.com/p/CpVEqQqNrkC/?img_index=1.

222 "I'm waiting for you": Ibid.

222 We have a Journalists' Day: "Journalists' Day in Iran in the Shadow of Imprisoned Journalists," *BBC Persian,* Aug. 8, 2023, www.bbc.com/persian/articles/cye5jxk17nxo.

222 Its title was "Your Absence, Your Empty Places": *Shargh,* YouTube, www.youtube.com/watch?app=desktop&v=CRRN0xwG0NY.

223 Everyone demanded their trials: "At the Same Time as the Wave of Requests for an Open Court, Nilofar Hamedi and Elaheh Mohammadi Met with Their Chosen Lawyers for the First Time," *BBC Persian,* May 28, 2023, www.bbc.com/persian/articles/cxxy2014j7yo.

223 They didn't let: Mohamadhosein Ajorloo, Instagram, www.instagram.com/p/CvHd12nNAQs/.

223 Niloofar responded: Mohamadhosein Ajorloo, Instagram, www.instagram.com/p/Cs8P2jJuRsv/.

224 "Respect and solidarity": Angelina Jolie, Instagram, www.instagram.com/p/CvJAkoFJ-Ns/.

224 "In the Name of the Pen": "Elaheh Mohammadi in Court: I Am Proud That I Stayed with the People to Be Their Voice," Radio Farda, July 26, 2023, www.radiofarda.com/a/the-final-session-of-Elaheh-mohammadi-court-was-held/32521173.html.

224 After fourteen months: "Two Iranian Journalists Jailed on Protest Charges Temporarily Released—State Media," Reuters, Jan. 14, 2024, www.reuters.com/world/middle-east/two-iranian-journalists-jailed-protest-charges-temporarily-released-state-media-2024-01-14/.

THE ROSES HAVE ALL GONE

226 In February 2023, Khamenei reportedly ordered: Leila Fadel and John Helton, "Despite Khamenei's Amnesty, Most Protesters in Iran Won't Go Free, Advocate Says," NPR, Feb. 14, 2023, www.npr.org/2023/02/14/1156115697/iran-amnesty-protests-arrests-khamenei.

226 In June, Iranian media: "Iranian Authorities Summoning and Re-Arresting Activists and Protesters," Human Rights Watch, June 26, 2023, www.hrw.org/blog-feed/iranian-society-under-crackdown.

226 On August 16: "Iran: Mass Arrests of Women's Rights Defenders," Human Rights Watch, Aug. 19, 2023, www.hrw.org/news/2023/08/19/iran-mass-arrests-womens-rights-defenders.

227 Then, on September 5: "Security Forces Arrest Uncle of Jina Mahsa Amini in Saqqez," Kurdistan Human Rights Network, Sept. 5, 2023, kurdistanhumanrights.org/en/news/2023/09/05/security-forces-arrest-uncle-of-jina-mahsa-amini-in-saqqez/.

227 Days later, security forces summoned: "Jina Mahsa Amini's Father Threatened for Family's Commemoration Plans," Kurdistan Human Rights Network, Sept. 13, 2023, kurdistanhumanrights.org/en/news/2023/09/13/jina-mahsa-aminis-father-threatened-for-familys-commemoration-plans/.

227 The family's lawyer: "Iran: Harassment, Reprisals, Continue for Mahsa Amini Family," *UN News*, Sept. 14, 2023, news.un.org/en/story/2023/09/1140777.

227 I spoke with Tara Sepehri Far: "About: People: Tara Sepehri Far," Human Rights Watch, accessed Oct. 21, 2023, www.hrw.org/about/people/tara-sepehri-far.

228 Her revolutionary action: Nilo Tabrizy, "Their Loved Ones Were Killed in Iran's Uprising. Then the State Came for Them," *Washington Post*, Sept. 15, 2023, www.washingtonpost.com/world/2023/09/15/iran-anniversary-protests-mahsa-amini/.

229 Their family home was surveilled: @heydari_____fatemeh, "They came again today, no matter how much my mother insisted, what permission and order did you have to enter my house?!," Instagram, Nov. 24, 2022, www.instagram.com/p/ClVZTwxt3E_/?igshid=MzRlODBiNWFlZA%3D%3D.

229 Even her two-year-old: @heydari_____fatemeh, "Did you arrest my two year old niece to change Javad's headstone for you?," Instagram, April 5, 2023, www.instagram.com/p/CqqL9FTNqoS/?igshid=MzRlODBiNWFlZA%3D%3D.

229 Four family members: @fatemehheydari8, "Now his wife, who is a nurse, was fired and told: Why did Javad participate in the protests?," Twitter, Aug. 29, 2023, twitter.com/fatemehheydari8/status/1696442111577530853.

230 I didn't quite get: "Iran's Path Forward: Civil Society's Lessons Learned on the Anniversary of Mahsa Amini's Killing," Center for Strategic & International Studies, YouTube, Sept. 14, 2023, www.youtube.com/watch?v=6jRGzmXDhkI.

230 NUFDI even cites: "Our Mission," National Union for Democracy in Iran, nufdiran.org/mission-and-vision/.
230 "The difference between Iran": "Iran's Path Forward: Civil Society's Lessons Learned on the Anniversary of Mahsa Amini's Killing," Center for Strategic & International Studies, YouTube, Sept. 14, 2023, 54:08, www.youtube.com/watch?v=6jRGzmXDhkI.
230 an interesting disconnect from protesters: Maryam Sinaee, "Over 60% of Iranians Want Transition from Islamic Republic," Iran International, April 1, 2022, www.iranintl.com/en/202204015794.
231 "Iranians, you know": "Iran's Path Forward," at 54:08[1/n]27.
231 death of his brother Azad: "Mahabad; A Protester Was Killed by the Repressive Forces," Kurdistan Press Agency, Nov. 18, 2022, kurdpa.net/en/news/mahabad-a-protester-was-killed-by-the-repressive-forces.
233 Hengaw, a local: "Ramin Fatehi Died Under Torture by the Authorities," Hengaw Organization for Human Rights, Oct. 22, 2022, hengaw.net/en/news/ramin-fatehi-died-under-torture-by-the-authorities.

GOODBYE, MY BELOVED HOMELAND

234 "What do I want": Sherko Bekas, delkaveh.blogfa.com/post/456.
236 The Ministry of Culture: "These Female Actresses Banned from Playing."
237 "I will not wear": "Taraneh Alidoosti: Blood Is Still Dripping from That Forced Scarf You Put on Our Head" (in Persian), IranWire, Oct. 28, 2023, https://iranwire.com/fa/news-1/121988-از-آن-روسری-زوری-که-سرمان-کردید-هنوز-خون-میچکد-ترانه-علیدوستی/.
237 Shortly after I left: Somayeh Malekian, "Imprisoned Iranian Activist Hospitalized as Hunger Strike Reaches 13th Day, Lawyer Says," ABC News, Sept. 12, 2023, abcnews.go.com/International/imprisoned-iranian-activist-hospitalized-hunger-strike-reaches-13th/story?id=103081762.
237 In a hunger strike: Dr. Mehbod Ebrahimi, "How Long Can You Survive a Hunger Strike?," BBC Persian, Jan. 3, 2017, www.bbc.com/persian/science-38498117.
237 Bahareh was imprisoned: "Bahareh Hedayat's Nine-and-a-Half-Year Sentence Was Confirmed in the Appeals Court," BBC Persian, Jan. 24, 2010, www.bbc.com/persian/iran/2010/07/100724_l17_hedayat_verdict.
237 Bahareh could not: "Bahareh Hedayat Was Sentenced to Four Years in Prison for Protesting the Destruction of the Ukrainian Plane," BBC Persian, Jan. 25, 2020, www.bbc.com/persian/iran-53537120.
238 The judiciary system sentenced her: Ibid.
238 "I strongly request": "Bahareh Hedayat, a Political Prisoner, Ended Her Hunger Strike After 13 Days" (in Persian), Iran International, Sept. 13, 2023, www.iranintl.com/202309135365.

WE WAIT FOR LIGHT AND DARKNESS REIGNS

239 A year after the protests: "Iran: New Hijab Law Adds Restrictions and Punishments," Human Rights Watch, Oct. 14, 2024, www.hrw.org/news/2024/10/14/iran-new-hijab-law-adds-restrictions-and-punishments.

239 The bill passed: "Parliament Passes New 'Hijab and Chastity' Bill," *Iran Primer*, United States Institute of Peace, Sept. 25, 2023, iranprimer.usip.org/blog/2023/sep/25/parliament-passes-new-%E2%80%9Chijab-and-chastity%E2%80%9D-bill.

239 This law contains: "Iran: New Hijab Law Adds Restrictions and Punishments."

239 Repeat offenders: Jiyar Gol, "Iran Pauses Controversial New Dress Code Law," BBC, Dec. 16, 2024, www.bbc.com/news/articles/c0mv83m4z7vo.

239 Even worse, other punishments: Center for Human Rights in Iran, "Iran Wages War Against Women with Draconian New Hijab Law," press release, Dec. 13, 2024, iranhumanrights.org/2024/12/iran-wages-war-against-women-with-draconian-new-hijab-law/.

240 Its Orwellian arm: "Iran: New Hijab Law Adds Restrictions and Punishments."

240 One article of the law: Center for Human Rights in Iran, "Iran Wages War Against Women with Draconian New Hijab Law."

240 during his campaign: "Masoud Pezeshkian's Frank Statements About the Hijab" (in Persian), *Donya-e Eqtesad*, June 21, 2024, اظهارات صریح مسعود پزشکیان درباره حجاب/ قطعا با زور نخواهیم توانست حجاب را بر سر زنان بپوشانیم+ فیلم, www.donya-e-eqtesad.com.

240 even days before: Masoud Pezeshkian (@drpezeshkian), X, Dec. 2, 2024, 2:21 p.m., x.com/drpezeshkian/status/1863664770882195608.

240 I verified the videos: Nilo Tabrizy, "Iranian Student Arrested in Her Underwear Is Latest Symbol in Fight for Rights," *Washington Post*, Nov. 15, 2024, www.washingtonpost.com/world/2024/11/15/iran-woman-underwear-arrest/.

241 The university's public: Seyed Amir Mahjob (@s_amirmahjob), X, Nov. 2, 2024, 11:31 a.m., x.com/s_amirmahjob/status/1852735195163582908.

241 A government spokesperson: "The Government Spokesperson in a Conversation with the Compatriot: A Girl's Subject Is Not Science and Security Research" (in Persian), *Hammihan Online*, Nov. 5, 2024, سخنگوی دولت در گفت‌وگو با همیمن: موضوع دختر علوم و تحقیقات امنیتی نیست, www.hammihanonline.ir.

241 Parastoo Ahmadi sang: Parastoo Ahmadi, YouTube, Dec. 11, 2024, www.youtube.com/watch?v=oYcaDHEnhbU.

242 Unsurprisingly, she was arrested: Andrea Tode Jimenez, "Iranian Singer Parastoo Ahmadi Released from Jail After Performing Without a Hijab," *International Business Times*, Dec. 18, 2024, www.ibtimes.co.uk/defiant-iranian-singer-parastoo-ahmadi-released-jail-after-performing-online-without-hijab-1729579.

242 "I am Parastoo": Parastoo Ahmadi, YouTube, Dec. 11, 2024, www.youtube.com/watch?v=oYcaDHEnhbU.

FOR RESISTANCE AND HOPE

244 There weren't any: Elnaz Mohammadi (@elnazmohammadii8), Instagram, May 2, 2023, www.instagram.com/p/CrvZOaMt6Rj/?igsh=MXVoZzU3NmdlZmNjNw==.

244 The judiciary system eventually had to give in: "Narges Mohammadi Once Again Left Evin Prison for the Hospital Without Compulsory Hijab," Iran International, Nov. 21, 2023, www.iranintl.com/202311211585.

244 "Yesterday I saw": Nooshin Jafari, Instagram, www.instagram.com/nooshinjafari?utm_source=ig_web_button_share_sheet&igsh=ZDNlZDcoMzIxNw==.

245 Elnaz, Elaheh Mohammadi's twin: Elnaz Mohammadi (@elnazmohammadii8), Instagram, Oct. 28, 2023, www.instagram.com/p/Cy8oXJONxcc/?igsh=dXJzZTZvOXN2and4.

245 Elnaz reflected on the experience: Ibid.

246 Elnaz ended her day: Elnaz Mohammadi (@elnazmohammadii8), Instagram, Oct. 28, 2023, www.instagram.com/p/Cy8oXJONxcc/?img_index=1.

246 Elnaz told Niloofar: Elnaz Mohammadi (@elnazmohammadii8), Instagram, Oct. 28, 2023, www.instagram.com/p/Cy8oXJONxcc/?igsh=dXJzZTZvOXN2and4.

246 Less than twenty-four hours later: Somayeh Malekian, "Hijab Judiciary Case Opened Against 2 Iranian Journalists 1 Day After Their Temporary Release," ABC News, Jan. 15, 2024, abcnews.go.com/International/hijab-judiciary-case-opened-2-iranian-journalists-day-after-release/story?id=106374187.

247 There's no better way: Narges Mohammadi (@narges_mohamadi_51), "Trial of the Oppressors: Evin's Symbolic Stand Against Injustice," Instagram, Dec. 30, 2023, www.instagram.com/p/C1eSoYNK4Ar/?igsh=MThrbTJ4eXp5aXB1eg%3D%3D.

247 "The name Mohsen": "Iran: Horrifying Execution of Young Protester Exposes Authorities' Cruelty and Further Risk of Bloodshed."

247 "The judges who had issued": "Female Political Prisoners Denounce Iran Officials During Prison Visit," Iran International, Dec. 30, 2023, www.iranintl.com/en/202312307601.

248 "Stop issuing": Ibid.

249 "Long live resistance": Narges Mohammadi (@narges_mohamadi_51), "The visit of authorities to the Evin prison," Instagram, Dec. 30, 2023, www.instagram.com/p/C1ee2VAKnPU/?igsh=ZWpieTIycTd4YmMy.

INDEX

abortion rights, 92, 96
actors, female, 25
ADHD medication, 175
Aeli, Safa (Jîna's uncle), 227
Afghanistan, 41, 222
Agha-Soltan, Neda, 141
agricultural reforms, 91
Ahmadi, Parastoo, 241–42
Ahmadinejad, Mahmoud, xii, 140
Ahvaz (town), 19, 123, 138–39
Aichi cemetery, Saqqez, 3
airports, hijab and, 142
Ajei, Gholam Hossein Mohseni, 212
Akbari, Mina (journalist), 37–38, 238, 253
Akbari, Reza H., 40, 201–2, 206–7, 228
Albania, 69, 70
Albright, Madeleine, 91
Algiers Agreement (1975), 115
Ali, Amir, 28

Ali, Bahareh, 28
Alidoosti, Hana, 38
Alidoosti, Taraneh, 36–38, 236–37
Alipour, Reza, 138
Al Jazeera, 150, 164
Allameh Tabataba'i University, 141, 142
Amaken Police, 145, 220
Amanpour, Christiane, 125
ambulances, 17, 53–56
American Christian missionaries, 84
Amini, Amjad (Jîna's father), 3–4, 30–31, 227
Amini, Ashkan (Jîna's brother), 198, 212
Amini, Mahsa Jîna
 anniversary of death, 226, 233, 235, 238
 death and funeral of, ix–xii, xiv, 3–4, 8, 10–12, 24, 30–32, 34, 40–41, 44–45, 64, 180, 191, 200, 202, 227, 230, 233, 244

Amini, Mahsa Jina *(continued)*
　Kurdish minority and, xn, 38, 40
　movement begun by, 10–11, 15, 36, 173
　photos of life of, 30–31
Amir Bakery, Canada, 167
Amir Kabir University of Technology
　(Tehran Polytechnic), 1, 218
Amir (lawyer), 181–82, 185, 234–35
Amiry, Suad, 170
Amnesty International, 31
Amouzad, Mohammad-Reza, 247–49
Andika County, 121
Anglo-Persian Oil, 108
Anglo-Persian War (1856–57), 78
Anna Karenina (Tolstoy), 137
"Another Birth" (Farrokhzad), 105–6
Ansarifar, Farzad, 163
anti-hijab activists, prostitution charges, 240
Arab ethnic groups, 47
Arab invasion of Iran, xii
Aram, Siamak, 230
Armenia, 78
Askarizadeh, Raha, 176
Atatürk, Mustafa Kemal, 86–87
athletics, 121–22, 127–29
Atlantic Council, 240
Azadi Stadium, ban on women, 149–51, 221
Azeri ethnic minority, 9, 12, 42, 60, 95, 101, 112–14, 231

Babol Noshirvani University of
　Technology, 197
Badawi, Zeinab, 125
Bahai'i religion, 227, 245
Bahareh (Fatemeh's friend), 237–38
Bahman (bookstore owner), 27
Bajoghli, Narges, 201
Bakhtiari, Bibi Maryam, 84–86, 89, 190, 198
Bakhtiari, Hossein Qoli Khan, 84

Bakhtiari, Masoud, 121
Bakhtiari, Sardar Asad, 86
Bakhtiari tribe, 65, 84–86, 89, 98–99, 108–9, 195–99
Baluchestan, 41–42, 61, 233
Baluchi ethnic minority, 39, 41–46, 57–61, 245
Bamdad bookstore, 136–37
Bandar-e Mahshahr (city), 47
bank concession of 1872, 79
Bank Sepah, 72
Baradari, Alam (Nilo's grandmother), 102–5, 115
Baraheni, Reza, xi
"Baraye" (Hajipour), ix, xii–xiii, 26–27
Barbod, 147
Basij (paramilitary unit), 8, 21–22, 24, 55, 56, 66, 205, 207, 220, 240–41
Basquiat, Jean-Michel, 104
Bayani, Niloufar, 181, 244–46
BBC, 6, 27, 125, 178
BBC Persian, 10, 147, 170–76
BBC World Service, 171
Beauvoir, Simone de, 137
Beheshte Sakineh cemetery, 202–3, 210
Behnoush (sex worker), 148–49
Behzadi, Mr. (interrogator), 178–80
Bekas, Sherko, 4, 35–36, 234
Bellingcat, 31–32
Benjamin, Daniel, 69–70
Bing search engine, 71
Bisheh Waterfall, 139
Black Lives Matter protests, 32, 186–87
Bloody Friday incident, 57
Bolton, John, 70
Boukan (city), 203
Bozorgmehr (Fatemeh's friend), 176
Britain (UK), 112–13, 115
　coup of 1953 and, 90–91
　oil and, 90, 108
　Persian concessions to, 78–83
　Revolution of 1979 and, 94

tobacco concession and, 79–80
WW II occupation by, 89
British MI6, 90
Browne, Malachy, 32
"By the Time You Read This, I Might Be in Jail" (Fatemeh), 14

Canada, 113–16, 125–26, 129–31, 133
   Flight 752 and, 167, 173
Carter, Jimmy, 94–95, 116
Caucasian provinces, 78
censorship, 8, 164, 171–72
   banned books, 136
   banned films, 37
Center for Human Rights in Iran, 47
Central Al-Khalil Mosque, 59
Central Intelligence Agency (CIA), 90
Chabahar (city), 43–44
Chaharlang, Ali Qoli Khan, 84–85
Chamran University, 138
Chao, Elaine, 70
Chelcheragh magazine, 136–38
child marriage, 5, 86, 107, 109
children's citizenship, 144
children's rights activists, 183
Chile, 32
China, 32
Cinema Organization, 236
citizen journalists, 53, 71, 140–41, 203
civil disobedience, 247
CNN, 63
Colombia, 32
Communists, 92–93
Constitutional Revolution (1905–11), 83–87, 89, 190
Constitution of 1906, 85
construction contracts, 146–47
coronavirus pandemic, 174, 180
corruption, 48, 78, 83, 145–46
Council of the Islamic Revolution, 146
counterterrorism, 69
coup of 1921, 86

coup of 1953, 90–92
currency devaluations, 220
Curzon, Lord, 79

"Daf" (Baraheni), xi
dancing, 38–39
Daneshvar, Habib, 213–14
Darvishpour, Mehrdad, 91
death penalty, 24, 59, 174
"'Death to the Dictator': What Is Iran's Future?" (Fatemeh), 165
Dehghanpisheh, Babak, 57
Democratic National Committee (DNC), 70
diaspora, 9, 68–73, 100, 141, 230–31
Divar (website), 173–74
divorce, women's right to, 86, 99
Doctors Without Borders, 149
Dolatabadi, Sedigeh, 83, 190
Dolatshahi, Mehrangiz, 92
domestic violence, 99, 107, 139
drug addiction, 148–49
Dubai, 116, 131, 220

Ebrahimzade, Farzaneh, 191
Ebtehaj, Hushang, 182–83, 225
economy, 27
   hardships and, 48, 70, 173–74
   IRGC control over, 146–47
   late nineteenth and early twentieth century, 78–79
   protests of 2017 and, 158
   protests of 2019 and, 162
   White Revolution reforms and, 91
education
   Reza Shah and, 86
   White Revolution and, 91
   women and girls and, 84, 86, 89, 92, 96, 139–140
Eftekhari, Mojgan (mother of Jina), 3, 238
Egypt, 94

elections, 136
	of 2009, 140–41
	of 2013, 220
	of 2020, 25
	of 2021, 155–56
Elyasi, Borhan, 206
employment and jobs, 174, 229
	restrictions on women's, 139–40
Engelbrecht, Cora, 44
Enlightenment, 78
environmental activists, 181
Eskandari, Mohtaram, 83–84
Esmaeilion, Hamed, 173
Espinas Palace Hotel, 27, 182
Estrabadi, Bibi Khanum, 84
Etemad (newspaper), 66
ethnic minorities, 40–43, 47, 203–5, 230–31
Eureka (film), 37
Evin Court, 161
Evin Prison, 29, 34–35, 38, 54, 150, 176, 181, 185, 237, 243–49
eyewitness testimony, 16, 31–32, 44–47, 54–55, 57–61, 66, 72–73, 188, 206–7, 209, 219, 240

Facebook, 7, 141, 147, 150, 176
family laws
	One Million Campaign of 2006, 142
	White Revolution and, 92
family members of murdered protesters, 227–29, 232
Family Protection Law (1968), 96, 98
FARAJA (national police), 205
	Special Unit, 205
Faraz Daily, 171
Farhad (wedding groom), 145
Farham (Fatemeh's nephew), 236
Fariba (Fatemeh's aunt), 123
Farrokhzad, Forough, 105–6, 157
Fars Bulletin (IRGC newsletter), 48
Fars shop strike of 2022, 48

Fatehi, Ramin, 233
Fatehi, Ramtin, 232–33
Fazli, Rahmani, 162
feminism, 10, 13, 183–84, 190–91. *See also* women's rights
Ferdowsi, xi–xii
films, 136, 157, 187–88
	banned, 37
Firouz, Dayi (Nilo's great uncle), 102
forced marriage, 107, 139
Foruhar, Leila, 121
France, 93, 94
freedom of speech, 136
fuel delivery, 43
fuel prices, 162–63
funerals and memorials, 64–65, 201–7, 227–28, 229

Garamendi, John, 70
García Márquez, Gabriel, 136
gender inequality, 5, 119, 121–23, 126, 128, 130–31, 136, 139–40, 161
gender segregation, xv, 86, 96
	universities and, 140, 142–43
	weddings and, 144–45
	women's rights protests and, 86
geo-locating, 44, 71–72
Germany, 86, 220, 232–33
Ghaemi, Hadi, 47, 57
Ghavami, Ghoncheh, 151
Ghobadlou, Mohammad, 212–14
Gholian, Sepideh, 248–49
Ghotbi, Mr., 163
Ghotbzadeh, Sadegh, 94
Gilan province, 54
Girls of Enghelab Street, 20, 67
Giuliani, Rudy, 70
Godar Café, 67
Golden Age, 200
Golestan, Hengameh, 97
Google, 71
Googoosh, 121

gozinesh (allegiance to Islam and Shia concepts), 42–44
Green Movement of 2009, 140–41, 158, 237
Guadeloupe Conference (1979), 94

Haalvsh (human rights organization), 45, 58, 60–61
Haar, Rohini, 54
Hafez, xi
hair cutting, 7, 228
Hajhosseinof, Azia, (Nilo's great-grandmother), 80–82
Hajhosseinof, Taghi (Daneshpouy; Nilo's great-grandfather), 80–82
Hajipour, Shervin, ix, xii–xiii, 26
Halparke (traditional dance), 30
Hamedi, Niloofar, x, 30, 34–36, 171–72, 221–25, 243–44, 246
Hamid, Molavi Abdul, 44
Ham-Mihan (newspaper), 3, 241
Handmaid's Tale, The (Atwood), 35
  TV series, 151
Hanieh (homeless mother), 149
Havel, Václav, 145
Hazrati, Mehdi, 203
Health and Knowledge Corps, 91
health care, 53–54, 56, 91
health care workers, 56, 59–60
Hengameh Golestan: Witness 1979 (exhibition), 97
Hengaw (human rights group), 206, 233
Herasat police branch, 142–43
Herat, 78
Herndon, Astead, 187
Heydari, Fatemeh, 200, 227–29
Heydari, Javad, 200, 227–28
Heydarian, Javad, 163
hijab, Islamic Republic and, ix, xiv–xv, 23–24, 26, 36–37, 62, 86, 120, 130, 141–42, 160, 173, 176, 236–37, 241, 244

black veil, 122–23
imposition of, 1981, 20, 86, 96–98
maghnaeh, 120, 122, 130, 143
makeup, 142–43
nail polish and, 142–43
new law of 2024 on, 239–40
protests of 1979 vs., 97–98
protests of 2022 vs. (*see* Woman, Life, Freedom protests)
sunglasses and, 142
hijab, pre-1979
Mohammad Reza Shah and, 89–90
Reza Shah and, 86–87
Kashf-e hijab (unveiling) law (1936), 87
HIV, 149
Hoda (Fatemeh's friend), 222
honor killings, 139
Hosein, Mohamad (husband of Niloofar Hamedi), 35–36, 221–23
hospitals, 51, 58
Hosseini, Seyyed Mohammad "Kumar," 210–12
Hosseinpouri, Azad, 229, 231–32
Hosseinpouri, Hiwa, 229–33
House Resolution 100, 70
human rights abuses, 16, 29, 32, 70
human rights activists, 155, 174, 204, 206
human rights organizations, 31–32, 45, 57
Human Rights Watch, 31, 227, 229, 241
hunger strikes, 237–38, 244
Hussein, Saddam, 69, 115–16, 146

I Am Taraneh, 15 Years Old (film), 37
"If within my poems" (Bekas), 35–36
Ilam province, 203
Imam Khomeini International Airport
  Flight 752 shot down, 167
  IRGC and, 146–47
India, 79
inflation, 27, 174–75, 220

Instagram, x, xii, xiii, 36, 54, 63, 65, 67, 163, 172, 191, 197–99, 202, 210, 212, 215, 218, 224, 238, 244–45
Institute for War and Peace Reporting, 40, 201
intellectuals, crackdown on, 136
internalized authoritarianism, 69
international human rights law, 53
internet, 7–8, 46, 54, 72, 162–64
Iran, Islamic Republic of. *See also* Persia; Revolution of 1979
   contacting for comment on investigative reports, 32–33
   diaspora and, 68–69
   founding of, 8, 18, 20, 93, 97–98
   hijab as cornerstone of, 97–98
   women athletes and, 109
Iran Human Rights Documentation Center (IHRDC), 41, 202, 206–7
Iranian Americans, 131–32
Iranian Canadians, 167
Iranian Ministry of Communications, 140
Iranian Ministry of Culture and Islamic Guidance, 141, 236–37
Iranian Ministry of Housing and Urban Development, 43
Iranian Ministry of Intelligence, 6, 11–14, 34, 55, 136, 143, 178–85, 213, 233
Iranian national youth karate team, 210
Iranian Parliament
   blocks oil concessions to USSR and Britain, 1951, 90
   closure of 1908–9, 85–86
   created in 1906, 85
   fuel price increases and, 162–63
   hijab code of 2023, 239–40
   One Million Campaign and, 142
   women elected to, 1963, 92
Iranian Permanent Mission to the United Nations, 32–33
Iranian students studying abroad, 92
Iranian Supreme Council of Economic Coordination, 163
Iranian Supreme Court, 210, 212–13
Iranian Supreme National Security Council, 173
Iran-Iraq War (1980–88), 42, 49, 64, 69, 115–17, 140, 144, 146, 212
Iran nuclear deal, 70, 217, 220
Iraq, 69, 70, 115–16, 146, 166–67, 204
Iraqi Kurds, 4
IRGC Intelligence Organization, 34, 143, 171, 181, 213
IRGC Salman Corps, 59
Isfahan (city), 85
   protests of 1891 and, 80
   protests of 2022, 212
Isfahani, Khosro, 240
Islam, xii, 13, 23
   Bakhtiaris and, 197 hijab and, 143
Islamic Azad University, 141
Islamic clerics, 93
Islamic religious groups, 84
Islamic Republic News Agency (IRNA), 140, 222
Islamic Revolutionary Court, 54
Islamic Revolutionary Guard Corps (IRGC), x–xi, 8, 14, 21–22, 24, 27–28, 72
   Baluchi province and, 42–43, 59
   corruption and, 145–47
   crackdown of 2000 and, 136
   established in 1979, 146
   gozinesh requirement and, 42
   hijab enforcement and, 142
   Iran-Iraq War and, 146
   Kurds and, 204
   as obstacle to free future of Iran, 147
   protests of 2017 and, 158
   protests of 2019 by, 47
   protests of 2022 and, 202, 205–6
   satellite TV dishes attacked by, 141

sexual harassment by, 181
shadow state, 146–47
shopkeepers strike of 2022 and, 48
Soleimani assassination and, 166, 172–73
Taraneh Alidoosti arrested by, 38
Ukraine International Airlines Flight shot down by, 32, 165, 173
violence vs. protesters by, 33, 47, 51–52, 57, 202, 205–6
Zahedan arrests of 2023 and, 59–60
Zahedan protests of 1994 and, 43
Islamic schools, 90
Islamic Students' News Agency (ISNA), 141–42, 144, 155–56
Islamists, 89–90
  seize power in 1979, 92–96
  women's right retracted by, 96
Ismay, John, 46
Israel, 170
Istanbul, 171, 235
Istanbul (Pamuk), 182
Izeh (city), 195

Jafari, Nooshin, 244–45
Jamalpour, Bijan, 184
Jamalpour, Ehsan (Fatemeh's brother), 121, 138–39, 144
Jamalpour, Fatemeh
  arrest and hunger strike of Bahareh and, 237–38
  arrest of, at Azadi Stadium, 149–50
  arrest of as protests of 2022, 14–15
  awards, 147, 171
  Bakhtiari background of, 84
  banned from producing content in 2021, 181
  bond with Nilo and, 154–56
  camping trip in Lorestan as student, 138–39
  challenges of being journalist in Iran and, 155–56

childhood and early life of, 117–24
childhood poverty and, 175
collaborates with Nilo during protests, 6–9, 14–15, 17–18
decides to become journalist, 135
education at Chamran University, 138, 140
education in journalism, at Allameh Tabataba'i University, 141–42
education in journalism, at Northwestern University, 152
education as young girl, 120–21
Evin Prison and, 29
executions of protesters and, 208–15
family stories and, 107–8
father and, 11, 119–20, 122, 137–39
father's cancer and return to Tehran of 2021, 6, 8, 153, 176–80, 185
first apartment in Tehran, 144
first article published, 137
impact of revolution on parents and, 109–10
interrogation of, by Ministry of Intelligence, 6, 8–9, 11–14, 132, 161, 178–85
job as reporter at ISNA Tehran, 141–42
job as reporter at *Shargh,* 144–50
Khatami reforms of 1997–2000 and, 135–38
Killing of Kian Pir Falak and, 195–99
lawyer Amir Raisan and, 213
leaves Iran for London in 2020, and writes for *BBC Persian,* 170–76
leaves Iran in 2023, 234–36
Mah Monir on Instagram with, 198
maternal grandfather and, 108, 109, 121
meets Nilo in person, 152–53
menstruation and, 123–24
mother, 108–9, 118–24, 137–38, 175
n+1 story with Nilo and, 164–66

302 · Index

Jamalpour, Fatemeh *(continued)*
  Nilo's love for Persian language and, 157
  Paris Review story with Nilo and, 154–55
  paternal grandfather, 108–9, 121
  protests of 2009 vs. fraud and morality police and, 140–41
  protests of 2017 and arrest of, 158–61
  protests of 2019 and threat of arrest warrant, 162–65
  protests of 2022 and, ix–xv, 3–5, 10–11, 19–28, 34, 48–52, 153–55, 195–99
  reading as teen and, 137
  reports on executions of protesters in 2022, 208–9
  reports on IRGC corruption, 145–46
  sexual abuse accusation vs. Khosravi and, 171
  Soleimani assassination and, 166
  stopped at airport by IRGC for improper hijab, 138
  teenage years and repression of parents, 138
  trials of Nilofar and Elaheh and, 221–25, 243–49
  visits US to study journalism, 153
  writes for *Los Angeles Times*, 164–65
Jamalpour, Hossein (Fatemeh's brother), 121–22
Jamalpour, Mohamed Mehdi (Fatemeh's brother), 158
Jam'iyat-e Nesvan-e Vatankhah (Society of Patriotic Women), 83–84
Japan, 65
Javanrud (city), 205–7
Jhaveri, Ishaan, 44, 54
"Jîna" (song), 22
Johns Hopkins University, 201
Jolie, Angelina, 65, 223, 224
journalists
  arrests of, 29–30
  death of parents while abroad or in prison, 176
  female, 136, 222
  objectivity vs. "speaking nearby" and, 186–89
  repression of, 173
  in U.S. vs. Iran and, 155–56
Journalists' Day, 222
judiciary system, 96, 145
  women judges abolished, 96
Jundallah (armed group), 42–43

Kafi, Sheikh Ahmad, 201
Kahrizak Morgue, 63
Kamyaran killings of 2022, 207
Karaj protests of 2022, 8, 202–3, 210
Karami, Borhan, 207
Karami, Mohammad Mehdi "Kian," 210–11, 249
Kashani, Ayatollah, 90
Kashani, Sepideh, 245
Kasra Hospital, ix–x
Kaveh (ancient Iranian hero), 211
Kayhan newspaper, 156
Kermanshah province 126, 203
Khadijeh (sex worker), 148–49
Khamenei, Ayatollah Ali, Supreme Leader, 37, 118–19, 135–36, 156
  amnesty of 2023 and, 226
  Khatami reforms ended by, 136
  protests of 2019, 162–63
  protests of 2022 and, 198
Khamenei, Mojtaba, 119
Khaneh Khorshid aid center, 147
Khansarinia, Cameron, 230–31
Khash deadly Friday protests of 2022, 57–59
Khatam-al-Anbiya Construction Headquarters, 146
Khatami, Mohammad, 136–38, 146
  reforms, 135–38
Khobregan (council of clerics), 118

Khodakarami, Sajjad, ix
Khodayari, Sahar (Blue Girl), 221
Khojasteh, Mansoureh, 118
Khomeini, Ayatollah Ruhollah, 69, 92–97, 117–18, 146, 204
Khorramabad (city), 63–64
Khosravi, Elaheh, xi
Khosravi, Maziar, 171
Khuzestan province, 116, 195
Kianarsi, Bibi Fatemeh, 84
Kianouri, Noureddin, 93
Koettl, Christoph, 32
Komala (Marxist-Leninist group), 204
Kourkour, Mojahed, 248
Kurdish Democratic Party of Iran (KDPI), 203–4
Kurdish ethnic minority, xn, 3, 4, 30, 36, 40, 204, 229–33, 245
  executions of 1979, 97
  killings of protesters of 2022, 202–7, 226
Kurdish liberation movement, 232
Kurdistan, 3, 41, 44, 97, 113, 232
  protests of 2022 and, 203, 206–7
  strike of 2022, 48
Kurdistan, Republic of, 1946, 203–4
Kurdistan Human Rights Network, 227, 229
Kurdpa (Kurdish news agency), 204
Kurds, 4

lasers, 21–22
leftists, 92–93, 135–36, 245
Leila's Brothers (film), 37
Le Monde, 94
LGBTQ+, 23–24
"life poem" (Ebtehaj), 182–83
literacy, 91
Lojei, Khodanur, 39
London, 170–78
Lorenzo (Nilo's friend), 133–34
Lorestan province, 63, 138

Los Angeles Times, 10, 94, 164–65, 237–38
Louise (Fatemeh's friend), 14, 223, 224
Lur ethnic minority, 63–65

Madreseh Doshizegan (Muslim girls school), 84
Mahabad (city), 203, 231–32
Mahshahr (city), killings of 2019, 47
Makki Mosque, 57
Mälardalen University, 91
Mamlekate (Telegram channel), 203
Manijeh (wife of Mr. Mashallah), 211–12
Marcolini, Barbara, 32
marriage laws on multiple wives, 98
martial rule of 2022, 21
Martina (Nilo's friend), 132–33
Marxists, 69, 92
Mashallah, Mr., 211–12
Mashhad
  protests of 1978, 201–2
  protests of 1891, 80
  protests of 2017, 158
  protests of 2022, 7
  Sunni mosque destroyed, 43
Mashhad Medical Society, 56
Masjedi, Mr., 161, 180–81, 183
Masjed Solyman (town), 107–8, 121, 137
Massacre of 1988, 212
media outlets, conservative control of, 156
Mehrnaz, 25–26
menstruation, 123, 175
#MeToo movement, 37, 173
Milad (Nilo's friend), 127, 129–30, 134, 216–20
Milani, Shahin, 202
mining concession, 79
Mirhadi, Touran, 252
Mirza, Atthar, 57
modernization, 86–87, 91–93
Mohamadi, Mr. (editor), 146
Mohammad, Qazi, 203

Mohammad Ali Shah, 85
Mohammadi, Elaheh, 3–4, 34–36, 52, 171
    trial and sentencing of, 221–25,
    244–46
Mohammadi, Elnaz, 171, 222–23, 225,
    245–46
Mohammadi, Foad, 207
Mohammadi, Narges, 174, 224, 244–48
Mohammad Reza Shah Pahlavi, 89–95
    Revolution of 1979 vs. 92–95
Molaverdi, Shahindokht, 149–50
Mona, 27
Monir, Moh, 196–99
morality police, x, 8, 32, 140–41, 149–50,
    159–61
mosques, 22–23, 93
Mossadegh, Mohammad, 90–93
Moulai-Rad, Pooya, 198
Mousavi, Mir Hossein, 140
Moussavi, Cyrus, 168
Movahed, Vida, 20, 67
Mozaffar ad-Din Shah, Qajar king of
    Iran, 77–78, 85
Muhhammad, Prophet, 42, 143
Mujahideen-e Khalq (MEK), 69–70

n+1, 15, 164–66
Nafiseh (bookstore employee), 27–28
Naghshbandi, Nahid, 241
Nahid (Fatemeh's friend), 36, 238
Najafi, Hadis, 202–3, 210–11
NAJA (Iranian national police
    force), 56
Narges (Fatemeh's friend), 23
Naroohi, Rafeh, 47
Naser al-Din Shah Qajar, 79–80
National Front Party, 90, 93
national identification cards, 58
national police, 22, 33, 45, 55–56
National Solidarity Group of Iran, 230
National Union for Democracy in Iran
    (NUFDI), 230

national work program, 96
Naval Postgraduate School, 56, 205
Negar, 25–26
New York Times, 6–7, 16–17, 29, 30,
    31–32, 46, 70, 72–73, 132, 152, 187,
    217
NHK (Japanese TV station), 223
Nikbakht, Saleh, 238
Niki (student), 54–55
Nikjoumand, Maliheh, 97–98
Nobari, Sakineh Soltan (Nilo's great-
    grandmother), 100–103, 115
Nobel Peace Prize, Narges Mohammadi
    wins, 174
Nobel Prize in Literature, Pamuk wins,
    182
Noor (Fatemeh's friend), 177
North Khorasan province, 203
Northwestern University, 152
Noshin (Fatemeh's friend), 185
Nothing to Lose but Your Life (Amiry),
    170
Nowruz (Iranian New Year), 122–23

Obama, Barack, 141
Öcalan, Abdullah "Apo," 4–5
Öcalan, Hawa, 5
oil, 90, 91, 94, 95, 108, 116, 121, 147
"O mother, O mother, it is wartime"
    (Luri song), 62
One Hundred Years of Solitude (García
    Márquez), 136
One Million Campaign, 142
open-source intelligence (OSINT),
    31–32, 56, 72–73
Operation Ajax, 90
Organization of the Petroleum
    Exporting Countries (OPEC), 94
Ostovar, Afshon, 56, 59, 205–6

Pahlavi, Farah, 95–96, 100
Pahlavi, Reza, 230

Pahlavi monarchy, 41, 89–95, 201
Pakistan, 41, 43
Pamuk, Orhan, 182
Paris Review, The, 15, 154
Parks, Rosa, xv
patriarchy, 37, 38, 99, 119, 137, 148, 190
Pejman (Fatemeh brother's friend), 122
Persian language, xii, 9, 17, 41, 43, 101, 113–14
Persia. *See also* Iran, Islamic Republic of
    ancient, 126–27
    Islam brought to, xii
    nineteenth century, 78–82
Pezeshkian, Masoud, 42, 240
Philadelphia Police Department, 32
Pir Falak, Kian, 195–99
plainclothes police, 33, 49, 58
poetry and verse, importance of, xi–xii
police brutality, 71, 165, 202
political prisoners, 174, 237, 243–47
poverty, 173–75
prisons, 29, 155, 174, 236
pro-monarchy groups, 230, 245
Protection of the Family through Promoting the Culture of Hijab and Chastity Law (2024), 239–42
protests of 1891–92 vs. tobacco concession, 79–82
protests of 1905–11, 83–84. *See also* Constitutional Revolution
protests of 1979 vs. mandatory hijab law, 97–98
protests of 2009, vs. election fraud and morality police, 7, 140–41
protests of 2017, 20, 158–59
protests of 2019, vs. fuel price increases, 15, 162–65, 233
protests of 2020, 237–38
protests of 2022–23. *See* Woman, Life, Freedom protests
Pyruz, Mark, 205–6

Qajar dynasty, 77–83, 85–86
Qalian, Sepideh, 245
Qarchak Prison, 34–36, 244
Qazvin, 200, 210, 228
Qom, 118, 149
Quran, 121, 123, 143

Rafsanjani, Akbar Hashemi, 146
Rahmani, Rebin, 229, 231–32
Rahmanian, Mahdi, 146–47, 150, 163
Rahnavard, Majidreza, 214–15, 219
Raisi, Ebrahim, 156
Raisian, Amir, 212–13
Rajavi, Maryam, 70
Ramadan, 143
rape, 26, 37, 184
Rashnu, Sepideh, xiv–xv
Rasht, protests of 2022, 54, 56
Razi University Hospital, 56
referendum of 1963 on White Revolution reforms, 91
reformist newspapers, 136, 155
reformist organizations, 136, 155–56
reform movement of late nineteenth century, 7, 78
Reham al-Farra Memorial Journalism Fellowship, 152
Rendell, Ed, 70
Reuter, Paul Julius, 79
Reuter concession of 1872, 79
Reuters news agency, 176
Revolutionary Court, 9, 181, 221, 247–49
Revolution of 1979, 8, 18, 69, 91–97, 109, 115, 146, 201–4, 218
"Revolution Is Woman, The" (Öcalan), 5
Rezaei, Reza, 248
Rezaian, Jason, 54, 132
Reza Shah Pahlavi, 86–89
riot police, x–xi, 20, 22–24, 26, 49–52, 158, 162, 202–3, 207, 209
Rolland, Romain, 137

Room of One's Own, A (Woolf), 137
Rouhani, Hassan, 149, 158, 220
Roya (Fatemeh's cousin), 123
Roya (Nilo's mother), 115
Rumi, xi
Russia, post-Soviet, 32
Russia, Tsarist
  concessions to, 78–79, 83
Russo-Persian Wars (1804–13, 1826–28), 78

Saadi (poet), 95
Saam (Nilo's friend) 127, 129
Saeed (Elaheh Mohammadi's husband), 223, 225
Safavid dynasty, 200
Salavati, Abolqasem, 224
Salehi, Toomaj, 213, 223–24
Salesman, The (film), 36
Salman, Saad, 235
Salman Corps (IRGC), 59
Samuels, Elyse, 60
Sanandaj (city), 232
Sangin Mah (Fatemeh's grandmother), 107–9, 138
Sanjabi, Karim, 93
Saqqez (city), 3, 31, 203
Saravan (village), 43
Sarvnaz (Elnaz's friend), 245
Saskatoon, 116
satellite imagery, 31
satellite television, 141
Schopenhauer, Arthur, 50
Second Sex, The (Beauvoir), 137
security forces, 1, 22, 23, 25, 55, 58–59, 154
  families of loved ones killed in protests, 201
  killings by, 63–64, 195–98, 202, 205–7
  Mousavi campaign attacked by, 140
  shootings and arrests by, 48–51
Sedaghat, Maryam, 11–14, 179–85

Sepehri, Fatemeh, 185
Sepehri Far, Tara, 227–29, 233
sexual assault, 37, 181
sexual harassment, 37
sex workers, 96, 147–49
Shafiei, Hamed, x
Shahkarami, Nika, 38–39
Shahnameh (Ferdowsi), xi–xii
Shahr Theater, 96
Shahrzad (editor), 223, 225
Shajarian (musician), 121
Shakarami, Aida, 65–66
Shakarami, Atash, 63–67
Shakarami, Nika, 62–67, 191
Shamlou, Ahmad, xiv
Shams beer factory, 96
Shargh (newspaper), x, 139, 142, 144–49, 155, 171, 222–23
sharia law, 137, 143
Sharif University, 55
Shatt al-Arab waterway, 115
Shekari, Mohsen, 36, 208–11, 219, 247–49
Sherdost, Saba, 35
Sherman, Brad, 70
Shia Islam, 42, 78–80, 115, 118, 201, 231
Shirani-Naroui, Shirahmad, 45, 57, 60–61
Shirazi, Mirza Hassan, 80
Shiraz (town), 79–82
Shirin (barista), 253
Shirin (Nilo's cousin), 126–27, 130, 216–17
Shokat (Fatemeh's friend, pseudonym), 19–21, 23–28, 49–52
Shokat Khanum (Nilo's grandmother), 115
Signa, 71, 152, 234–35
Sina (Amir Ali's friend), 28
Sistan and Baluchestan, 41–44, 57–61
social media, 7, 16, 31, 33, 38, 63, 68, 71–73, 162–63

Soleimani, Qasem, 166–68, 172–73
solitary confinement, 29, 35
Somayeh (Fatemeh's friend), 172
Soraya, Queen, 98–99
Soraya (Fatemeh's aunt), 98–99
Soul Enchanted, The (Rolland), 137
South Palestine Street, 22
Soviet Union, 89–90, 203
Storyful, 31–32
strikes, of 2022, 7, 48–49
Suits (TV show), 125
Sunday Times, The, 14, 223–24
Sunni Arabs, 245
Sunni Muslims, 41–42
Supreme Leader, 118
Syrian Kurds, 4

Tabriz, 47, 60, 84, 101–2
   Nilo's father and, 9, 112–13
   protests of 1891, 80
   protests of 2022, 7
Tabrizy, Ahmad (Nilo's uncle), 112
Tabrizy, Nargess (Nilo's sister), 113
Tabrizy, Nilo
   athletics as girl and, 127–29
   birth and early life of, in Iran, 111–12, 116
   birth of, 116
   Black Lives Matter and, 186–87
   bond with Fatemeh and, 154–56
   breaks in Iran coverage at *Washington Post* and, 60
   breaks writing on Iran in 2020, 168–69
   challenges of, as journalist, vs. Fatemeh's, 155–56
   childhood and early life of, in Canada, 125–26, 129–31
   childhood visit to Iran, of 2000, 126–31, 134
   collaborates with Fatemeh on protests of 2019, 164–65
   collaborates with Fatemeh on protests of 2022, 14–17, 153–55
   cousin's friend Milad and, 127, 129–30, 216–20
   death of grandmother and, 176
   decision to report on Iran, and loss of ability to return, 131–33
   family history and, 100–102
   family losses in tobacco concession and, 80–82
   Fatemeh's arrest during protest of 2017, 159–61
   Fatemeh's return to Iran in 2021 and, 153, 177
   Fatemeh's rubber bullet wound photo and, 52
   father and, 111–16, 125
   father's brother Ahmad and, 112
   grief at not being able to return to Iran, 29–30, 156
   Iranian Americans and, 131–32
   IRGC strike on Ukraine International Flight 752 and, 31, 167–69
   Iranian ethnic minorities and, 203–5, 230–31
   Iranian women's movement as heritage of, 190–91
   Jina's anniversary of death and, 227–28
   journalistic objectivity vs. "speaking nearby" and, 186–89
   love of poetry by Farrokhzad and, 105, 157
   maternal grandmother and, 100, 127
   meets Fatemeh in person, 152–53
   mother and, 104, 111–12, 115, 125–26, 130–31, 166, 217–18
   n+1 story with Fatemeh and, 164–66
   Paris Review article with Fatemeh and, 154–55
   Persian language study and, 17, 157

Tabrizy, Nilo *(continued)*
   reporting tool OSINT and, 31–33, 56–57, 72–73
   reports on killing of Mehdi Hazrati in Karaj and, 203
   reports on killings of Kurds, 205
   reports on violence at funerals, 226
   Soleimani assassination and, 166
   verifies reports and videos of protests, 16–17, 44–45, 71–73
   writes for *New York Times*, 6–7, 20, 30–32, 70
   writes for *Washington Post*, 20, 56–57, 60
Takht-e Jamshid, 126
Talbot, Gerald F., 79
Taliban, 222
tarof (politeness norms), 114
Tasnim News Agency, 156
Taymouri, Ebrahim, 82
tear gas, 22, 32, 49, 51–52, 55, 59
Tehran, x–xi
   American Christian girls schools in, 84
   Constitutional Revolution of 1909 and, 85–86
   ethnic minorities and, 41
   executions of protesters and, 215–16
   Farah Pahlavi and, 95–96
   Fatemeh arrested attempting to attend volleyball championships in, 149–51
   Fatemeh arrested in protests of 2017, 158–61
   Fatemeh leaves, in 2020, 170–71
   Fatemeh moves to, as graduate student and reporter, 141–45
   Fatemeh reports undercover as street vendor in, 147–48
   Fatemeh returns to, in 2021, 6–8, 176–79
   honor killings in, 139
   IRGC corruption in, 145–47
   killing of Mahsa Jîna Amini by morality police in, ix–xi
   nightlife during Ramadan, 143
   Nilo's family and early childhood in, 115–17, 131
   Nilo's trip to, at age 10, 126–31, 134, 216
   protests of 1891 and, 80
   protests of 2022 in, 6–8, 10–11, 14–16, 19–28, 40–41, 48–56, 62–66, 216–19
   Ramadan and, 143
   red coloring added to fountains, 14
   Revolution of 1979 and, 96–98
   sex workers and, 96–97, 148–49
   shop strike of 2022 and, 48
   suburbs of, 25
   trade in newborn babies in, 149
   women street vendors in, 148
Tehran (Bekas), 4
Tehran Journalists' Association, 173
Tehran Municipality, IRGC contract and, 145–47
Tehran Museum of Contemporary Art, 96
Tehran University, 51, 66, 98, 115, 158, 218
Telegram, 8, 31, 44, 47, 53, 58, 71, 203, 219, 238
television
   dancing banned on, 39
   protests of 2019 and, 162
text messages, 140–41, 162–63
   encrypted, 71, 218, 222
TikTok, 202
Time, xn
Tobacco Boycott, the First Passive Resistance in Iran, The (Taymouri), 82
tobacco concession and boycott of 1890–92, 79, 80–82
Tolstoy, Leo, 137
trade embargo of 1980, 116

Trans-Iranian Railway, 86
Triebert, Christiaan, 32
Trinh T. Minh-ha, 187–89
Trump, Donald, 70, 132, 163, 166, 220
Turkey, Republic of, 86–87
Turkish Kurds, 5
20:30 (TV program), 49
Twelver Shia Islamic law, 42
Twitter, ix, xii, 7, 30, 35, 56, 73, 141, 147, 150–51, 163–64

Ukraine International Airlines flight 752, missile strike, 31–32, 60, 165, 167–69, 173, 237
Umebinyuo, Ijeoma, 110
United Nations
   journalism fellowship award and, 152
   Iranian Permanent Mission to, 32–33
United States
   Fatemeh visits, in 2017, 152
   Iranian coup of 1953 and, 90–91
   Iranian oil and, 94
   Iranian Revolution of 1979 and, 94–95
   police and, 32
   sanctions vs. Iran and, 220, 235–36
   Soleimani assassination and, 166, 168
   travel ban and, 132
U.S. embassy, Tehran, occupation of, 95, 116
U.S. foreign terrorist organizations (FTO) list, 69–70
U.S. Navy, 46
U.S. State Department, 69
universities
   closed, 1979–81, 98
   gender segregation in classes and, 142–43
   Herasat police and, 142–43
   protests of 2022 and, 197
   Ramadan and, 143
   restrictions on women in, 140, 143
   student activists banned from, 237
   woman stripped by security forces at, 250–51
University of Art, Tehran, 75
University of California, Berkeley, 31, 54
Urmia (town), 84

Vahid, Mr., 178–81, 183
Vancouver, 116, 128
Vanity Fair, 187
velayat-e faqih concept, 42, 93
Vice, 132
videos, 31, 32, 53–54, 57, 58, 63
   geo-locating, 44–45, 59
   social media and, 53, 71
   verification of, 16, 71–73
Vietnam, 187
violence against women, 139–40
virginity, 124, 141
Visual Forensics team, *Washington Post*, 56
Visual Investigations team, *New York Times*, 31–32

Washington Post, 29, 54, 56, 60, 132, 202, 231
weddings, 144–45
welfare system, 91
West Azerbaijan province, 203, 231
Westernization, 87
Western media, 93–94
West Germany, 94
WhatsApp, 152–53, 166
White Revolution, 91–92
White Scarves campaign, 149
"Why It's Vital to Center Kurdish Voices in the 'Woman, Life, Freedom' Movement" (Zandi), xn
Willis, Haley, 32, 72–73
Wisdom of Life, The (Schopenhauer), 50

Woman, Life, Freedom (*Jin/Zan, Jîyan/Zendegi, Azadî/i*) protests of 2022–23, xn, xii–xiii, xiv, 4–5, 7–11, 14–31, 36, 48–52, 55, 174
   ambulances used for arrests and, 53–55
   arrest of Niloofar and Elaneh and, 36
   death of Jîna triggers, 10–11, 31, 36, 173
   end of, in 2023, 226
   Enghelab Street as center of, 19–21, 19–26, 48–52, 54, 56, 62–63, 66
   ethnic rights and, 40–42
   executions of protesters and, 208–15, 219
   Fatemeh and Nilo decide to write about, 14–18
   Fatemeh films, 14
   Fatemeh's arrest at, 14–15
   Fatemeh writes first story on, 14
   Hadis Najafi killing and, 202–3
   Iranian journalists and, 155–56
   Javad Heydari killing and, 200–201
   Khamenei and, 118–19
   Kian Pir Falak killing and, 195–99
   killings by security forces and, 205–7
   Kurds killed during, 204–5, 231–32
   leaders and, 190–91
   Nika killed during, 62–67
   Nilo's contact with Fatemeh during, 153–55
   Nilo's contact with Milad during, 217–19
   OSINT method and, 32–33
   protesters shot on Enghelab Street, 50
   secret notes and, 19–20, 23
   shopkeepers strike and, 48–49
   song of, 193
   U.S. media coverage on causes of, 70–73
   Zahedan massacre and, 39, 41
woman's movement of 1891–92, 81–82
woman's movement of 1906, 77–78
Women's Awakening of 1936–41, 86–87
women's rights, 176
   activist arrests of 2023 and, 226–27
   Atatürk and, 86–87
   ban on women at sports stadiums and, 149–51
   ban on women singing in public and, 241–42
   Constitutional Revolution and, 83–86
   Fatemeh's role models and, 137
   first Persian association for, 83–84
   forced unveiling law of 1936 and, 87–88
   hijab violation enforcement and, 138, 142
   Islamic Republic and restrictions on, 94, 117–18
   job discrimination and, 139–40
   leaderless nature of, 190–91
   mandatory hijab law protests of 1979 and, 97–98
   Mossadegh and, 90
   Nilo's role models and, 80–82
   One Million Campaign of 2006 and, 142
   protests of 2022–23 and (*see* Woman, Life, Freedom protests)
   protests vs. morality police of 2009 and, 140–41
   Reza Shah and, 86–87
   sharia law and, 137
   travel restrictions and, 138

university women, and Ramadan and, 143
voting rights and, 90–93, 96
White Revolution and, 91–92
women defying hijab rules and, 12, 17
Woolf, Virginia, 137
World Food Programme, 174
World Volleyball Matches of 2014, 149–50

Yandex search engine, 71
Yazdi, Ebrahim, 94
Yerahi, Mahdi, 1
"Your Absence, Your Empty Paces", segment, 222

Youth of the Neighborhoods of Tehran, 219
YouTube, 7, 241–42

Zaban-e Zanan (*Women's Voice* magazine), 83
Zahedan (city), 41, 59–61
  Bloody Friday massacre of 2022, 39, 41–42, 44–47, 53, 56–57, 60
  riots of 1994, 43
Zahhak, King of Persia, 211
Zandi, Jiyan, xn
Zan-e rooz (*Modern Woman* magazine), 100
Zardkoh (village), 43
Zeinab (Fatemeh's aunt), 109

ABOUT THE AUTHORS

FATEMEH JAMALPOUR IS a feminist freelance journalist banned from working in Iran by the Ministry of Intelligence. She has contributed to *The Sunday Times, The Paris Review,* and the *Los Angeles Times* and previously worked with BBC World News in London and *Shargh* newspaper in Tehran. Fatemeh was a 2024–25 Knight-Wallace Fellow at the University of Michigan.

NILO TABRIZY IS an investigative reporter at *The Washington Post*. She works for the Visual Forensics team, where she covers Iran using open-source methods. Previously, she was a video journalist at *The New York Times,* covering Iran, race and policing, abortion access, and more. She is an Emmy nominee and the 2022 winner of the Front Page Award for Online Investigative Reporting. Nilo received her MS in journalism from Columbia University and her BA in political science and French from the University of British Columbia.

A NOTE ON THE TYPE

This book was set in Arno, a typeface designed by Adobe principal designer Robert Slimbach in 2007. Its namesake is the Arno River, which flows through Florence, the city at the heart of the Italian Renaissance. Inspired by the humanist letterforms of the fifteenth and sixteenth centuries, Slimbach designed Arno with the vitality and readability of Venetian and Aldine book typefaces in mind.

Composed by North Market Street Graphics,
Lancaster, Pennsylvania

Designed by Marisa Nakasone